BETWEEN TEXT AND ARTIFACT

Society of Biblical Literature

Archaeology and Biblical Studies

Andrew G. Vaughn,
Editor

Number 8

BETWEEN TEXT AND ARTIFACT
Integrating Archaeology in Biblical Studies Teaching

BETWEEN TEXT AND ARTIFACT

Integrating Archaeology in Biblical Studies Teaching

Edited by
Milton C. Moreland

Society of Biblical Literature
Atlanta

BETWEEN TEXT AND ARTIFACT
Integrating Archaeology in Biblical Studies Teaching

Copyright © 2003 by the Society of Biblical Literature

Library of Congress Cataloging-in-Publication Data

Between text and artifact : integrating archaeology in biblical studies / edited by Milton C. Moreland.
  p. cm. — (Archaeology and biblical studies ; no. 8)
  Includes bibliographical references (p.) and index.
  ISBN 1-58983-044-X (paper binding : alk. paper)
  1. Bible—Antiquities—Study and teaching—Congresses. 2. Bible—Evidences, authority, etc.—Study and teaching—Congresses. 3. Bible—Study and teaching—Congresses. 4. Excavations (Archaeology)—Middle East—Study and teaching—Congresses. 5. Middle East—Antiquities—Study and teaching—Congresses. I. Moreland, Milton C. II. Series.
  BS621 .B48 2003b
  220.9'3—dc22   2003019714

1 10 09 08 07 06 05 04 03   5 4 3 2 1

Printed in the United States of America on acid-free, recycled paper conforming to ANSI/NISO Z39.48-1992 (R1997) and ISO 9706:1994 standards for paper permanence.

CONTENTS

Acknowledgements

The recognition that there was a need to provide biblical scholars and teachers with practical tools for integrating archaeology into the teaching of the Bible grew out of meetings at Duke University and the University of Oregon in 2000–2001. The Wabash Center for Teaching and Learning in Theology and Religion supported these meetings with a grant and encouraged the publication of the papers. Melissa Aubin organized the meetings and initiated the efforts to collect the papers; without her hard work and planning, this volume would not have come to fruition. Andy Vaughn offered exceptional advice and encouragement throughout the process of preparing the volume for publication. His attention to detail is greatly appreciated. Rex Matthews at the Society of Biblical Literature was also a patient advocate and advisor for the volume, and Bob Buller expertly guided the volume through to publication. Most of all, the contributors are to be thanked for their efforts. Each essay was written specifically for this volume and appears in print for the first time.

ABBREVIATIONS

AASOR	Annual of the American Schools of Oriental Research
AB	Anchor Bible
ABD	*Anchor Bible Dictionary.* Edited by D. N. Freedman. 6 vols. New York: Doubleday, 1992.
Arch	*Archaeology*
BA	*Biblical Archaeologist*
BAR	*Biblical Archaeology Review*
BARIS	British Archaeological Reports International Series
Bib	*Biblica*
BMes	Bibliotheca mesopotamica
BASOR	*Bulletin of the American Schools of Oriental Research*
BTB	*Biblical Theological Bulletin*
BibSem	The Biblical Seminar
CANE	*Civilizations of the Ancient Near East.* Edited by J. M. Sasson. 4 vols. New York: Charles Scribner's Sons, 1995.
CRINT	Compendia Rerum Iudaicarum ad Novum Testamentum
DSD	*Dead Sea Discoveries*
ErIsr	*Eretz Israel*
HSM	Harvard Semitic Monographs
HSS	Harvard Semitic Studies
HTR	*Harvard Theological Review*
IEJ	*Israel Exploration Journal*
JNES	*Journal of Near Eastern Studies*
JSOTMS	Journal for the Study of the Old Testament Monograph Series
JSOTSup	Journal for the Study of the Old Testament Supplement Series
JSPSup	Journal for the Study of the Pseudepigrapha Supplement Series
NEA	*Near Eastern Archaeology*
NEAEHL	*The New Encyclopedia of Archaeological Excavations in the Holy Land.* Edited by Ephraim Stern. 4 vols. Jerusalem: Israel Exploration Society and Carta; New York: Simon & Schuster, 1993.
NTS	*New Testament Studies*

OBO	Orbis biblicus et orientalis
OEANE	*The Oxford Encyclopedia of Archaeology in the Near East.* Edited by E. M. Meyers. 5 vols. New York: Oxford University Press, 1997.
PEQ	*Palestine Exploration Quarterly*
QC	*Qumran Chronicle*
RB	*Revue Biblique*
RevQ	*Revue de Qumran*
SNTSMS	Society for New Testament Studies Monograph Series
SBLABS	Society of Biblical Literature Arachaeology and Biblical Studies
SBLDS	Society of Biblical Literature Dissertation Series
SBLSP	Society of Biblical Literature Seminar Papers
SBLSymS	Society of Biblical Literature Symposium Series
STDJ	Studies on the Texts of the Desert of Judah
TA	*Tel Aviv*
VTSup	Supplements to Vetus Testamentum

Introduction: Between Text and Artifact

Milton C. Moreland, Shannon Burkes, and Melissa Aubin

For those who study the world of the Bible, the primary corpus of data is comprised by the biblical texts themselves. From these writings, we first acquaint ourselves with the social and literary surroundings presumed in biblical texts and the traditions they record. We relate the biblical materials to other ancient documents that, through comparison, might illuminate philological, historical, or theological problems. We trace motifs, explicate poetry, and observe characterization so that we might deepen our appreciation of how literary traditions were crafted. Depending on a scholar's expertise, he or she might look for seams within the text to understand why and how redactors conducted their work. Alternatively, a scholar might examine distinctions among manuscripts themselves in order to determine which texts carry the greatest probability of providing earliest available readings. We perform these types of tasks because historical and literary-critical methods occupy the bulk of our training. Understanding the context of biblical literature with these tools provides some sense of the great cultural gap that separates contemporary readers from the texts' initial producers and readers. Nevertheless, academic study of the Bible, largely achieved through historical-critical methods, omits a corpus of evidence that is germane to the task of contextualizing the generation and use of the texts and traditions that comprise the Bible.

Given the strong motivation in much of our training to understand the social-historical context of biblical literature, to grasp something of the world in which it was created, and to reconstruct the historical scenarios that these texts presume, it is strange that we habitually exclude the immense corpus of archaeological data from our course of inquiry. After all, more than a free-floating network of documents and ideas, the cultures of the biblical world were ensconced in a rich mixture of objects. Some of these objects of material culture have been recovered and interpreted in the archaeological process.

Archaeological data contemporaneous to the texts that we study can allow us to visualize the items, environments, and landscapes taken for granted in the texts. Visual and material data can help us to unfold political

1

and social motivations for events described in the written material. Artifacts can remind us of the voices left out of texts and alert us to biases that authors and editors exhibit. When viewed alongside biblical literature, the archaeological record can help create new knowledge that leads to a richly textured set of historical reconstructions for the cultures of the biblical world.

As attractive as such results might be, the fact remains that we are products of bounded disciplines, and the taxonomy of disciplines results in the bifurcation of text and artifact that discourages us from bringing archaeological evidence to bear in our interpretive questions. Unlike the discipline of classical studies, which, despite its split into classical archaeology and classical philology, categorized its material and textual sources within the same greater rubric, biblical studies is dominated by the texts. At least from the perspective of a literary scholar, textual and archaeological studies of the Bible are largely distinct fields. Unlike the classicist, who could conceivable study archaeology and text in the same academic rubric, to study the archaeology of Syro-Palestine, the realia of biblical studies, one might have to work within biblical studies and outside the field as well. At present, the tools for educating oneself in the archaeology of Syro-Palestine might lead one to departments of Near Eastern studies or anthropology.

To some extent, the division between the two approaches seems to have been widening in recent decades as part of the general trend of intensifying specialization across the academy between areas and even sub-areas. As specialized journals have increased in number and the urgency to publish has become more acute for recently minted scholars, there is a tendency to tighten one's focus on familiar territory rather than to stray into pastures where one's mastery of the material might not be as strong.

Moreover, it seems that to some extent, at least, graduate programs also reflect and even solidify a division between the two fields. Candidates for the Ph.D. degree in biblical studies might have to include works by prominent archaeologists on doctoral exam reading lists, ensuring some exposure to relevant scholarship in the area. Nevertheless, training remains heavily based on the study of written texts and understanding these as far as possible in their historical settings. The historical interest has obvious links to the data produced by archaeologists, and to that extent, biblical studies training can be said to have been informed by the field. However, for many, exposure to it has been through books and articles that generally digest the bits of data to produce analyses of historical events and movements. Due to the nature of their training, biblical studies scholars often lack experience in confronting unprocessed archaeological evidence, and they might be ill at ease with the technical language and techniques of the field.

In the case of archaeology in particular, the fact that the scholar (from outside Israel, Jordan, or Palestine) physically relocates for fieldwork on a regular basis, often under demanding conditions, is another element that feeds into the separation of the archaeologist from the nonarchaeologist. Those who do not relish the physical nature of the work, the travel, the organizational demands, and so on are by definition lacking in the kind of personal experience that is probably the most direct resource on which a teacher can draw in the classroom. Without the hands-on experience, the biblical scholar has to be content as an "armchair" archaeologist, which in itself is not necessarily a bad thing. Not everyone can be an archaeologist, and getting training through publications produced by the specialists in the field is one time-honored method of preparation for the classroom.

Perhaps the most important factor in this regard is that in the case of ancient Israel, the culture developed into communities that ultimately produced written canons for various traditions. Because of this, much of the literary evidence for a course such as Hebrew Bible/Old Testament or New Testament is already conveniently prepackaged into one handy volume, and the teacher steps into the classroom with a ready-made textual framework. This framework provides a sense of a discrete subject matter, free standing and ready for examination within received boundaries. The Israelites, in their transformation after the exile and ongoing development into what would become an array of Jewish and Christian communities, produced a book-based tradition.

Egyptian literary culture provides a useful point of comparison. While the Egyptians produced plenty of written materials of all kinds, at no point in the history of the civilization is there evidence that it was selectively reduced into a "canon." The result is that when one teaches a course on Egyptian religion, one is forced to draw on a much more loosely organized body of textual evidence, evidence that is not inherently privileged in the field compared to the archaeology. Then there is the fact that the languages of the Egyptian texts had died and the code was not cracked again until the nineteenth century, which meant that the modern Western experience of the ancient civilization up to that point was by necessity mediated through physical remains, which may also be a contributing factor in the relatively lesser role of text in Egyptology as a whole. When teaching a course defined by a "testament," however, the structure is to some extent already shaped by and weighted toward the text. The very existence of a canon, then, is a significant factor in the emphasis on literature at the expense of archaeology in such courses, not just because of an implied prestige or authority of the canon, but simply because of convenience.

Related to this issue, of course, is the fact that in biblical studies the teacher has to be conscious that, whichever canon one uses, it relates to currently active religious traditions for many students. This fact means that an instructor is sometimes confronted with questions about the truth of the text and the truth of the archaeological data, and how the two relate, in a way that the Egyptologist simply need not consider. Moreover, in many religious communities, the New Testament and the Hebrew Bible enjoy the status of hallowed texts that purport to be readily understandable on their own, in no need of explanatory data that might come from the environs of the texts' production. This adds a layer of complexity for the instructor who may not feel that he or she has an advanced grasp of the archaeological field to begin with. In the average student's mind, there seems to be a predisposition to regard archaeology as a tool that either proves or disproves the biblical narrative; this requires the teacher to spend additional time trying to introduce some level of methodological sophistication to the class and to untangle issues that simply are not present in other fields.

The selfsame disciplinary boundaries that discourage biblical scholars from studying material culture are embedded in the structuring of the courses we offer to undergraduates. Rather than teaching "Biblical Cultures," "The World of the Bible," or some such class, we teach and construct courses along canonical boundaries, offering, for example, introductions to New Testament or Hebrew Bible. Indeed, if a Hebrew Bible course were conceived not as a strictly literary enterprise, but as a course on Israelite religion or Israel and the ancient Near East, the need and opportunity for bringing in archaeological evidence would expand dramatically. It requires no argument that the Hebrew Bible is not an accurate or complete picture of religious practices of the Israelites, since it was collected and edited with specific ideologies in mind, for the most part long after the events narrated, with little interest in providing a neutral account of Israel, its activities, and its interactions with its neighbors.

The situation is somewhat different when one is teaching an introduction to the Bible course. By definition, such a course is an introduction to a literary collection rather than a study of a culture as a whole. The Bible itself becomes in some sense an artifact, and rather than attempting to understand a particular culture, one instead is attempting to understand a literary corpus within its cultural setting. The distinction may seem to be hair-splitting, but it looms large in the tendency to focus on text rather than physical data in this kind of course. The emphasis lies on the themes and worldviews that emerge in the literary collection, which certainly can and ought to be illuminated by some attempt to identify related historical events, actual practices, and so on. Nonetheless, in the limited time of a single semester, with a large literary corpus to handle, and in view of the inhibiting factors discussed above, it does become seductively easy for the instructor to let the text bear most of the weight of the course.

Difficulties accessing the data are quickly compounded by interpretive problems. After reading archaeological information, how does one interpret

the data that constitute the archaeological record, and how does one evaluate this data vis-à-vis the claims of biblical literature? How does one
present these types of questions in the classroom? How does one move
beyond the relatively simplistic use of archaeological data and realia as
"visual aids" that often characterizes inappropriate attempts to verify the
historicity of biblical claims?

Finally, apart from these considerations, there is also the basic problem
of the mechanical difficulties sometimes involved. Slides, video, and computer resources are all effective tools for introducing archaeology into the
classroom, but the awareness of specific resources in these media is hit and
miss for many nonarchaeologists. The facilities at different institutions for
using such media also vary in convenience, and probably at least a part of
the hesitation to make use of these things is related to the physical difficulty
of getting the equipment to the right place at the right time.

The sum of all of the above factors—tendency toward specialization;
graduate training; the nature of biblical studies, which has a literary canon;
religious predispositions of some students; interpretive questions—results
in maintaining circumstances that routinize the distancing of realia from
text in the task of teaching a course in biblical studies. To be sure, prefer-
ence of texts to realia in academic study and teaching is a tendency that
appears in all manner of disciplines. One could say that religious studies in
general focus on the written media of religious messages, as opposed to
the remaining materials that comprise the environment in which religious
instruction and ritual are conducted.

The opening of traditional biblical studies pedagogy to archaeological
data and, moreover, demonstrations of the richness and texture of the
resulting reconstructions could provide a useful impetus for other reli-
gionists to attend to artifacts and texts alike. Now more than ever, we are
subject to academic impulses that wish to repair this division. We exist in
an environment that values interdisciplinary work and encourages one to
transcend disciplinary boundaries and to employ the tools of multiple
fields, producing results that are meaningful to a variety of audiences. In
such an academic environment, it is becoming increasingly counterintuitive to neglect the realia contemporary to biblical society when
reconstructing biblical history. A growing number of disciplines need to
be consulted when attempting to contextualize biblical voices and to
sharpen our understandings of social, political, and economic dimensions
of biblical literature. Interdisciplinary work pushes textual scholars to turn
up archaeological data made accessible through reference materials, journals, study trips, documentaries, and textbooks. In addition, the benefits
of bringing archaeological resources to students in the classroom are
exciting for instructors and students alike. The use of images that include
visual and material evidence engage students and readily work to

enhance historical-critical instruction, encouraging use of media that provide an alternative to "chalk and talk" lecture teaching. When viewed alongside the growing popularity of "biblical archaeology" in nonacademic spheres, current interdisciplinary sensibilities make the absence of visual and material culture rather conspicuous.

The obvious large-scale answer to the difficulty is a structural reshaping of the field, starting with graduate training and extending to more integrated scholarly activities at conferences.[1] For the present, the approach more likely to be effective is probably at the grass-roots level and in situations that can produce some practical assistance for those already in the classroom.

Fully aware of the many types of obstacles for textual scholars wishing to ask questions of material remains, the organizers of this volume have drawn together voices who encourage and exemplify the fruitful integration of archaeological data and biblical literature in teaching the religion and culture of the biblical world. The essays collected here are designed to articulate the value of historical reconstructions that draw from many media, to provide guidance for those who would like to do the same, and to offer case studies and models for readers to use as starting points.

The work represented in this volume issues from a consultation series entitled "Integrating Archaeology and Biblical Studies" that was conducted in Durham, North Carolina, and Eugene, Oregon, during the 2000–2001 academic year. The meetings, funded by a grant from the Wabash Center for Teaching and Learning in Theology and Religion, occasioned presentations and exchanges devoted to integrating knowledge from the field of biblical (or Syro-Palestinian) archaeology into biblical studies courses that have been traditionally limited to the literature (not the realia) of biblical cultures. As archaeologists and humanists, the participants in these consultations understand how pedagogy in biblical literature can be deeply enriched by the importation of archaeological data and wish to introduce the possibilities of this integration to biblical scholars.

In order to facilitate the connection between the traditionally distinct subdisciplines of biblical archaeology and literary studies of the Bible, we specifically explored cogent and practical examples that will persuade biblical studies instructors to consider incorporating visual/archaeological data into their courses. We indicate pedagogical strategies for using visual and material culture in courses that traditionally focus on biblical literature only, producing a variety of options for revising different types of biblical

---

[1] Thus, one might suggest that the increasing separation of the Society of Biblical Literature and the American Schools of Oriental Research in this regard is unfortunate.

studies courses through the integration of visual/material culture. We hope to help readers to find practical approaches for integrating such data into a syllabus in meaningful ways for students and instructor alike. In addition, the contributors to this volume express a common concern to make explicit certain implicit agendas that have figured both in the reconstruction of the history of biblical cultures generally and in the use of archaeological evidence to further certain ideological positions.

The essays included here cover a wide range of subject matter designed to prove useful for instructors in both New Testament and Hebrew Bible. Of course, the history of Palestine need not be marked by New Testament/Hebrew Bible divisions, but because this book is designed with a readership of biblical studies instructors in mind, the essays are presented in ways that demonstrate the particular contributions of archaeology in instruction for these fields.

The first essay, "Between Heaven and Earth: Educational Perspectives on the Archaeology and Material Culture of the Bible," sums up the difficulties in using both archaeological and literary data for historical reconstructions in contexts that are infused with political and spiritual claims to the lands under study. By examining the classic publications on archaeology and the Bible, Ann E. Killebrew comments on selected aspects of the political, theological, and ethical issues at hand when one teaches reconstructions of Israelite history that are sometimes counter to biblical claims.

Two essays in particular illustrate how archaeological evidence can, in conjunction with literary data, provide textured reconstructions of elements in Israelite culture. Carol Meyers's contribution to this volume, "'Where the Girls Are': Archaeology and Women's Lives in Ancient Israel," indicates the biases in the biblical record that result in the silencing of women and the undervaluing of women's contributions to Israelite society. Meyers reviews resources in secondary scholarship that profitably use archaeological evidence to indicate women's roles and discusses the impact of such roles on the dynamics of daily life in households of the period of the Hebrew Bible.

Beth LaRocca-Pitts's essay, "'These Are Your Gods, O Israel': The Challenge of Reconstructing Israelite Religion Using Both Text and Archaeology," explores the methodological issues encountered when one seeks to account for archaeological remains linked to Israelite religion, discusses relevant archaeological finds germane to a historical reconstruction of Israelite religion, and suggests ways of approaching such reconstructions when teaching the cultural contexts of the Hebrew Bible.

Four essays are devoted to providing overviews of available tools and strategies for profitably using the fruits of archaeological research in classroom situations. J. P. Dessel's "In Search of the Good Book: A Critical Survey of Handbooks on Biblical Archaeology" contextualizes the variety of "biblical archaeology" textbooks available within the shifting intellectual currents that have dominated the interpretation of archaeological evidence vis-à-vis the Bible. Along the way, Dessel provides an informative overview of those textbooks that Hebrew Bible teachers might consider as supplements to their courses, exposing the intellectual biases and scope of each.

Scott R. A. Starbuck's essay, "Why Declare the Things Forbidden? Classroom Integration of Ancient Near Eastern Archaeology with Biblical Studies in Theological Context," is a exemplary contribution to the discussion of archaeology and its relation to theological issues. Writing particularly for scholars who teach in theological seminaries or church-related colleges, Starbuck begins by considering the epistemological ethos that is often implicit in the biblical studies classroom in theological contexts. He then offers a particular theological hermeneutic ("the Chalcedonian hermeneutic") with a test case that uses the material remains of Kuntillet ʿAjrûd (Horvat Teiman) in order to show a positive relationship between theology and archaeology.

Of particular practical use for instructors in Hebrew Bible is John C. H. Laughlin's "On The Convergence of Texts and Artifacts: Using Archaeology to Teach the Hebrew Bible." In this essay Laughlin demonstrates how archaeology can be used both positively and negatively in biblical studies when teaching the "conquest" of Canaan according to Numbers, Joshua, and Judges, the development of an "Israelite" state, and the nature of "Israelite" religion. Drawing on his many years of successful teaching in undergraduate settings, Laughlin packs his essay with practical advice and relevant resources for teaching.

One analogous essay for the early Roman period provides an introduction to teaching tools and texts and explicated syllabi. In "Archaeology in New Testament Courses," Milton C. Moreland provides a critique of facile uses of material culture that function, consciously or not, to concretize the historicity of events narrated in the New Testament for students. Suggestions for more sophisticated incorporation of archaeological data into New Testament teaching permit a richer understanding of social and economic considerations during the period of the Jesus movement and obviate reliance on archaeology as a visual aid that might be used to enforce uncritically biblical claims. The essay presents several points of contact between archaeology and introduction to New Testament courses to illustrate how archaeology can be used both to explain the texts and to encourage critical thinking in the classroom.

Other chapters will be especially useful for understanding the cultural environment of Second Temple period Syro-Palestine through sources from within and outside the biblical canon. In "Teaching Second Temple Judaism in Light of Archaeology," Eric M. Meyers demonstrates not only the central importance of Persian and Hellenistic archaeological materials for an appreciation of the period after the return from exile but also how to navigate through the mass of potentially useful resources for this task.

Daniel Falk's essay, "Text and Artifact: The Dead Sea Scrolls and Qumran," presents a case in which a body of textual evidence (the scrolls from Caves 1–11) and archaeological data (the site of Qumran material finds, skeletons) are evaluated together to create a historical reconstruction for the generation and use of the Dead Sea Scrolls. Falk adds to the discussion external texts about the Essenes and the site of Qumran in order to discuss how one presents interpretive decision making with the use of text and artifact in the pedagogical process.

The essay by Jürgen Zangenberg turns attention to a widely neglected aspect of the population of ancient Syro-Palestine, the so-called "pagan" groups who shared the land with the people of Judah and, much later, with nascent Christian communities in the region. "Realizing Diversity: Reflections on Teaching Pagan Religion(s) in Late Hellenistic and Early Roman Palestine" explains the importance of teaching nonbiblical cultures in biblical studies classes and argues that the best way to teach "paganism" is by importing archaeological evidence into one's pool of data. The essay ends with a select bibliography that suggests further reading on the topic at hand.

In the conclusion to the volume, Byron R. McCane contends that the best way to integrate archaeology and biblical studies is to involve students in the actual work of archaeology by taking them into the field for a season of excavation. To that end, his essay, "'Here I Am At Khirbet Cana': Integrating Biblical Studies and Archaeology" evaluates fieldwork alongside other methods of integrating archaeology and biblical studies (e.g., incorporating archaeological information into the biblical studies course, teaching courses on archaeology and biblical studies) and concludes that field excavation provides an ideal environment to appreciate the important contributions that both disciplines make to our knowledge of the past.

The volume concludes with an extended, annotated bibliography that includes texts, videos, and slide collections arranged in general categories ranging from interpretive questions that impact the correlation of archaeological and textual data to reference materials, such as atlases and encyclopedias, and to teaching subject areas, such as Dead Sea Scrolls, New Testament, and Hebrew Bible. This bibliography provides a broad sampling of the resources deemed useful tools for instructors who would allow their teaching to benefit from archaeological data.

There is a need in the field of biblical studies for the integration of archaeological and literary studies. The authors of these essays, archaeologists and biblical scholars alike, are advocates for the fact that the academic study of biblical literature can be deeply enriched by the importation of archaeological data. This volume seeks to show both why this integration

is useful and how the areas of research can be integrated by biblical scholars who are not formally trained in Near Eastern archaeology. Given the
great divide between archaeology of Syro-Palestine and biblical studies, the
authors recognize a special need to create awareness of the great enhance-
ments material culture provides for biblical studies instruction in a variety
of institutional settings, from seminaries to secular institutions.

Between Heaven and Earth: Educational Perspectives on the Archaeology and Material Culture of the Bible

Ann E. Killebrew
The Pennsylvania State University

As a field archaeologist and academic whose research is focused on second and first millennia B.C.E. Canaan and Israel, one of my greatest challenges as an educator has been the integration of archaeology and Bible into our understanding of both the past and contemporary worlds. Most scholars have traditionally considered archaeology as a subdiscipline of biblical studies, usually closely aligned with a more historical approach to the study and analysis of the biblical texts. From my archaeological perspective, I see the relationship somewhat differently: that the archaeology of biblical lands is an autonomous discipline (albeit an interrelated discipline) with spheres of interest that overlap with the various subfields of biblical studies and other disciplines such as history, anthropology, theology, Near Eastern studies, religious studies, and modern Middle East studies. The Bible and related texts constitute only one of many the essentials in our archaeological material-culture tool kit that we use in our reconstruction of the past and its significance to us today.

Much of the difficulty in successfully integrating the fields of archaeology and biblical studies lies in the nature of the evidence. Archaeology is the study of humanity's past and its interpretation based on a stratified but incomplete and complex material-culture record. The Bible is also a multilayered historical, literary, political, theological, and spiritual document comprised of "stratified" texts that were composed during different periods of time. Up until the just several decades ago, the connection between artifact and text seemed fairly straightforward. Archaeology was an additional tool to be utilized in the illustration and historical reconstruction of the biblical world.[1] However, during the past thirty plus years, the relationship

---

[1] For a summary of the historical approach to the Bible, see, e.g., J. Maxwell Miller, "Reading the Bible Historically: The Historian's Approach," in *To Each Its Own Meaning: An*

between biblical studies and the archaeology of biblical lands has become less clear-cut and increasingly ambiguous. Much of the reason for the ambiguity is the result of the development of new directions in biblical studies. These new directions include approaches to the Bible that are ahistorical, literary, or postmodern in nature.[2] In many of these subfields of biblical studies, archaeology is seen as irrelevant and useful only in relation to more traditional and historically based approaches to the text. Corresponding to this trend and in response to the ever-increasing level of expertise required to adequately master the massive amounts of incoming data and material culture, archaeology reached maturity and achieved independence, while at the same time acknowledging its biblical roots. In my discussion of the integration of text and artifact, I address three main issues regarding the role of archaeology in biblical studies and academic curricula.

1. I define "biblical archaeology" and its integration in academic programs during the 1920s–1960s.
2. I trace the development of biblical archaeology into a separate, professional discipline and examine its relevance to biblical studies during the 1970s through the present at institutes of higher learning.
3. I address the future of a broader-based approach to biblical archaeology and its potential role in educational curricula, especially its integration in the fields of biblical studies and other liberal arts disciplines.

Through the discussion of these three topics in this essay, I explore how the earthly world that produced the biblical texts still has a significant role to play, not only in the historical-critical approach to the Bible, but in broader fields of the ancient Near East, anthropology, and the general curricula of institutes of higher learning.

"BIBLICAL ARCHAEOLOGY" IN ACADEMIA AND CURRICULA:
THE ALBRIGHTIAN PERIOD

Over the past two centuries, archaeology of the lands associated with the Bible has captured the imagination and support of foreign and local

---

Introduction to Biblical Criticisms and Their Application (ed. S. L. McKenzie and S. R. Haynes; rev. and exp. ed.; Louisville: Westminster John Knox, 1999), 17–34.

[2] For general overviews of the new developments in biblical studies and criticism, see, e.g., Leo G. Perdue, *The Collapse of History: Reconstructing Old Testament Theology* (Minneapolis: Fortress, 1994); Steven L. McKenzie and Stephen R. Haynes, eds., *To Each Its Own Meaning: An Introduction to Biblical Criticisms and Their Application* (rev. and exp. ed.; Louisville: Westminster John Knox, 1999).

governments, faith-based organizations, academic institutions, and private philanthropists. It is a pursuit that has attracted a large and diverse audience of adventurers, scholars, theologians, and collectors, and it has always held a special appeal to the public. Many books and articles are devoted to the history of archaeological exploration in the modern Middle East and its development into a scholarly discipline usually termed "biblical archaeology."[3] Equally numerous publications discuss and deconstruct "biblical archaeology" and its contemporary political implications.[4]

During the first half of the twentieth century, American archaeological activities in the modern Middle East were conducted under the banner of "biblical archaeology" as envisioned by Albright[5] and further developed in academic circles by more than a few of his students, most notably

---

[3] For a classic work dealing with the early years of archaeological exploration in the "Holy Land," see Neil Asher Silberman, *Digging for God and Country: Exploration, Archeology, and the Secret Struggle for the Holy Land, 1799–1917* (New York: Knopf, 1982). For a general history of archaeological exploration in biblical lands, see Peter R. S. Moorey, *A Century of Biblical Archaeology* (Louisville: Westminster John Knox, 1991); for a review of American archaeological activity in the Middle East, see Philip J. King, *American Archaeology in the Mideast: A History of the American Schools of Oriental Research* (Philadelphia: American Schools of Oriental Research, 1983).

[4] See, e.g., Neil Asher Silberman, *Between Past and Present: Archaeology, Ideology, and Nationalism in the Modern Middle East* (New York: Holt, 1989); Amy Dockser Marcus, *The View From Nebo: How Archaeology Is Rewriting the Bible and Reshaping the Middle East* (New York: Little, Brown & Company, 2000); Nadia Abu El-Haj, *Facts on the Ground: Archaeological Practice and Territorial Self-Fashioning in Israeli Society* (Chicago: University of Chicago Press, 2001).

[5] In any discussion of "biblical archaeology" and the relationship between text and artifact, the starting point must be the legendary William F. Albright, "orientalist" and archaeologist. Under his effective guidance and inspiration, biblical archaeology became an integral element of mainstream academic curricula and scholarly attempts to write a history of ancient Israel based on the Bible and related texts. Although Albright viewed archaeological fieldwork as a scientific and empirical endeavor, his interpretation of the evidence and message appealed especially to evangelical communities, seminaries, and theologians, in addition to more traditional biblical students and scholars. There are numerous articles and books that document Albright's background, career, scholarly work, and legacy; see, e.g., Leona Glidden Running and David Noel Freedman, *William Foxwell Albright: A Twentieth-Century Genius* (New York: Two Continents, 1975); Gus W. Van Beek, ed., *The Scholarship of William Foxwell Albright: An Appraisal* (HSS 33; "Papers Delivered at the Symposium 'Homage to William Foxwell Albright,' The American Friends of the Israel Exploration Society, Rockville, Maryland, 1984; Atlanta: Scholars Press, 1989); a series of articles that appear in the *Biblical Archaeologist* 56 (1993): Jack M. Sasson, "Albright As an Orientalist," 3–7; Neil A. Silberman, "Visions of the Future: Albright in Jerusalem, 1919–1929," 8–16; William W. Hallo, "Albright and the Gods of Mesopotamia," 18–24; William G. Dever, "What Remains of the House that Albright Built?" 25–35; Burke O. Long, "Mythic Trope in the Autobiography of William Foxwell Albright," 36–45; idem, *Planting and Reaping Albright: Politics, Ideology, and Interpreting the Bible* (University Park: Pennsylvania State University Press, 1997).

G. Ernest Wright.[6] "Biblical archaeology" as advocated by Albright and Wright was a subfield of biblical studies in the United States that reached its greatest intellectual impact in the early to mid-twentieth century. The role of archaeology in biblical research as defined by Albright was "the systematic analysis or synthesis of any phase of biblical scholarship which can be clarified by archaeological discovery."[7] Wright further refined Albright's definition of biblical archaeology as

> a special "armchair" variety of general archaeology. The biblical archaeologist may or may not be an excavator himself, but he studies the discoveries of the excavations in order·to glean from them every fact that throws a direct, indirect or even diffused light upon the Bible.... His central and absorbing interest is the understanding and exposition of the Scriptures."[8]

The Albrightian School's enthusiastic embrace of biblical archaeology was due in no small measure to both a personal and professional reaction against higher criticism, especially Wellhausen's Documentary Hypothesis and Gunkel's form criticism.[9] For Albright and many of his followers, archaeology was a scientifically based discipline that could provide an independent and neutral standard by which to verify the historicity of the biblical texts and to confront higher criticism's skepticism regarding a literal reading of the Bible as history.[10] These conflicting historical approaches to

---

[6] G. Ernest Wright can be considered the true architect of "biblical archaeology" in its American context. He is defined by his critical Protestant perspective to biblical and theological studies combined with a strong interest in the potential of hard and social sciences to conclusively resolve historically based biblical questions. He served as a mentor to two generations of archaeologists and biblical students, many of whom are still active in academic institutions today. Numerous articles have been written about Wright and his contribution to biblical archaeology. See, e.g., William G. Dever, "Biblical Theology and Biblical Archaeology: An Appreciation of G. Ernest Wright," *HTR* 73 (1980): 1–15; Philip J. King, "The Influence of G. Ernest Wright on the Archaeology of Palestine," in *Archaeology and Biblical Interpretation: Essays in Memory of D. Glenn Rose* (ed. L. G. Perdue, L. E. Toombs, and G. L. Johnson; Atlanta: John Knox, 1987), 15–30.

[7] William F. Albright, "The Impact of Archaeology on Biblical Research–1966," in *New Directions in Biblical Archaeology* (ed. D. N. Freedman and J. C. Greenfield; Garden City, N.Y.: Doubleday, 1971), 4.

[8] G. Ernest Wright, *Biblical Archaeology* (rev. ed.; Philadelphia: Westminster, 1962), 17.

[9] For a discussion of the significance of archaeology in Albright's conception of a historically based approach to biblical studies as an answer to Wellhausen's "higher criticism," see, e.g., Moorey, *A Century of Biblical Archaeology*, 54–84.

[10] For an insightful and affectionate evaluation of Albright, see Peter Machinist, "William Foxwell Albright: The Man and His Work," in *The Study of the Ancient Near East in the Twenty-First Century: The William Foxwell Albright Centennial Conference* (ed. J. S. Cooper and Glenn M. Schwartz; Winona Lake, Ind.: Eisenbrauns, 1996), 385–403, esp. 394–400. See also Long, "Mythic Trope" and idem, *Planting and Reaping Albright*, esp. 111–48.

the biblical texts during the first half of the twentieth century were at times similar to the debates, often highly polemical in nature, between the "minimalists" and "maximalists" of today.[11]

The period between the two world wars through the mid-twentieth century is considered to represent the "golden age" of biblical archaeology and Albright's historically based vision of biblical studies. Fifty-seven students completed their doctoral studies under the tutelage of Albright, who held the W. W. Spence Chair in Semitic Languages at the John Hopkins University from 1929–58. During these years, the graduate studies curriculum in Oriental Seminar included Akkadian, Egyptian, Ugaritic, Ethiopic, advanced Hebrew, and seminars in the biblical texts. Several part-time professors taught comparative Semitic grammar, Hebrew grammar, Arabic, and Judaica. As summarized by Van Beek in his short biography of Albright, the graduate program's "core curriculum indoctrinated students in all fields of study, and engendered a respect for the contribution of each field; a philologian understood the importance of archaeology, and an archaeologist understood the basic structure and relationships of languages."[12] Graduate students participated in four three-year courses: Hebrew grammar, comparative Semitic grammar, ancient Near Eastern history, and archaeology of the ancient Near East (including Egypt, Mesopotamia, and the Levant). Biblical archaeology was studied at the graduate level as part of an academically oriented program designed to produce theologians and scholars. Written examinations were given upon completion of the entire course of study, followed by the dissertation, where a specialization was pursued.[13] Albright's "universalist" approach to the Bible and the ancient Near East in general and its later impact on educational curricula in the United States cannot be underestimated and, as we will discuss below, is still evident today.

None of Albright's books can be considered a "textbook" per se of biblical archaeology. Albright's publications reflect his more philosophical and historical integration of archaeology into larger biblical themes. In *The Archaeology of Palestine and the Bible*,[14] he divides his treatment of the

---

[11] For a recent survey and summary of the debate, the issues involved, and relevant bibliography, see William G. Dever, *What Did the Biblical Writers Know and When Did They Know It? What Archaeology Can Tell Us about the Reality of Ancient Israel* (Grand Rapids: Eerdmans, 2001).

[12] Gus W. Van Beek, "William Foxwell Albright: A Short Biography," in Van Beek, *The Scholarship of William Foxwell Albright*, 15.

[13] Van Beek, "William Foxwell Albright," 14–15; for a description of Albright as professor, see Running and Freedman, William Foxwell Albright, 194–220.

[14] William Foxwell Albright, *The Archaeology of Palestine and the Bible* (New York: Revell, 1932).

topic into three parts. In the first section Albright recounts the discovery of ancient Palestine, where he places the emphasis on development of methods rather than results. In the second chapter, he presents a popularized account of his excavations at Tell Beit Mirsim. His third chapter summarizes the Bible in light of archaeology, specifically, the age of the patriarchs, the law of Moses, and the age of the exile and restoration. Today most scholars would agree that archaeology is ill-equipped as a discipline to deal with such nonmaterial culture–based dilemmas and has very little to contribute to the discussion.

From Stone Age to Christianity is considered by many to be Albright's most important and influential book. In it he surveys the state of the discipline and integrates archaeological discoveries in the ancient Near East with the biblical texts, covering a range from the "stone age" through Roman (New Testament) times. The book was reprinted numerous times, and Albright confidently proclaims in his 1957 edition:

> Turning to Israel, I defend the substantial historicity of patriarchal tradition, without any appreciable change in my point of view, and insist, just as in 1940–46, on the primacy of oral tradition over written literature. I have not surrendered a single position with regard to early Israelite monotheism but, on the contrary, consider the Mosaic tradition as even more reliable than I did then. . . . I recognize that the Covenant is not only fully as ancient as I had thought, but was much more pervasive in its effect on the religious and political life of Israel."[15]

Again, archaeological discoveries during the last thirty years have seriously challenged these Albrightian views, and few scholars would support such statements today.

More than any other of Albright's students Wright, advanced his teacher's agenda of biblical archaeology with a focus on "biblical theology." From 1939 to 1959 he taught Hebrew Bible at McCormick Seminary in Chicago, culminating in his 1957 landmark book *Biblical Archaeology*.[16] This publication presented archaeology as a resource for biblical history and religion. It is the best example of the utilization of archaeology in the service of social history and to illustrate the historicity of the biblical texts. Wright's book served as a textbook of the period for two decades, reflecting his integration of text and artifact in his courses as well as a publication with a broad popular appeal.

---

[15] William F. Albright, *From Stone Age to Christianity: Monotheism and the Historical Process* (Garden City, N.Y.: Doubleday, 1957), 2.

[16] Wright, *Biblical Archaeology*. See also the condensed version: G. Ernest Wright, *Biblical Archaeology* (abridged ed.; Philadelphia: Westminster: 1960).

In 1959 Wright accepted the Parkman Chair of Divinity at Harvard University Divinity School, where he mentored a new generation of biblical archaeologists in addition to a host of biblical specialists. Wright's greatest contribution to archaeology during his tenure at Harvard Divinity School was the practical field training of a third generation of American biblical archaeologists at Shechem and later Gezer and Idalion. The development of the "archaeological field school" as part of the educational program for students was the first step in the creation of a professional approach to archaeology. Philip King summarized the impact of the field school at Shechem under Wright's directorship as being "responsible directly or indirectly for establishing a number of other excavations such as Gezer, Taanach, Ai, Tell el-Hesi, Heshbon, Shema, and Caesarea. The directors and several staff members of these digs were trained at Shechem, and in all cases Wright continued to confer with the core staff of these satellite projects."[17] Many of Wright's students entered academic teaching fields at seminaries, colleges, and universities during the 1960s and 1970s, with a significant number still teaching today. Although, as will be discussed below, their approaches to archaeology at times diverged from those of the "Albrightian School," they were still largely operating on an "essentialist" or "super-dogmatist" model."[18]

The American attitude to the archaeology of Palestine was not unique. In Europe, biblical archaeology was also generally part of biblical studies but usually was based in schools of theology. As with early American archaeological activities in Palestine, French archaeological activities in the Holy Land were closely associated with Christian institutions. The first archaeological school in Palestine, the École Biblique, was founded by the Dominican Fathers in 1890. Its curricula included the study of the geology, ancient history, oriental languages, archaeology, epigraphy, and cultures of the Holy Land and ancient Near East. The École Biblique dominated French archaeological exploration in the region and conducted several significant excavations at Tell el Far'ah (N), throughout Jerusalem, and most notably at Qumran. Other Catholic institutions in Jerusalem also conducted archaeological excavations and established educational programs in biblical studies. One of the most notable is the Pontifical Biblical Institute of Jerusalem, closely affiliated with the Vatican. The influence of these institutions continues until today with the addition of the government-supported and nonsectarian

---

[17] King, "The Influence of G. Ernest Wright," 21.

[18] For overviews and appraisals of G. Ernest Wright's life and career, see note 6 above and Edward F. Campbell, "Wright, George Ernest," *OEANE* 5:350–52 and bibliography there.

"French Mission" (Centre national recherche scientifique [CNRS]) to Israel in 1950.[19]

The twentieth century started off on an optimistic note for German biblical scholarship with the establishment of the German Institute for the Archaeology of the Holy Land in 1900, the same year that the American School in Jerusalem was founded. Although German academics have traditionally played a major role in biblical studies, their archaeological activities in the Holy Land suffered a serious setback due to the political situation during World Wars I and II that continued well into the mid-twentieth century. In spite of the decline in its archaeological field activities, biblical archaeology remained part of biblical studies—a tradition that was and continues to be stronger than the American model. Throughout the twentieth century, German academic curricula clearly define archaeology as part of biblical studies. Programs in biblical archaeology in German-speaking countries academically belong to Protestant or Roman Catholic theology departments until today, although Syro-Palestinian archaeology occasionally is taught in Near Eastern studies departments as part of the degree curriculum. Historically, biblical archaeology was closely related to church-sponsored organizations and seen as a subfield of Old Testament and New Testament exegesis. In Germany, biblical archaeologists are still defined as biblical historians or theologians who approach material-culture studies in light of their relevance to the Bible.[20]

The British model differed significantly from the American, French, and German experience during the period from the end of World War I until the 1967 Six Day War. Noteworthy is the key role British archaeologists played during the British Mandate period until 1948. Archaeology in Palestine developed as a separate discipline in British academic circles and subsequently was less closely intertwined with biblical studies. The British Mandate period ushered in the golden age of British archaeology in Palestine, coinciding with the establishment of a British School of Archaeology in 1919 in Jerusalem. During this period, several leading British archaeologists of this generation, including John Garstang, W. J. Phythian-Adams, and G. Lankester Harding, served as directors of the Palestine Department of Antiquities under British administration. A number of archaeologists who trained under Flinders Petrie, including James L. Starkey and Olga Tufnell, also played significant roles in the development of archaeology between the two

---

[19] Pierre Benoit, "French Archaeologists," in *Benchmarks in Time and Culture: An Introduction to Palestinian Archaeology Dedicated to Joseph A. Callaway* (ed. J. F. Drinkard Jr., G. L. Matthingly, and J. M. Miller; SBLABS 1; Atlanta: Scholars Press, 1988), 63–86.

[20] Manfred Weippert and Helga Weippert, "German Archaeologists," in Drinkard, Matthingly, and Miller, *Benchmarks in Time and Culture,* 87–108.

world wars. Starkey's and Tufnell's excavation work at Lachish and the subsequent site reports are still considered a standard today.[21]

Katheleen M. Kenyon was the most influential British archaeologist whose work changed the direction of archaeology in Israel, Jordan, and Palestine as it developed academically and professionally during the 1960s and later.[22] An accomplished field archaeologist, her first practical experience was under the guidance of the legendary British archaeologist Mortimer Wheeler. She later excavated several major sites in Palestine, including Samaria, Jericho, and Jerusalem. In the 1930s, Wheeler's protégé was involved in the administration of the newly established Institute of Archaeology at University of London. This institute, founded by Wheeler in 1934, set the tone for the British approach to archaeology in the ancient Near East as a discipline separate from biblical studies.

After World War II, Kenyon served as honorary director of the British School of Archaeology in Jerusalem between 1951 and 1966, during which time she conducted excavations at Jericho and Jerusalem. These two sites later formed her core interpretation of the archaeology of Palestine during biblical periods. Archaeology of the Holy Land, as coined by Kenyon, was one of the topics included in the curriculum at the Institute of Archaeology, University of London. Kenyon's book, *Archaeology in the Holy Land,* first published in 1960, reflected this more professional attitude to archaeological studies.[23] However, Kenyon also assumed an essential reality and a "positivist" view with regard to the ability of a scientific archaeology to define and reconstruct a history of ancient Israel. Her book was noteworthy for its focus on material-culture studies and its detailed technical drawings, architectural plans, and descriptions of pottery and other artifacts.[24] It is the model for numerous other textbooks in the archaeology of Israel, Palestine, and Jordan that were to follow in the 1970s through the 1990s.

Albright's influence on local archaeologists working in Palestine and his impact on Israeli archaeology are well documented. During Albright's

---

[21] For a summary of British archaeological activities in Palestine, Jordan, and Israel, see Graham I. Davies, "British Archaeologists," in Drinkard, Matthingly, and Miller, *Benchmarks in Time and Culture,* 37–62.

[22] Peter R. S. Moorey, "Kathleen Kenyon and Palestinian Archaeology," *PEQ* 111 (1979): 3–10; A. D. Tushingham, "Kenyon, Kathleen Mary," *OEANE* 3:279–80; see bibliography there for a summary of Kenyon's contributions.

[23] London: Benn, 1960.

[24] A second, largely ignored, textbook by Dimitri C. Baramki (*The Art and Architecture of Ancient Palestine: A Survey of the Archaeology of Palestine from Earliest Times to the Ottoman Conquest* [Beirut: Palestine Liberation Organization Research Center, 1969]) also approaches the archaeology of Palestine from a professional archaeologist's perspective. His book is innovative in its approach, discussing the Palaeolithic through Islamic periods. It is the only archaeological book to this day that deals with such a broad chronological scope.

term as director of the American School of Oriental Research in Jerusalem in the 1920s, Eleazar L. Sukenik, a young scholar and one of the early Jewish archaeologists in Palestine, was closely associated with the American School and developed a close friendship with Albright. In 1927 he was appointed "archaeologist" on the faculty of the newly established Hebrew University of Jerusalem and later founded its Institute of Archaeology.[25] However, it was Sukenik's son, Yigael Yadin, who was most instrumental in developing a uniquely Israeli version of "biblical archaeology."[26] Yadin was the first Israeli archaeologist to mount large-scale excavations on a biblical tel, Hazor, from 1955 to 1958. Hazor proved to be the training grounds for an entire generation of archaeologists, similar to the impact of Shechem and later Gezer on American biblical archaeology. However, Israeli biblical archaeology differed significantly from the Albrightian American version. In Israel, archaeology not only deserved its own department but also merited its own research institute. Yadin and the following generations of archaeologists defined the *biblical* in biblical archaeology as a chronological term referring to the periods broadly related to the Bible (Early Bronze through Iron Ages, ca. 3000–sixth century B.C.E.). Emotional, nationalist, and, to a lesser degree, religious ideologies that reinforced Jewish claims to the land of Israel distinguished the Israeli version of biblical archaeology from the American and European counterparts. As expressed by Israeli archaeologist Amihai Mazar, there was and remains a conscious or "probably subconscious motivation to relate modern Israeli culture to its ancient roots."[27] Yadin was one of the last of the traditional biblical archaeologists, who as late as 1984 and shortly before his death promoted an approach to "biblical archaeology" that followed closely in Albright's footsteps.[28]

However, what is less noted in the literature is that archaeology in Israeli university curricula was much closer to the British example. The Israeli academic approach created departments or institutes of archaeology at the major Israeli universities that teach archaeology as the focal point, with cross-disciplinary connections to biblical, Near Eastern, Egyptological, and classical studies. From the days of Yadin until the present, the curriculum in these departments has changed little in its general approach to

---

[25] For a short biography of Sukenik, see Neil A. Silberman, *A Prophet from amongst You: The Life of Yigael Yadin: Soldier, Scholar, and Mythmaker of Modern Israel* (New York: Addison-Wesley, 1993), 7–23.

[26] For a detailed biography of Yigael Yadin, see ibid.

[27] Amihai Mazar, "Israeli Archaeologists," in Drinkard, Matthingly, and Miller, *Benchmarks in Time and Culture,* 127.

[28] See, e.g., Yigael Yadin, "Biblical Archaeology Today: The Archaeological Aspect," in *Biblical Archaeology Today: Proceedings of the International Congress on Biblical Archaeology, Jerusalem, April 1984* (ed. J. Amitai; Jerusalem: Israel Exploration Society, 1985), 21–27.

educating future archaeologists. In addition to material-culture studies, students are encouraged to enroll in courses in archaeometry, geology, epigraphy, Assyriology, Egyptology, geography, and Bible. With the completion of the undergraduate degree, a student is considered a trained archaeologist. Graduate programs are designed to produce scholars who are fully trained professional archaeologists and academics. In Israel, the terms *biblical archaeology, Syro-Palestinian archaeology, archaeology of the Levant, archaeology of the land of Israel, archaeology of the land of the Bible,* and *archaeology of the Holy Land* are basically interchangeable, lacking the American ideological connotations.[29]

By the 1970s, Albright's vision of biblical archaeology was under fire in the United States, in part due to more professional approaches to field archaeology that demanded practitioners to devote full-time energies to mastering the exponentially multiplying areas of expertise and data. The biblical and theological communities became increasingly disillusioned with archaeology as the "savior" of a noncritical historical reconstruction focused on the biblical account. At the same time, archaeology in Israel witnessed the rising influence of local, professionally trained Israeli archaeologists who began to dominate the field. This was best reflected in the peculiarly American debate regarding the pros and cons of "biblical archaeology" versus Syro-Palestinian archaeology.[30]

What, then, is "biblical archaeology"? It encompasses a wide range of definitions depending on its context. For American, French, and German scholars, it has traditionally been part of biblical studies, while for most Israeli and British academics it has been treated as a related but distinct discipline from biblical studies. In this essay, following the Israeli definition, I use the term *biblical archaeology* in its broadest meaning that encompasses various approaches to the material culture of the land of

---

[29] For a further discussion of these terms and biblical archaeology in Israel, see Ephraim Stern, "The Bible and Israeli Archaeology," in Perdue, Toombs, and Johnson, *Archaeology and Biblical Interpretation,* 31–40.

[30] There have been numerous articles written on this topic, most notably by William G. Dever. He proposed the term *Syro-Palestinian archaeology* as the preferred term to indicate a professional version of biblical archaeology. See, e.g., William G. Dever, "Retrospects and Prospects in Biblical and Syro-Palestinian Archeology," *BA* 45 (1982): 103–7; idem, "Syro-Palestinian and Biblical Archaeology," in *The Hebrew Bible and Its Modern Interpreters* (ed. D. A. Knight and G. M. Tucker; Chico, Calif.: Scholars Press, 1985), 31–74; idem, "Biblical Archaeology: Death and Rebirth?" *in Biblical Archaeology Today, 1990: Proceedings of the Second International Congress on Biblical Archaeology, Jerusalem, June–July 1990* (ed. A. Biran and J. Aviram; Jerusalem: Israel Exploration Society and the Israel Academy of Sciences and Humanities, 1993), 706–22; idem, "Biblical Archaeology," *OEANE* 1:315–19 and bibliography there. For additional perspectives, see Lawrence E. Toombs, "The Development of Palestinian Archeology As a Discipline," *BA* 45 (1982): 89–91.

Israel within its biblical and Near Eastern context and the belief that archaeology can write a history of ancient Israel. Chronologically, it includes the archaeology of the land of the Bible during periods of time that are directly or indirectly related to the Hebrew Bible (Early Bronze through Iron Ages; ca. 3000–sixth century B.C.E.). I define Syro-Palestinian archaeology as the archaeology of Syria, Israel, Jordan, and Palestine from the Paleolithic through the Ottoman periods, thus also including biblical archaeology.[31]

"SYRO-PALESTINIAN ARCHAEOLOGY" AND ITS IMPACT ON BIBLICAL STUDIES AND CURRICULA

Parallel to developments and new challenges facing biblical studies, a similar intellectual and disciplinary split occurred in the archaeological world in the 1960s and 1970s. During the first half of the twentieth century, archaeology was often defined as the "handmaiden of history" or what is sometimes referred to as "culture history" (i.e., the mapping of cultures and cultural influences as a tool in reconstructing the past). As archaeology became more closely affiliated with anthropology, new methods and theories challenged previous culture-history approaches. These include "New Archaeology" (or processual archaeology in its mature stage) and, more recently, postprocessual archaeology. Somewhat belatedly these developments influenced biblical archaeology. The impact of these new ideas on biblical archaeology was best exemplified in Dever's term "Syro-Palestinian" archaeology as part of his efforts to promote a more systematic and scientific professional "biblical archaeology" that encouraged closer ties to the larger world of an anthropologically based archaeology.[32] However, these attempts to integrate biblical archaeology into anthropological studies have not significantly changed how biblical archaeology was and is being taught in the United States. In fact, as a result of attempts to redefine Albrightian biblical archaeology, it was often

---

[31] I consider the term *Syro-Palestinian archaeology* to be interchangeable with the terms *archaeology of the land of the Bible, archaeology of the Holy Land,* and *archaeology of the Levant.* It is my opinion that archaeology of the Levant is probably the most neutral and preferred designation of the archaeology of the land of Israel and its neighboring countries; however, it is probably a term that will generate little widespread student or public interest.

[32] For his most recent comments, see William G. Dever, "Impact of the 'New Archaeology,'" in Drinkard, Matthingly, and Miller, *Benchmarks in Time and Culture,* 337–52; idem, "Syro-Palestinian and Biblical Archaeology," in Knight and Tucker, *The Hebrew Bible and Its Modern Interpreters,* 31–74; idem, "Biblical Archaeology," 1:315–19 and bibliography there. See also Lawrence E. Toombs, "A Perspective on the New Archaeology," in Perdue, Toombs, and Johnson, *Archaeology and Biblical Interpretation,* 41–52.

considered a less essential element of course curricula in some seminaries, colleges, and universities. This gradual parting of the ways between text and artifact in the later decades of the twentieth century is perhaps best represented symbolically by the breakaway of the American Schools of Oriental Research from the Society of Biblical Literature and American Academy of Religion's annual meetings in 1997, resulting in two separate, back-to-back conferences each November.

When archaeology was retained on the course listings, biblical archaeology generally remained intellectually in Near Eastern, biblical, ancient history, theology, religion, or Judaic studies programs or departments. Biblical archaeology seldom entered mainstream programs such as anthropology or archaeology departments that are generally responsible for the training of professional archaeologists. Thus in the American context, although many courses in biblical archaeology are more concerned with material culture and archaeology proper (rather than simply as a tool to illustrate and illuminate biblical history as conceived by Albright and Wright), it is still considered to be part of a larger world of culture history rather than a topic or subfield in archaeology or anthropology departments. Syro-Palestinian archaeology in an academic curriculum taught as a competitive professional field, as envisioned by Dever and as it appears in curricula at most Israeli universities, has not transpired in the American context. When compared to the highly specialized Israeli approach to the professional training of archaeology students, where each department of archaeology includes ten to fifteen faculty members who are all archaeologists, it is understandable that this degree of concentrated expertise is simply not possible in American seminaries, colleges, and universities.

In spite of the fact that biblical archaeology remains situated in Near Eastern, Judaic, or biblical studies, over the past thirty years the course syllabus has changed. This is best illustrated by the many textbooks devoted to biblical archaeology that have appeared in the post-Wright period. Several of these textbooks follow the approach first explored by Kenyon in her *Archaeology in the Holy Land,* where archaeology is the focus and the Bible illustrates the historical setting for archaeological discoveries. In other textbooks archaeology is integrated into a historical-geographic or biblical context. One textbook incorporates an anthropological perspective.

Yohanan Aharoni, founder of the Institute of Archaeology at Tel Aviv University in 1969 and Yadin's nemesis during the 1960s and 1970s, authored two textbooks that became standards during the 1970s and 1980s. His first, *The Land of the Bible,* initially published in 1967,[33] is a masterpiece

---

[33] Yohanan Aharoni, *The Land of the Bible A Historical Geography* (trans. A. F. Rainey; London: Burns & Oates, 1967).

in its integration of historical geography, Bible, and archaeology and is still occasionally used in classrooms today. His broad geographical approach to biblical archaeology sets the stage for the establishment of the "Tel Aviv School" that pioneered the potential of systematic regional archaeological survey and that became the hallmark of Aharoni and several generations of his students. Aharoni's second book, *The Archaeology of the Land of Israel,* was a standard in numerous biblical archaeology classes in the 1980s.[34] Although Miriam Aharoni, writing in the preface, compares it to Albright's *The Archaeology of Palestine,* I contend it is more similar in structure and archaeological focus to Kenyon's *Archaeology of the Holy Land,* though it offers different interpretations of the archaeological evidence.

During the 1990s several prominent archaeologists published updated versions of Kenyon's classic archaeology textbook that focused on the material culture from the Neolithic through the Iron Ages. Amihai Mazar's *Archaeology of the Land of the Bible: 10,000–586 B.C.E.* first appeared in 1990 and immediately became the favored textbook for many courses in biblical archaeology. Mazar describes the purpose of his book and its significance for biblical history as follows: "Although this book is written as a straightforward introduction to the archaeology of Palestine, wherever possible I discuss the implications of the discoveries for biblical history. Hopefully this work will serve to narrow the ever growing fissure between archaeologists and other scholars of disciplines relating to biblical studies."[35]

Two years later Amnon Ben-Tor, a colleague of Mazar's at the Hebrew University of Jerusalem, published his edited textbook, *The Archaeology of Ancient Israel.* This book contains nine chapters authored by some of the most prominent Israeli archaeologists in the field. It is the English version of a Hebrew textbook prepared for an introductory archaeology course, "The Archaeology of the Land of Israel in Biblical Times," offered at the Open University of Israel.[36] Although these two books differ in details, both share a general material-culture and archaeological perspective. For introductory archaeology courses in Israel that tend to concentrate on material-culture studies, both of these books are ideally suited for the task. However, in an American context where lower and midlevel courses in archaeology are broader in focus and are geared to a more general student

---

[34] Yohanan Aharoni, *The Archaeology of the Land of Israel from the Prehistoric Beginnings to the End of the First Temple Period* (trans. A. F. Rainey; Philadelphia: Westminster, 1982).

[35] Amihai Mazar, *Archaeology of the Land of the Bible: 10,000–586 B.C.E.* (ABRL; New York: Doubleday, 1990), xvi.

[36] Amnon Ben-Tor, ed., *The Archaeology of Ancient Israel* (trans. R. Greenberg; New Haven: Yale University Press; Tel Aviv: Open University of Israel, 1992).

enrollment, all of the books discussed above tend to be overly technical for the average nonmajor undergraduate.

In 1992 Trinity Press International published one of the few textbooks written by an American biblical archaeologist. This slim and highly readable volume by Walter E. Rast, titled *Through the Ages in Palestinian Archaeology,* lacks the technical detail of the two above-mentioned books but covers a longer chronological range (prehistoric through the Islamic periods).[37] Its style and general approach are appropriate for more general undergraduate survey courses in biblical archaeology that deal with an overview of prehistoric through Islamic periods of time. A second recently published general handbook, *Doing Archaeology in the Land of the Bible* by John D. Currid, introduces the basic fundamentals of archaeology to novice students, the largest potential student audience at most universities that include biblical archaeology in their course listings.[38]

In Thomas E. Levy's edited interdisciplinary textbook, *The Archaeology of Society in the Holy Land,* the authors undertake the daunting task of linking ethnohistory, anthropology, and archaeology in each of its thirty-two chapters. This is undoubtedly the most ambitious of all the textbooks and includes sections dealing with approaches to the past, covering the Paleolithic through the end of the Ottoman period.[39] It is the most anthropologically oriented of all the published volumes and is best suited for more advanced-level Syro-Palestinian courses based in anthropology departments.

Other textbooks that have appeared during the past ten years are directed to a more traditionally defined and biblically oriented archaeology. One textbook representing this genre, targeting a more evangelical approach to biblical archaeology, is Alfred J. Hoerth's *Archaeology and the Old Testament.* Hoerth, the former director of archaeology at Wheaton College, describes the relationship between archaeology and the Bible as follows: "The most important contributions of archaeology to biblical studies are the various ways it illuminates the cultural and historical setting of the Bible; adds to our knowledge of the people, places, things, and events in the Bible; and aids in translation and exegesis of biblical passages."[40] Hoerth's well-illustrated book follows in the footsteps

---

[37] Walter E. Rast, *Through the Ages in Palestinian Archaeology: An Introductory Handbook* (Philadelphia: Trinity Press International, 1992).

[38] John D. Currid, *Doing Archaeology in the Land of the Bible: A Basic Guide* (Grand Rapids: Baker, 1999).

[39] Thomas E. Levy, ed., *The Archaeology of Society in the Holy Land* (New York: Facts on File, 1995).

[40] Alfred J. Hoerth, *Archaeology and the Old Testament* (Grand Rapids: Baker, 1998), front flap.

of Wright and can be considered as an updated version of his *Biblical Archaeology.*

One of the most recent textbooks to integrate archaeology with the Hebrew Bible and the New Testament is *The Oxford History of the Biblical World,* edited by Michael D. Coogan.[41] This book, although a more traditional approach to archaeology as part of a larger world of biblical studies, is unique in its reconstruction of a social and political history of the biblical world within its larger ancient Near East context. It is a scholarly and well-written tome that is suitable to undergraduate courses in Near Eastern or biblical studies departments that integrate archaeology with biblical and Near Eastern texts, with a focus on the textual evidence.

The last example of the variety of publications that could be used as a textbook is Israel Finkelstein and Neil Silberman's highly popular and best-selling *The Bible Unearthed.*[42] Although written for a popular audience and somewhat controversial in its presentation, its entertaining style and readable overview of the current issues and problems in biblical archaeology make it a popular textbook in general nonspecialist introductory courses. It can be used as basic background reading to more specific and detailed assignments and discussions or as a supplement to several of the more conventional textbooks.

This brief overview of the variety of textbooks demonstrates biblical archaeology's diversity and cross-disciplinary appeal in educational contexts. Still lacking is a basic textbook that gives equal time and attention to text and artifact in an academic but readable and interesting format. The need for such a textbook is doubtless the main challenge facing us as educators and scholars in the twenty-first century.

THE FUTURE OF BIBLICAL ARCHAEOLOGY IN EDUCATIONAL CURRICULA: BETWEEN HEAVEN AND EARTH

The redefinition and subsequent fragmentation of biblical archaeology described above closely parallels developments in biblical studies. In an insightful article entitled "On Listening to the Text—and the Artifacts," William G. Dever convincingly proposes that the history of scholarly interpretation of both archaeology and the Bible shares a similar and parallel

---

[41] Michael D. Coogan, ed., *The Oxford History of the Biblical World* (New York: Oxford University Press, 1998).

[42] Israel Finkelstein and Neil Asher Silberman, *The Bible Unearthed: Archaeology's New Vision of Ancient Israel and The Origin of Its Sacred Texts* (New York: Free Press, 2001).

intellectual development.[43] As Dever maintains in this article, and as I have long argued in archaeology courses tailored for students of Bible, material culture should also be considered a "language" with a vocabulary and grammar that can be translated and read using both a historical or literary approach in much the same way as biblical Hebrew or any other language. Rather than mourn the "death" of a narrowly defined "biblical archaeology" dominated and controlled by a handful of prominent biblical scholars, we should rejoice in the "new and expanded" version of archaeology with its broader definition, diversity of interpretation, and more inclusive attitude.

Today the renewed and vibrant field of "biblical archaeology" manifests itself in many different pedagogical settings. For those who yearn for a return to the past, an updated version of archaeology in its Albrightian tradition is still being taught at many seminaries and colleges. Coexisting with more traditional approaches, Syro-Palestinian archaeology has been integrated into many more secular-oriented curricula of Near Eastern studies, biblical studies, Eastern Mediterranean studies, and anthropological programs. While it is true that the "greats" of American biblical archaeology have departed and that fieldwork is no longer dominated by Americans (or other foreign nationals), in its stead there is a democratization that has engendered a greater diversity of expression evidenced by its integration into a number of educational curricula. The health and potential future of our field can be measured by the increasing number of individuals who are participating in professional archaeology (ASOR) and biblical (e.g., SBL) annual meetings, including significant numbers of graduate students.

However, we should not underestimate the challenges that we are facing. Waning institutional and governmental financial support for archaeological research has been paralleled by cuts in educational budgets. Over the last few decades, students are taking a more practical approach to higher education and pursuing a curriculum oriented to specific career goals and the job market. Lastly, there is an increasing emphasis at many public universities on teaching large core or crowd-pleasing courses with student enrollment numbering in the hundreds. Even at liberal arts colleges where enrollments are much reduced, there are administrative pressures to keep the course fully enrolled.

There are also a number of additional challenges specific to biblical studies. Fewer and fewer students are raised in traditional Judeo-Christian traditions. As a result, many students (even those who grow up in families that sometimes attend church or synagogue) have little or no background

---

[43] William G. Dever, "On Listening to the Text—and the Artifacts," in *The Echoes of Many Texts: Reflections on Jewish and Christian Traditions: Essays in Honor of Lou H. Silberman* (ed. W. G. Dever and J. E. Wright; Atlanta: Scholars Press, 1997), 1–23.

in the Bible. In recent years, it became increasingly clear to me that I could not assume any general knowledge of the Hebrew Bible or New Testament among students in my classes. There also seems to be a decreasing interest in history and the past, perhaps as a result of primary- and secondary-school educational curricula or simply as a result of our postmodern early twenty-first-century cultural attitudes.

Simultaneously, there are also more opportunities and new possibilities than ever for biblical archaeology in its broadest meaning. As we have been forced to face the reality that the "genius generalist" does not and will not exist, a renewed and healthy dialogue between academics from diverse subfields of biblical studies is increasingly taking place. The crisis in biblical archaeology has heightened our awareness of its relevance to an array of fields in biblical and Near Eastern scholarship that can be integrated in the classroom setting in an unending and creative variety of contexts.

The question I often ask myself is: Who is our student audience, and how do we reach them? The largest and most enthusiastic student audience remains students of Bible, in particular at evangelical seminaries and colleges, and students who feel a personal connection to the State of Israel. In this context, archaeology is closely integrated into a study of the biblical texts and is examined through the lens of the Bible. When instructing courses tailored for the needs of this audience, it is important carefully to delineate the boundaries and limitations of what the material-culture world can and cannot do and what it can say about the Bible. Essential to teaching biblical archaeology in more traditional contexts is the need to emphasize that archaeology can never be used to prove or disprove faith—archaeology belonging to the "earthly" realm and faith belonging to the "heavenly" sphere.

A second audience is biblical archaeology in its broader Near Eastern contexts. Here biblical archaeology is integrated with the general history and written texts of the region with the goal of reconstructing the cultural and social history of the ancient world. The various disciplines are complementary, with each field—text and artifact—making its own unique contribution. In these types of courses, the past should also be a basis for discussing contemporary political events in the Middle East and its impact on the present. In this framework, it is even possible to introduce post-processual approaches and concepts into the course content. Unfortunately, no textbook exists with this type of integration of text and artifact.

Anthropology students are a third target audience. In courses where a majority of the participants are anthropology majors, the emphasis must shift from gazing through the lens of culture history to a more theoretical and sociological examination of the biblical past. The Bible certainly plays a role as part of the material culture of biblical archaeology, although its role is far less central. Levy's edited textbook, *The Archaeology of Society in the Holy Land* (cited above), serves as a helpful and appropriate resource for more anthropologically oriented courses.

Perhaps the most fertile ground to increase student interest in the topic is through the introductory core or general-education courses that typify many of the large public universities. All of us who work in the field of archaeology are aware of the fascination archaeology holds for the general public and its potential appeal to students. These courses could be an effective means of introducing biblical archaeology in its wider regional context to large numbers of students. A textbook suitable for this type of course is lacking.

Thus far I have addressed undergraduate education. Graduate-level studies in biblical archaeology cannot be sufficiently addressed solely in a United States context. Most of the leading graduate programs where biblical archaeology can be studied include only one faculty member who can be considered a professional biblical archaeologist. Generally, graduate studies in the United States are a combination of historical, biblical, and philological studies with a dose of archaeology. At a few American graduate programs it is possible to study Syro-Palestinian archaeology within the framework of anthropology; however, these students tend to focus more on prehistoric periods. Proper training in this field requires long-term residence in the country of specialization, and fluency in the local language is advisable. Many years of active "in situ" field experience and an in-depth knowledge of material culture are necessary in order to gain the level of expertise required to be a "professional biblical archaeologist."

The most encouraging recent trends in biblical archaeology include a revival of interest in a dialogue between text and artifact. This can be observed in the increased number of cross-disciplinary sessions at professional meetings, both American and international, such as those sponsored by the Society for Biblical Literature, the American Schools of Oriental Studies, and the European Association of Biblical Studies.[44] The true challenge to us as academics and professors is the successful and innovative integration of this ongoing dialogue between text and artifact into our research and in the classroom setting. We must be aware that in

---

[44] Noteworthy is the recent increase in the number of cross-disciplinary sessions at the Society of Biblical Literature annual meetings that encourage dialogue between the related fields of biblical archaeology, Bible, Assyriology, and Egyptology. These sessions tend to be some of the best attended, often attracting up to three hundred people. The papers from one of these sessions, "Jerusalem in Bible and Archaeology," have been published in a volume coedited by Andrew G. Vaughn and Ann E. Killebrew: *Jerusalem in Bible and Archaeology: The First Temple Period* (SBLSymS 18; Atlanta: Society of Biblical Literature; Leiden: Brill, 2003).

our "post-modern" and "postprocessual" twenty-first-century intellectual milieu, text and artifact take on multiple meanings and contexts. As outlined above, both "biblical" and "Syro-Palestinian" archaeology today are cross-cultural and cross-disciplinary with a multitude of meanings in their various settings. Our obligation to the future of our profession as educators and scholars will be the ability to adapt a multivocal approach to both the biblical past and its contemporary significance in a multicultural present.

WHERE THE GIRLS ARE: ARCHAEOLOGY AND WOMEN'S LIVES IN ANCIENT ISRAEL

Carol Meyers
Duke University

INTRODUCTION

Mentioning "women" and "the Bible" in one sentence can evoke a variety of responses from students. Most of what they say consists of unexamined and ill-founded assumptions; their notions are probably rooted in traditional understandings of the biblical world that are part of institutional religion and that also appear in general cultural productions, including the contemporary media. Let me provide a few examples of comments that I collected recently from students at the beginning of a course I teach on "Women in Biblical Tradition":

- When I told my father I was taking this course, he said, "Women in the biblical tradition? Huh? Is there even one woman?"
- Women were to be seen, not heard.
- Women were shrouded and quiet.
- Are women as devalued in the Bible as they seem?
- I have very few impressions of women's roles.... However, subservience is what comes to mind.
- I have always assumed that women were vastly inferior to men in biblical times.
- I think of women in the biblical period as being oppressed.
- I think husbands would leave the household for the day and only come home at the end of the day.
- Women were primarily care-givers.
- Women were mainly [i.e., only] wives and mothers.

The images provided in these quotations from my students reflect three overlapping problems. First, the first three statements indicate the matter of invisibility, the sense that women are absent from the biblical

31

record or were invisible in Israelite society or both. Second, the next four statements concern the issue of status, the idea that women were subservient and submissive, if not oppressed. Third, the last three statements reflect the ignorance of what women did and how their roles were valued in their Iron Age context.

Clearly, as an aggregate, these remarks depict a failure to see the presence, albeit limited, of women in the Bible and, even more important in some ways, an inability to understand what life was like for women in ancient Israel and what their roles entailed. How can we educators rectify these misperceptions? How can we provide information about biblical and Israelite women that will create a more accurate and less demeaning picture of women's lives in the period of the Hebrew Bible? I will provide some suggestions for that. However, first I want to stress how important it is for instructors of introductory Bible courses to confront the tendency of students to be present-minded in their consideration of an ancient text and its culture.

Because the Bible is still so much a part of the lives of many of our students, they tend to forget that it arose in a part of the world and in a time period that are both very distant from the twenty-first-century West. One must constantly remind students (and oneself) that the meaning and value of what women contributed to their households and the larger community in ancient Israel cannot be measured on the basis of our experience in contemporary middle-class cultures.[1] Despite the objections of many second- or third-wave American feminists, women's household activities are often undervalued. Because work in the home in today's world, still largely the responsibility of women, is typically considered secondary and supportive, it tends to be trivialized and marginalized. Consequently, household work in the biblical world is likewise considered less important than whatever the men did. At the same time, activities associated with men—such as the heroes and prophets and kings and sages of the Bible—tend to be imbued with power and prestige, just as are formal leadership roles in the modern world. We must help students first become aware that the idea that women's work has less value and prestige than that of men is a contemporary ethnocentric perception on the part of the Western viewer of biblical antiquity. Only then can we perhaps replace that notion with a better understanding of the real value and status of women and their work in a vastly different premodern context.

Similarly, we must help our students contest the conventional wisdom that women were passive and powerless in ancient Israel (and in virtually

---

[1] See Sarah M. Nelson, *Gender in Archaeology: Analyzing Power and Prestige* (Walnut Creek, Calif.: Altamira, 1997), 13–21, 88.

all premodern societies). Women's household activities, which we shall discuss below, had major economic value in ancient Israel—as in virtually all premodern, small-scale, horticultural and agrarian societies, in which all productive labor is based in the household and in which the contributions of women and men, though differentiated, are seen as equivalent.[2] Thus women's contribution to the "domestic mode of production" contributed to female power in ways that challenge our persistent and often unexamined notions of patriarchal dominance and female dependence.[3]

Another aspect of the problem of present-mindedness is our tendency to conceptualize our contemporary world as divided into public and private domains. This analytical construction, which originated in changes to the concept of the workplace brought about by the industrial revolution, considers the public (economic and political institutions) and the private (family or domestic life) as separate domains. This construct was popular in the last few decades of the twentieth century for assessing women's roles in traditional societies.[4] However, it is no longer considered a useful or even accurate analytical framework, especially for assessing societies that pre-date the industrial revolution.[5] A more integrated approach now recognizes that, at least in ancient agrarian societies if not also in the modern world, the "public" and "private" are really overlapping domains. Therefore, we must remind our students, and ourselves, that what happens in the Israelite household has significance not only for the household but also for the larger community in which it is embedded. What women did and said in household contexts had implications beyond their immediate families.

Having set forth the conceptual barriers that we must continually struggle to overcome in examining the lives of women in the period of

---

[2] Ülku U. Bates et al. (Hunter College Women's Studies Collective), *Women's Realities, Women's Choices: An Introduction to Women's Studies* (2d ed.; Oxford: Oxford University Press, 1995), 458–62.

[3] It would be useful for both instructors and students to read my critique of the concept of "patriarchy" as applicable to premodern societies in chapter 2 of Carol Meyers, *Discovering Eve: Ancient Israelite Women in Context* (New York: Oxford University Press, 1988), 24–46.

[4] See Michelle Z. Rosaldo, "Women, Culture, and Society: A Theoretical Overview," in *Women, Culture, and Society* (ed. M. Z. Rosaldo and L. Lamphere; Stanford, Calif.: Stanford University Press, 1974), 23–35; and Peggy Sanday, "Female Status in the Public Domain," in Rosaldo and Lamphere, *Women, Culture, and Society*, 189–206.

[5] So Janet Sharistanian, *Beyond the Public/Private Dichotomy* (Westport, Conn.: Greenwood, 1987); Dorothy O. Helly and Susan M. Reverby, eds., *Domains: Rethinking Public and Private in Women's History* (Ithaca, N.Y.: Cornell University Press, 1992); Louise Lamphere, "The Domestic Sphere of Women and the Public Sphere of Men: The Strengths and Limitations of an Anthropological Dichotomy," in *Gender in Cross-Cultural Perspective* (ed. C. B. Brettell and C. F. Sargent; Englewood Cliffs, N.J.: Prentice Hall, 1993), 67–77.

the Hebrew Bible, we can turn now to the complicated problem of finding those women, reconstructing their roles, and then theorizing the dynamics of their relationships with each other as well as with their families and other members of their communities. There can be no question about the value of archaeology for these tasks. Indeed, it is precisely because of the relative invisibility of women in the Hebrew Bible—for example, women's names account for less than 8 percent of the personal names[6]—that archaeology becomes critical to the task. We look to the material culture for information that the incomplete and androcentric biblical record does not provide.

ENGENDERING ARCHAEOLOGY: PROBLEMS AND PROSPECTS

Turning to archaeology—in particular to the archaeology of the household, in which virtually all women and men lived and worked in ancient Israel's agrarian settlements—for information about women and their lives in ancient Israel is essential, but it is easier said than done. There are several factors involving the way archaeology is practiced in the lands of the Bible and also in the way archaeological materials are interpreted that make it difficult to use archaeological materials directly for this task. In order to consider the practice of archaeology with respect to the archaeological materials to be used for gender-sensitive study, it is important first to understand what is meant by "household."

The household is not simply a structure in which people lived. It is that and more: it involves people and their "hardware" (their domicile and all its associated installations and artifacts), and it involves the activities and interactions of daily life.[7] The household is fundamental to human society, for it is the basic unit of society, the level at which premodern social groups articulate directly with the environment in order to survive. Although studies of ancient Israelite society may consider the household the *tertiary* aspect of society, with the tribe or nation as primary and the clan secondary,[8] I would argue the opposite: the household is *primary* and fundamental because it involves the daily life of every member of society and because it is the site of the economic production necessary for people

---

[6] Karla G. Bohmbach, "Names and Naming in the Biblical World," in *Women in Scripture: A Dictionary of Named and Unnamed Women in the Hebrew Bible, the Apocrypha/Deuterocanonical Books, and the New Testament* (ed. C. Meyers, T. Craven, and R. S. Kraemer; Boston: Houghton Mifflin, 2000), 33–34.

[7] Amos Rapoport, "Spatial Organization and the Built Environment," in *Companion Encyclopedia of Archaeology* (ed. T. Ingold; London: Routledge, 1994), 461.

[8] E.g., Norman K. Gottwald, *The Tribes of Yahweh: A Sociology of the Religion of Liberated Israel, 1250–1050 B.C.E.* (Maryknoll, N.Y.: Orbis, 1979), 237–92.

to survive. One can study the state or the clan, with all the attendant political and religious operations, and ignore women; one cannot ignore women if one studies the household.

Unfortunately, the importance of the household has made little impact on the practice of archaeology in the land of the Bible. A major reason for this is the Bible itself. We have been seduced by the compelling biblical narrative and its authoritative role in Judeo-Christian culture to use archaeology to trace the large-scale political, social, and religious processes and practices described or alluded to in the Bible. Since the very beginning of "biblical archaeology," most explorations, surveys, and excavations have had an eye to the Bible—to prove it, disprove it, illustrate it, or understand its rhetoric and themes. Archaeology has been primarily concerned with the peoples and polities of the Bible and their relationships with each other over time, not with family groups and especially not with their female members.

To put it another way, archaeologists working in the Near East and especially in Israel are rarely concerned with the *micro* level of analysis. That is, their focus has almost never been on the examination of domestic structures and activity areas and the associated artifacts with the intent of reconstructing family activities and dynamics. Rather, archaeological projects have historically focused on the *meso* level, which entails the developmental history of a site, and of course the *macro* level, which can provide insight into regional changes and connections. These blatantly diachronic interests mean that the household almost never appears on the radar screen of archaeological plans, projects, and publications. For example, a recent textbook edited by Thomas Levy and called *The Archaeology of Society in the Holy Land,* while worthwhile in many respects,[9] explicitly and unabashedly focuses "on the macro scale of investigations, primarily because our interest is in fleshing out the dynamics of the structure and changes affecting the larger issue of past social organizations which existed in the Holy Land."[10] The contributors to Levy's book, as is true for most other works on the archaeology of the lands of the Bible, want to explore change over time in relation to the social, political, and religious history presumably reflected in the Bible.

I do not mean to give the impression that households are never excavated. They indeed are. However, the recovery of materials, the extent to which they are published, and the way they appear in publications all

---

[9] See the comments on this text in J. P. Dessel, "In Search of the Good Book: A Critical Survey of Handbooks on Biblical Archaeology," 83–85 in this volume.

[10] Thomas E. Levy, "Preface," in *The Archaeology of Society in the Holy Land* (ed. T. E. Levy; New York: Facts on File, 1995), xiv.

make it difficult to recover in a useful and systematic way the artifacts of daily life, especially as they pertain to gender. Despite the ubiquity and abundance of households, the buildings themselves and their associated artifacts are excavated, recorded, and published in ways that serve interests in typology and chronology, that is, in relative constructs, rather than in ways that serve the interests of knowing about the people who lived in the houses and used the objects. As Michèle Daviau has noted in the introduction to her book on houses in Bronze Age Palestine, publications in Syro-Palestinian archaeology tend to illustrate ceramic and artifactual materials in stylistic groupings rather than in locus groups.[11] Without being able to recover the presence, amount, and spatial distribution of artifacts that can be associated with women's activities, the task of reconstructing women's roles in and contributions to their households and communities is challenging at best.

For example, the artifacts of textile production, such as spindle whorls and loom weights, are arguably the remains of a female-dominated economic activity carried out in households.[12] However, usually only a few examples of such artifacts are presented in the publications of most sites, and the total number of such objects is rarely mentioned. Moreover, their find spots and the nature of the loci in which they were found are almost never reported or, at best, are difficult to recover given the organization and interests of most archaeological publications, which are geared to typologies rather than synchronic features. A number of years ago, I had a modest grant to work on the artifacts of textile production. In her written report of her search for data, the graduate student who assisted me in this project stated that "it's shocking the amount and kind of information that are left out."

Using archaeological data to inform our interests in women's lives in the biblical period is difficult not only because of the nature of the excavated materials and the way they are reported but also because of the interpretive process necessary to move from artifact to person. To begin with, that move is almost never attempted. The artifacts and buildings of daily life somehow remain disembodied—separated from those who used them and evoking almost no interest in *who* (female or male) used them

---

[11] P. M. Michèle Daviau, *Houses and Their Furnishings in Bronze Age Palestine* (JSOT/ASOR Monograph Series 8; Sheffield: JSOT Press, 1993), 26–7.

[12] Carol Meyers, "Material Remains and Social Relations: Women's Culture in Agrarian Households of the Iron Age," in *Symbiosis, Symbolism, and the Power of the Past: Canaan, Ancient Israel, and Their Neighbors from the Late Bronze Age through Roman Palestine* (ed. W. G. Dever and S. Gitin; Winona Lake, Ind.: Eisenbrauns, 2003), 432–34; Elizabeth Wayland Barber, *Women's Work—The First 20,000 Years: Women, Cloth, and Society in Early Times* (New York: Norton, 1994).

and what the gendered patterns of use might reveal about the social dynamics of a household and community. The individual is usually not part of the investigative scope of the interpreters of data in Syro-Palestinian archaeology. With artifacts seen as keys to chronology, the humans who used them are virtually ignored. Interpreting artifacts in a way that is useful for gender studies and for finding the women of Iron Age households thus means focusing on those artifacts in a new way: considering the gender of those who used them. This involves, assuming that the function of objects is correctly assessed (for example, that a donut-shaped ceramic or stone object is in fact a loom weight used in textile production), identifying the gender of the objects' users.

Here the present-mindedness I mentioned earlier can be an obstacle. How can we know that women rather than men used specific artifacts? Artifacts are not intrinsically gender noisy, and associating a set of objects with one gender rather than the other involves explicit operations toward establishing gender specificity. However, most biblical archaeologists, if they do assign gender to objects, do so intuitively, anachronistically, and perhaps erroneously. If gender is ever indicated, it has probably been assigned by unexamined assumptions about women's or men's work or, worse, by a tendency to see men everywhere unless proven otherwise, rather than by an examination of all the resources that would lead to a reasonable suggestion about the use of artifacts, given the possible range of the gendered division of labor in household activities. Such considerations are now part of the discourse in the archaeology that is part of anthropological research.[13] However, they are not part of the discourse of Syro-Palestinian archaeology, and the theoretical issues involved in interpreting data with an eye toward women's lives are rarely explored, though they can be explored by attending to the methods and theory of anthropologists practicing the archaeology of gender.

As such anthropologists have shown, the gendered use of artifacts can be established with reasonable certainty by using: *written sources, ethnography* and *ethnoarchaeology,* and, of course, *archaeological remains* (including iconography). All of these sources are actually already used in interpreting the data of Syro-Palestinian archaeology on the meso

---

[13] See, e.g., Joan M. Gero and Margaret W. Conkey, eds., *Engendering Archaeology: Women and Prehistory* (Oxford: Basil Blackwell, 1991); Roberta Gilchrist, *Gender and Archaeology: Contesting the Past* (London: Routledge, 1999); Nelson, *Gender in Archaeology;* Rita P. Wright, ed., *Gender and Archaeology* (Philadelphia: University of Pennsylvania Press, 1996). I will be publishing an article reviewing the materials from anthropology that might help engender Syro-Palestinian archaeology in a forthcoming issue of *Near Eastern Archaeologist:* "Engendering Syro-Palestinian Archaeology."

and macrò levels, although not always explicitly,[14] but they have almost
never been combined in the interest of recovering the lives of individuals.
The use of comparative information from ethnography is especially
important, given the availability now of gender-sensitive studies made in
the last few decades, in which feminist critiques have led to better report-
ing of gendered activities. When it comes to attributing gender to
household activities, the information provided by the direct observation
of human societies can help determine the range of possibilities and thus
help in the interpretation of archaeological and textual data with respect
to the gender of the users.[15] However, beyond that, ethnographic observations provide ideas about the *meaning* of the household activities with
respect to the interactions of the female and male household members
and their relationship with people in the larger community.

Another interpretive tool—experimental archaeology—also is noteworthy. This aspect of archaeology, practiced far more by anthropologists who
are archaeologists than by Syro-Palestinian archaeologists dealing with the
biblical periods, involves controlled attempts to re-create or reproduce
ancient artifacts and technologies and to determine how they would have
been used. Such experiments provide data about, for example, how long it
would have taken to carry out a basic household activity using the available
technologies. Thus if a particular activity can be deemed a woman's task,
then the amount of time that activity would take on a daily basis can be
ascertained. Such information, in turn, can help reconstruct the activity patterns and attendant social relations of the female members of a household.

Because of the availability of these interpretive tools, I believe that a
gendered biblical archaeology is possible and that one can use archaeology to locate the "girls" of our biblical past. However, as I have gone to
some lengths to explain, most research in Syro-Palestinian archaeology
has not been designed to produce such results, nor have researchers
attempted to use the results of excavation projects to reconstruct the gendered use of artifacts and buildings. I may be one of the few who believe
that a gendered biblical archaeology is possible and who has actually
attempted it. This brings me to a somewhat awkward situation in that the
two examples I will describe will be my own studies. Both deal with

---

[14] The use of ethnography is often debated, with critics claiming that the analogical rea-
soning, which is at the core of ethnoarchaeological work, is overly subjective and unreliable.
Despite such concerns, ethnographic observations remain invaluable for interpreting the past.
For a useful discussion of the prospects and limitations of ethnoarchaeology, see Charles E.
Carter, "Ethnoarchaeology," *OEANE* 2:280–84.

[15] Cathy Lynne Costin, "Exploring the Relationship between Gender and Craft in
Complex Societies: Methodological and Theoretical Issues of Gender Attribution," in Wright,
Gender and Archaeology, 114–40.

aspects of women's roles in household life: one with the household economy, the other with household religion. I am not certain how accessible
these studies are to undergraduates.[16] Perhaps parts of them could be
read, and the instructor could explain the rest. In any case, I will summarize these two studies so that I can demonstrate the use of archaeology for
recovering all those invisible women of ancient Israel and for understanding something about their lives.

CASE STUDY 1: WOMEN AND FOOD PREPARATION

A recent issue of my college alumnae association featured several articles on food and food-ways. One of them is called "Food Matters." The
author, a prominent food journalist, asserts that those who control the
preparation and allotment of food have "both actual and symbolic
power."[17] If that is true in 2002, how much more so in the Iron Age, when
there was no recourse to grocery stores, microwaves, and refrigerators!
Thus any attempt to understand women's history—or human history, for
that matter—without considering the crucial role of food cannot succeed.
Feminist research is finally picking up on that fact. By turning aside the
present notion that kitchen work is menial and marginal, important aspects
of women's roles in food preparation in premodern societies can be ascertained. I have done so for Israelite women in an article called "Having
Their Space and Eating There Too—Bread Production and Female Power
in Israelite Households," appearing in *Nashim*.[18]

Cereal products were arguably the most important nutritional sources
in the biblical period. Indeed, it has been estimated that people obtained
some 50 percent of their daily caloric intake from bread. So important
were cereal crops that the word for "bread" in the Hebrew Bible, *leḥem*, is
often used for food more generally. Because daily grain-processing activities were essential to the survival of virtually all families in Iron Age
Palestine, I decided that an examination of bread production as a gendered activity would allow me to identify a central contribution of women
to the household economy. I then would take the interpretive process further by considering the implications for female power of the role of
breadmaker—very different from the idea of breadwinner, a role that

---

[16] However, I can report that I recently visited a small liberal arts college and met with
an undergraduate class studying the family in ancient Israel. The students had read these
papers before I met with them and apparently had no difficulty with them

[17] Nancy Harmon Jenkins, "Food Matters," *Wellesley* 85 (2002): 24.

[18] The entire issue of *Nashim* 5 is devoted to "Gender, Food, and Survival." See Carol
Meyers, "Having Their Space and Eating There Too: Bread Production and Female Power in
Ancient Israelite Households," *Nashim* 5 (2002): 14–44.

would not have existed in ancient Israel, where most productive labor was done in the household and without monetary compensation.

Bread production was not a simple matter. Only the seeds of cereal crops are edible, and they cannot be digested in raw form. The processing activities required to transform the harvested grain into edible form are manifold: parching or soaking, milling or grinding, heating and/or leavening. Unlike the activities (planting, plowing, sowing, reaping) required to produce the grain, which were seasonal, bread production was a daily activity, taking as much as three work hours a day per household.[19] In addition, as one might have expected (though could not assume), bread production can indeed be as identified as a female activity.

Biblical texts that mention the tools (such as grinders, millstones, ovens) and processes (grinding, kneading, baking) of bread preparation, if they happen also to indicate the persons using those tools or carrying out those activities, indicate that women were bread producers in ancient Israel. Such texts are Exod 11:5; Lev 26:26; Eccles 12:3; Isa 47:2; and Jer 7:18; although it is post-Israelite, see also Matt 24:41.[20] The Leviticus text is especially significant in that it indicates female responsibility for portion control as well as bread production. It also suggests, as does the Matthew passage, that some of the work of bread making was cooperative. Other relevant texts identifying women as bakers (and cooks) are 1 Sam 8:13 and 28:24. Furthermore, the dramatic story of the woman of Thebez (Judg 9:53–54; 2 Sam 11:21), who rescues her city by tossing an upper millstone at the enemy, shows a woman putting to military use an object that was part of her inventory of tools for daily usage. In fact, this story may be the one biblical text for which an artifact can be used for direct illumination of the text; for that, I would recommend having students read "A Watermelon Named Abimelech."[21]

That women worked together to produce bread is perhaps the most salient feature of the biblical texts and one that can be directly related to archaeological materials. For example, when the location of grinding stones can be ascertained, it is not unusual to find more than one such implement in a household, indicating that the time-consuming and tedious

---

[19] It has been estimated that it took about an hour to prepare 4/5 kg. of flour. With daily per capita consumption of flour calculated at about 1/2 kg., it would have taken almost three hours to produce enough edible grain for six persons (from an unattributed article titled "Common Roots" in the April-May 1999 issue of *Neot Kedumin News*).

[20] See also the remark of Rabban Gamaliel that "three women knead together, bake it [bread] in one stove" (*y. Pesaḥ.* 3:30b). Written sources from ancient Egypt and Mesopotamia similarly link bread production with women.

[21] Denise Dick Herr and Mary P. Boyd, "A Watermelon Named Abimelech," *BAR* 28/1 (2002): 34–37, 62.

task of grinding was done simultaneously by several women from one household, neighboring households, or both. Similarly, ovens were often positioned in ways that indicate they were shared across households, providing evidence that women from several households coordinated their bread-baking work. Iconographic remains dramatically point to the same cooperative work. Small terra-cottas of the late Iron Age depict several women kneading dough in tandem, and a Boetian terra-cotta of a group of women bent over a kneading trough has led the excavators of a Palestinian site to identify an installation in an Iron Age dwelling as a bread-kneading trough.[22]

Having established the likely dominance of women as bread producers, typically working together, I turned to ethnographic data for further evidence. I hoped that such information would support my claim that women were the household bread producers in ancient Israel and my sense that they often gathered together to carry out at least some of the constituent tasks. More important, I hoped that ethnographic data would suggest what the dynamics of bread production, involving groups of women rather than individuals, would have been. Indeed, I did find that women are bread producers in a high percentage of premodern societies and that bread production is often a social endeavor. The ethnographic literature abounds with descriptions of women lightening the hard and time-consuming process of grinding and kneading by working together, talking and singing. I suggest with some confidence, therefore, that the women of one Israelite household—and there could have been several adolescent and adult women in the complex or extended family households that were part of Iron Age agrarian settlements[23]—and even of neighboring households would have gathered together for many hours of the day to grind, knead, and bake and probably also to perform other household activities.

To take this claim about women's work one step further and to evaluate the significance of the control of the central economic activity of household (bread production) by women, I again turned to ethnography while reminding myself not to succumb to the problems of present-mindedness or of assuming a separation between households and the

---

[22] For references to these archaeological materials, see Meyers, "Having Their Space and Eating There Too."

[23] See Lawrence E. Stager, "The Archaeology of the Family in Ancient Israel," *BASOR* 260 (1985): 1–35; Carol Meyers, "The Family in Early Israel," in *Families in Ancient Israel* (by L. G. Perdue et al.; Louisville: Westminster John Knox, 1997), 1–47; Paula M. McNutt, *Reconstructing the Society of Ancient Israel* (Knoxville: Westminster John Knox, 1999), 90, 166–67; and Avraham Faust, "The Rural Community of Ancient Israel in the Iron Age," *BASOR* 317 (2000): 17–39.

larger community. Ethnographic research has demonstrated that gender-associated activities signify gender-associated power. Thinking about power usually means examining formal institutions, but in traditional societies informal power is the concomitant of the control of economic activities and is often just as important, if not more important, than formal relations of power.[24] That is, issues of household power in premodern agrarian societies are typically resource based and involve labor output, expertise in technologies, and control of foodstuffs.

I discovered that various kinds of informal power would have accompanied women's dominance of bread making in ancient Israel. I identified three of them: social power; personal power; and sociopolitical power.

Social power within households, specifically decision-making powers, accrue to women by virtue of their dominance of essential household processes.[25] The virtual exclusivity of women in Israelite households as producers and distributors of cereal foods (and probably other foods as well), which could not be obtained in any other way, would have privileged women in terms of internal household power differentials.

Personal power, or a valued sense of self, is contingent upon the importance of the set of tasks someone performs. The technological skills required for food production (and textile production) are, in the aggregate, more complex than those required for the growing of staple crops (which is arguably a male task). Furthermore, providing food is a daily event, with food immediately consumable, whereas bringing in a harvest is seasonal and somewhat unpredictable. Thus the process and results of women's labor in Israelite households would have produced gratification and the attendant sense of personal worth in a more immediate and consistent way than might have been possible for many men.

Sociopolitical power across households would have been held by Israelite women because of the communal nature of many of their activities. The gathering of women to carry out daily tasks means the formation of informal female networks. The time spent together gives women access to information that is unavailable to men and that is critical for forging suprahousehold social and political alliances. This social knowledge embedded in women's informal networks helps form essential community

---

[24] A useful definition of power is that of Szinovacz: power is the "net ability or capability of action to produce or cause intended outcomes or effects, particularly on the behavior of others, or on others' outcomes" (Maximiliane E. Szinovacz, "Family Power," in *Handbook of Marriage and the Family* [ed. M. B. Sussman and S. K. Steinmetz; New York: Plenum, 1987], 652).

[25] Carole M. Counihan, "Introduction—Food and Gender: Identity and Power," in *Food and Gender: Identity and Power* (ed. C. M. Counihan and S. L. Kaplan; Amsterdam: Harwood Academic Publishers, 1998), 2, 4.

solidarity. Such networks may provide a less visible and more diffuse form of agency and power than do men's (formal) groups, but they are hardly casual affairs. In ancient Israel, they would have contributed in manifold and often subtle ways to the viability of the community. For example, ethnographic evidence suggests that women's community connections helped to solve economic problems (such as deploying labor or other resources to households where there was illness or hardship); they would also have functioned to identify suitable spouses for marriageable offspring, and they would have provided information to male leaders about quarrels that needed formal adjudication.

It may be a long way from grinding stones to social and personal power, within and across households, but the journey is worth taking with students to help combat the notions that women were "only wives and mothers" and were powerless and led uninteresting lives. "Wife" clearly has built-in economic and thus sociopolitical features for Iron Age women, features that we cannot easily recognize in the twenty-first century. With this in mind, it is worth noting that traditional translations of Prov 31:10 as "capable wife" (NRSV; NJPS) do a disservice to the Hebrew, *'ēšet ḥayil*. Just as *'îš ḥayil* denotes a "warrior" or "mighty man of valor," the phrase denoting the female head of household in Proverbs should more accurately be translated "strong woman" or "powerful woman."[26] Indeed, it would be worthwhile having students give some attention to Prov 31, a biblical text that could serve as an entrée into considering women's household roles.

CASE STUDY 2: WOMEN AND RELIGION

Many students decide to take introductory Bible courses because of their own involvements in institutionalized religion. They are interested in biblically based beliefs and praxis. Thus, examining the lives of women with respect to religion would be an appealing aspect of an attempt to bring archaeology into a gendered consideration of the Hebrew Bible. I have tried to do just that in another paper, "From Household to House of Yahweh: Women's Religious Culture in Ancient Israel," and I will draw from that in describing what might be called "women's religion" for the period of the Hebrew Bible.[27]

---

[26] Carole R. Fontaine, "Wife (Prov 5:18–19; 12:4; 18:22; 19; 13–14; 21:9,19; 25:24; 27:15–16; 30:23; 31:10–31)," in Meyers, Craven, and Kraemer, *Women in Scripture*, 303.

[27] Carol Meyers, "From Household to House of Yahweh: Women's Religious Culture in Ancient Israel," in *Congress Volume: Basel, 2001* (ed. A. Lemaire; SupVT 92; Leiden: Brill, 2002), 277–303.

Note that the name of my essay uses the phrase "religious culture" rather than the term "religion." That phrase allows for a broad understanding of what is involved in religion in a premodern society. It acknowledges the fact that religion involves not only belief in one or more supernatural beings but also appropriate "responses" to them. Such responses can be activities or actions, with or without accompanying words. Indeed, women's religious lives in traditional societies, more often than those of men, are characterized by nonverbal or nontextual activities.[28] Thus, our contemporary Judeo-Christian focus on scripture and liturgy, on spoken prayer and homiletical discourse, should not be allowed to privilege verbal religious behaviors over performative ones in considering women's religious lives in ancient Israel. Nor should we side with the biblical text and assume that the public temple/tabernacle/high place rituals represent the most important aspect of Israelite religious activities.

Considering religious culture also allows us to include behaviors that might be termed magic and thus today would be considered marginal, quasi-religious, or even deviant. Again, we must not apply the values of the present to the praxis of the past, even if the formal texts of the past are likewise negative toward certain practices. In traditional societies magical behaviors often play a vital role in helping people deal with life-death issues that we now resolve primarily through medicine. Performing magical ritual acts affords people some sense of control and thus mental ease as they face danger and death, and women in premodern societies are often the ritual experts who carry out such procedures. However, too often the study of magic and religion is genderized, with higher religion considered masculine and debased magic labeled feminine.[29] The richness and importance of informal religious culture as practiced by women (and also men) are thus overlooked or even negated.

This brings us to the question of whether there could be anything distinctly female, as opposed to male, in informal religious culture. Although I am generally reluctant to essentialize behaviors and claim that any religious activity is intrinsically female or male, I would nonetheless suggest that religious activities associated with women's reproductive capacity can be considered largely female. Israelite women, like those of women in traditional societies everywhere, would have marked the life processes and problems associated with childbirth with behaviors performed only

[28] Rita M. Gross, *Feminism and Religion: An Introduction* (Boston: Beacon, 1996), 81; Nancy A. Falk and Rita M. Gross, eds., *Unspoken Words: Women's Religious Lives* (Belmont, Calif.: Wadsworth, 2001).

[29] Melissa A. Aubin, "Gendering Magic in Late Antique Judaism" (Ph.D diss., Duke University, 1998).

by them. Such behaviors typically surround pregnancy, labor, and birth; they are meant to achieve fertility (and thus there are some procedures prescribed for men as well), ensure healthy gestation and delivery, and secure lactation and protect newborns. The rituals of human reproduction may indeed be the most common of women's religious behaviors and probably the least studied, perhaps because of their characteristic atextuality.[30]

Precisely because women's religious culture involves activities and thus almost certainly objects, it can be investigated by considering archaeologically recovered artifacts, by consulting ethnographic data, and by attending to a few allusions in biblical texts. Before looking at these sources of information, I want to emphasize that I am not particularly concerned with whether the ritual behaviors I identify were part of the worship of Yahweh, Asherah, other deities, or some combination thereof. It is more important to acknowledge the existence of ritual practices surrounding reproduction and to consider their dynamics. Indeed, the behaviors associated with women's religious culture, apart from whatever meanings were attached to them or to whatever deities they were directed, were conservative and probably remained relatively constant throughout the Iron Age and beyond, whatever the identity of the deity or deities to which they were directed. The conservative nature of such "folk religion" means that ethnographic evidence gathered from traditional Middle Eastern societies by nineteenth- and early twentieth-century travelers is likely to be relevant.[31]

The archaeological remains that can most directly be associated with rituals of female reproduction are iconographic, namely, the small terracotta figurines representing women in some stage of the reproductive process. Sometimes they are called "pillar figurines," a term preferable to the designation Astarte or Asherah figurines, both of which make the assumption, perhaps unwarranted, that these objects were meant to represent certain female deities rather than their worshipers. I do not rule out the possibility that they symbolize goddesses, but, in the absence of clear markings denoting a divinity, the possibility that these are votary objects representing women striving for fertility, safe pregnancy and birth, and/or

---

[30] Nancy A. Falk and Rita M. Gross, "In the Wings: Rituals for Wives and Mothers," in Falk and Gross, *Unspoken Words*, 57.

[31] E.g., Lucy Garnett, *The Women of Turkey and Their Folklore* (2 vols.; London: Nutt, 1890–91); Hilma Granqvist, *Birth and Childhood among the Arabs: Studies in a Mohammedan Village in Palestine* (Helsingfors: Sodörström, 1947); cf. Julian Morgenstern, *Rites of Birth, Marriage, Death and Kindred Occasions among the Semites* (Cincinnati: Hebrew Union College Press, 1966); Michele Klein, *A Time to Be Born: Customs and Folklore of Jewish Birth* (Philadelphia: Jewish Publication Society, 1994).

successful nurturance seems more compelling.[32] These objects have been found by the hundreds in tenth–sixth century B.C.E. strata from over one hundred sites east and west of the Jordan. What is striking is that they are virtually absent from communal cultic contexts; rather, they appear primarily in the household,[33] the primary domain of women. In fact, it can be calculated that there were one or more pillar figurines per household.[34] They may or may not have been connected to the worship of a particular deity, but almost certainly their function, because of what they depict, was to help women with the concerns of reproduction. A similar distribution pattern and function can be assigned to another kind of archaeological object, namely, Bes images, though they are found in much smaller quantities than the pillar figurines.

Both pillar figurines and Bes images are typically found in what may be termed "cultic assemblages," that is, groups of objects that apparently played a role in household rituals.[35] Such objects include lamps, beads, amulets, rattles, inscribed seals, vessels—especially miniature ones—for food, pendants, and iron blades. In other words, objects of everyday secular use, when associated with pillar figurines or Bes images, are arguably part of a household religious culture surrounding women's reproductive processes. Both biblical texts and ethnographic data support such a possibility.

Although no biblical texts deal directly and specifically with women's cultic activities surrounding reproduction, there are allusions to acts and utterances that may have been part of women's religious culture. Indeed, the fact that women were called upon to engage in purification rites after childbirth (Lev 12:1–8)[36] indicates that reproduction and ritual existed together in ancient Israelite life with respect to extrahousehold ceremonies.

---

[32] Meyers, *Discovering Eve,* 162–63; Karel Van der Toorn, *From Her Cradle to Her Grave: The Role of Religion in the Life of the Israelite and the Babylonian Woman* (trans. S. J. Denning-Bolle; BibSem 23; Sheffield: JSOT Press, 1995), 91.

[33] Raz Kletter, *The Judean Pillar-Figurines and the Archaeology of Asherah* (BARIS 636; Oxford: Archaeopress, 1996), 45–46, 141, and appendices 1–5.

[34] John S. Holladay Jr., "Religion in Israel and Judah under the Monarchy," in *Ancient Israelite Religion: Essays in Honor of Frank Moore Cross, Jr.* (ed. P. D. Miller Jr., P. D. Hanson, and S. D. McBride; Philadelphia: Fortress, 1987), 276; Daviau, *Houses and Their Furnishings,* 202–3.

[35] For an example of cultic assemblages in domestic contexts, see P. M. Michèle Daviau, "Family Religion: Evidence for the Paraphernalia of the Domestic Cult," in *The World of the Arameans II: Studies in History and Archaeology in Honour of Paul-Eugène Dion* (ed. P. M. M. Daviau, J. M. Wevers, and M. Weigl; JSOTSup 325; Sheffield: Sheffield Academic Press, 2001), 199–229.

[36] See Rhonda Burnette-Bletsch, "Women after Childbirth (Lev 12:1–8)," in Meyers, Craven, and Kraemer, *Women in Scripture,* 173–74.

This would lead us to believe that household rituals linked with reproduction were likewise present. Securing fertility, for example, occasioned prayers no doubt accompanied by rituals. Hannah (1 Sam 1–2) and Samson's mother (Judg 13:3) are both plausible examples of this. Moroever, the practice of using medicinal substances—mandrake roots (Gen 30:14–17)—can be considered a household magical act intended to promote fertility, as is the use of certain plant substances specified in Babylonian texts.[37]

The rituals of childbirth are typically carried out by midwives and the other women in attendance at a birth. Students may be familiar with the fact that Israelites used midwives, as in the exodus story (Exod 1:15–21) or in the stories of Benjamin's birth (Gen 30:17) and probably that of Ichabod (1 Sam 4:20). However, they may not be aware that those women were ritual as well as medical experts and that medicine and religion were inextricably related in the biblical world. The red thread used by the midwife at the birth of Tamar's twins sons (Gen 38:28–30) may be an example; both the apotropaic color red and the fact that it is bound on the infant's hand contribute to magical protective powers of such threads, as both Mesopotamian and Hittite texts indicate.

Ethnographic evidence from the Middle East contributes to such a function for red threads, with its examples of red caps placed on infants, red threads tied around the hands of newborns, and red veils or kerchiefs worn by women in childbirth. Also relevant, although rarely examined because it is embedded in the horrific text depicting Israel and Judah as adulteresses to be punished, a verse in Ezekiel (16:4) refers to three procedures (washing the newborn, rubbing it with salt, and swaddling it) performed on a baby at birth. All of these procedures can be termed medical-magical acts. Again, ethnographic data are replete with examples of these three procedures as apotropaic actions to prevent harm to the newborn by keeping evil spirits at bay.

Neither the midwife texts nor the Ezekiel verse can be tied directly to archaeological data, although the ceramic vessels that are part of the assemblages I mentioned above are likely to have been used in birthing rituals. However, there is one artifact that does appear in a biblical text as well as in ethnographic data. I am referring to the lamps that are part of these household religious assemblages. In Prov 31:18, the "strong woman" (*'ēšet ḥayil:* NRSV, "capable wife") keeps a light burning continuously, even though she herself is not awake all night (31:15). If the lamp had no pragmatic, light-giving value during nighttime, it may well have been necessary

---

[37] Marten Stohl, *Births in Babylon and the Bible: Its Mediterranean Setting* (Cuneiform Monographs 14; Groningen: STYX, 2001), 52–59.

for the safety of the young children—by keeping evils spirits away—an interpretation supported by the fact that light is seen as protective in several other biblical passages, such as Job 29:3 and Prov 6:20–21. The Prov 6 passage also alludes to protective amulets worn day and night around the necks of children.

In this respect, we recall that amulets as well as lamps are often found in the household cultic assemblages, and the use of both lamps (or candles) and amulets, along with pieces of metal and metal jewelry (which are also part of household cultic groups) is widely attested in traditional societies of the Middle East. These artifacts appear in the households of Jews, Christians, and Muslims; they give or reflect light, thus keeping at bay the demons or night spirits believed to be lurking about, ready to pounce upon vulnerable infants and young children or to interfere with the milk supply of mothers. Such information should make us aware of the fact that metal jewelry, often called "items of personal adornment" in our archaeological publications, may be important items in the religious culture of households. The lamps, in addition to warding off evil demons, may also have played a role in the procedures for calling upon the dead to serve the living, a practice particularly associated with women (as in the biblical Medium of Endor) and often used in traditional societies to enlist the aid of ancestors in order to secure fertility, protect women during pregnancy and childbirth, and safeguard the health of newborns.[38]

Clearly, the allusions to women's household religious culture in biblical texts can be understood and expanded by reference to archaeological remains in relation to ethnographic sources, but it is not enough simply to make these connections. They must be interpreted with respect to their meaning for women's lives as well as for their meaning in the religious lives of all Israelites. I suggest three ways in which women's roles in household religious rituals were dynamic and essential aspects of Israelite life.

Ritual expertise. The rituals associated with the reproductive process, like those at major community shrines, represent a substantial body of knowledge. Students should be reminded that rituals are stereotyped behaviors that must be learned from experts. Thus ritual activities involving materials and artifacts depend upon the knowledge of specialists who prepare the materials and use them in prescribed ways; otherwise, they would not be efficacious. Women were the ritual experts for the overlapping physiological and material aspects of reproduction; they were responsible for securing pregnancy and for safeguarding mother and child. Who were

---

[38] Susan Starr Sered, *Women As Ritual Experts: The Religious Lives of Elderly Jewish Women in Jerusalem* (Oxford: Oxford University Press, 1992), 18–29; Phyllis Bird, "The Place of Women in Israelite Cultus, in Miller, Hanson, and McBride, *Ancient Israelite Religion*, 397–419.

these ritual experts? They would have been older women—mothers, neighbors, or other relatives—serving as mentors, transmitting knowledge across generations. Sometimes outside experts were brought in: midwives, necromancers, and others. The role of such volunteer or professional (paid) experts would have afforded them status and prestige.

Female solidarity. Individual women may have performed some of the rituals of reproduction as part of their daily routine, but groups of women, such as those attending the birth of Oded (Ruth 4:17), also carried out others.[39] Just as the communal bread-producing activities contributed to female solidarity in and across households in Israelite settlements, so too the performance of religious rituals in the intimate circumstances of childbirth would have created solidarity among women and contributed to the informal women's networks mentioned above.

Socioreligious power. The status and solidarity of women surrounding reproductive rituals were hardly trivial aspects of their religious culture. The rituals of reproduction were concerned with matters of life and death, not as abstract theological issues but rather as immediate and direct problems. Women's ritual praxis was focused on the well-being of themselves and their families, with their specialized behaviors deemed essential to the creation and sustenance of new life. Such female control of vital socioreligious functions may seem marginal when viewed from the top down (i.e., from the perspective of elite, male, formal structures), and perhaps this is why women's religious culture is largely invisible in the Bible. However, when seen from the bottom up, that culture represents female access to the supernatural on a daily basis; it was surely an integral and essential part of the lives of ancient Israelites. Cultural practices of such enormous value to the survival of a family carry a sense of worth and power. Indeed, because it would have been experienced as vital to the life of families and communities, the religious culture of Israelite women would have afforded them significant self-worth and group recognition.

The archaeological recovery of pillar figurines, amulets, metal jewelry, and the like can thus take us on a long journey, full of interpretive procedures and multidisciplinary perspectives, that allows us to reconstruct aspects of the religious lives of Israelite women that would otherwise have been invisible. Moreover, acknowledging the vital function of the rituals they performed—even if we lack descriptions of them or texts to go with them—allows us to rescue women from the notion of second-class status as well as obscurity. Status is hardly a uniform and unitary quality; it varies according to the dynamics of differing arenas of activity.

---

[39] See Carol Meyers, "Women of the Neighborhood (Ruth 4:17)," in Meyers, Craven, and Kraemer, *Women in Scripture,* 254.

CONCLUDING COMMENTS

I began this essay by providing comments about women in the period of the Hebrew Bible made by some of my undergraduate students, both male and female, before they had the opportunity to delve into this subject. It is therefore fitting that I conclude with several statements that they made at the end of their course work, which afforded them to see how many of their notions were misperceptions.

- There are so many notions that I clung to that now seem so obviously incorrect and ridiculous to me. It kind of makes me wonder about all those other things that I am so sure about.
- Now I realize that the context of the Bible extends far beyond the biblical texts themselves. . . .
- While I still believe that men have more of the dominant roles and stories, I now would be extremely hesitant to label the majority of women as subservient.
- I now realize how many ideas of women's work as inferior to men's work outside the home would not have fit in the biblical period.
- The importance of women as household managers had never occurred to me.
- My stereotype [of secondary roles and helpless women] has lost its validity.
- By critically analyzing texts and artifacts, I can now see how many different activities women did, activities that made them strong and powerful.

Clearly, despite the paucity of biblical texts that mention women, it is possible to rectify the imbalance of information in the Bible about women and men and the concomitant distortions by turning to archaeology and ethnography. Such data can compensate for the strong likelihood that most of the biblical texts are the product of elite males and thus do not provide a balanced view of gender roles and relationships in the biblical world. Moroever, it is possible to overcome the inability of students to imagine the variety of roles that they played, their central place in the household economy, their vital place in household religious culture, and the consequent power that they exerted in the decisions of daily life that affected their families and their communities.

Precisely because of the relative absence of ordinary peasant women from the biblical narrative, recovering their lives in an introductory Bible class is not a straightforward matter. Although archaeology can play a significant role, using artifacts is also not a straightforward enterprise.

Interpretive processes are necessary, and learning about the methodology for doing this kind of work can be just as important for undergraduates as is the kind of reconstruction that multidisciplinary analysis makes possible. I believe that it is worth the effort. I hope that some of the texts and artifacts—and how we might use them to understand Israelite household life—that I have mentioned will suggest possibilities for this task. As long as the Bible continues to be a current document as well as a relic of the past, and as long as distorted and even erroneous notions about women in the Bible and the biblical world continue to influence negatively the possibilities for gender equality in our culture, it is incumbent upon us as "experts" in biblical scholarship to make the new scholarship on women in the biblical past available to undergraduates. We should be able to help them discover where the "girls" are, what they were doing, and what their activities meant for themselves and their families.

"THESE ARE YOUR GODS, O ISRAEL": THE CHALLENGE OF RECONSTRUCTING ISRAELITE RELIGION USING BOTH TEXT AND ARCHAEOLOGY

Beth LaRocca-Pitts
University of Georgia

INTRODUCTION

Because we live in a culture that constantly has its mythic corpus as well as its religious history narrated back to it through the media of television and film, teaching each successive generation of students about the religious life of ancient Israel often necessitates clearing the air of images gained from exposure to Indiana Jones, *The Relic Hunter,* and *Hercules: The Legendary Journeys.* Nothing is more fascinating to the citizens of our modern age than the "actual facts" behind ancient ritual objects fabled to contain supernatural power. Whether one is dealing with the ark of the covenant, the temple of Solomon, the Holy Grail, or the wood of the true cross, ritual objects described in ancient religious texts stir the imagination of professionals and lay readers alike. Much is written about them, and most of it is largely fanciful.

This does not mean, however, that we should cease to investigate ancient cult life or dismiss discussion of religious artifacts as so much hokum. Contemplation of religious issues and the practice of cultic ritual are key components of virtually all ancient and traditional cultures. A study of ancient Israel, therefore, cannot hope to be complete without analysis of ancient Israelite religion. Although the process of rediscovering and correctly labeling religious structures and artifacts known from the archaeological record is fraught with difficulties, no reconstruction of ancient Israelite religion can hope to be accurate without accounting for and including certain archaeological remains.

THE SIGNIFICANCE OF ARCHAEOLOGICAL DATA FOR TEACHING THE HEBREW BIBLE

One of the main things that biblical scholars want archaeology to be able to do for them is to match physical objects recovered from excavations with descriptions of cultic objects described in the biblical text. Unfortunately, with the possible exception of altars whose use is fairly obvious, this is usually a difficult if not impossible task. Archaeologists often claim to have found examples of particular cultic objects such as standing stones, high places, or images of specific deities. However, when their methodological assumptions are explored, one often finds flaws that make the identification of these objects suspect.

In the main, archaeological finds come out of the ground with no explanatory material to accompany them. To quote my first archaeological field supervisor, Leslie J. Hoppe, "You don't get what you want. You get what you get." In other words, you dig and you uncover artifacts that are pieces of a larger puzzle, some of the pieces of which may be missing. It is a rare thing to uncover an ancient artifact, particularly a religious one, and know immediately what it is and what it meant to those who once possessed it. However, if one teaches the Hebrew Bible using only the text, there is some vital information missing from the puzzle that archaeology may provide. Below are just a few examples.

A clearer understanding of the doctrine of aniconism. If one thinks that ancient Israelites had no representational art, both the text (1 Kgs 6) and the archaeological record demonstrate otherwise. Small metal and ceramic figurines, paintings on pots, ivory carvings, stone carvings, and illustrated inscriptions are all to be found in the repertoire (see discussion of specific items below). However, one thing that has not been found to date in Israel is any attempt to represent the person of Israel's God in art. Art is to be found everywhere, yet in keeping with textual commands regarding aniconism (Deut 4:15–20), religious art and artifacts *do* appear to avoid making pictures of the primary deity of Israel. Other deities and their companion animals appear in artistic representations. Israel's God, so far, does not.

Challenges to the biblical claim of monolatry. As noted above, many small depictions of gods and goddesses are present in the archaeological record of ancient Israel. If one excludes images of gods found in strata that date prior to any proposed presence of Israelites in the land, one is still confronted with a huge number of metallic and ceramic representations of deities both male and female. Virtually every excavation of a site that has occupation during the periods related to Israel's monarchy produces such objects.

One way of seeing this is that it supports the biblical contention that Israelites were regularly worshiping, or at least revering, gods other than Israel's God (2 Kgs 17). Another way of seeing this is that it makes false the biblical description of Israelite religion as one that worshiped a single God and no other. Another way of interpreting this material is to posit a division between a "state-level" or "official" religion and the "personal" or "popular" religion of the average Israelite. Without this data, however, one would be missing a very important piece of the puzzle of Israelite religion, namely, that many Israelites, independent of their belief in or beliefs about Israel's high God, viewed the possession of small charms, statuettes, and amulets as a normal and desirable thing.

Challenges to the doctrine of cultic centralization. Archaeology also makes clear that, although the centralization of worship in the Jerusalem temple is presented by the text as a hard and fast doctrine (particularly by the Deuteronomist, as in 1 Kgs 12:25–33), other shrines continued to exist and were used both in preexilic and postexilic Israel, a fact also implied in the text (1 Kgs 14:21–24). The most famous preexilic shrine outside Jerusalem is found at Arad (see discussion below). In the postexilic era there was a famous Israelite shrine on the island of Elephantine that existed contemporaneously with the restored temple in Jerusalem.[1]

In short, archaeological evidence can present an important diachronic witness to the practice of Israelite religion that we most frequently see synchronically through the text. The fact that the text took shape over many generations, with each successive generation framing the issues at hand in keeping with its own perspectives, makes it difficult for us to know if what we are reading in the text is an accurate description of the way Israelite religion was practiced or merely a vague cultural memory recorded by successive generations long after the original practitioners had turned to dust. Archaeology can help recapture what was real for a given generation of Israelites. Unfortunately, we do not always understand completely what we are seeing in those slices of Israelite life that have been frozen in time for us. Below are some suggestions for how to view this material that can help one make the most of the evidence that we do have and to bring it to bear on the text as we have it as well.

METHODOLOGICAL SUGGESTIONS

When selecting archaeological examples to illustrate lectures on Israelite religion, it is best to be circumspect with regard to certain issues, including whether or not something that is found in the field is actually cultic. With the exception of one exceedingly small ivory pomegranate and one very large but largely empty stone structure, we have virtually no remains from the national cultic installations said to have existed in the biblical period, namely the First Temple in Jerusalem, and the state shrines at Dan and Bethel. What we do have are small objects, small shrines,

---

[1] Werner Kaiser, "Elephantine," *OEANE* 2:235.

pre-Israelite shrines, and a few inscriptions. This is not much with which to reconstruct a religion; however, if one is careful about method one can greatly enrich the material gained from the textual record without disseminating misinformation.

Several methodological pitfalls are described below, and following each description are suggested ways to avoid them. By offering some more cautious models of interpreting this material, the remainder of this essay seeks to help the reader discover the ways in which archaeological remains can make the study of ancient Israelite religion more accessible and more critically grounded for students. Although it remains true that "X never, *ever* marks the spot," there are ways to be true to the text and still uncover the treasures of Israel's religious past.

PITFALL 1: READING THEORETICAL RECONSTRUCTIONS OF ANCIENT RELIGION INTO THE ARTIFACTS

It was a common methodological failing of previous generations of scholars first to make up their minds about the theoretical nature of ancient religion and then to point out how artifacts uncovered in the field illustrated such theories. Just one case in point is the way standing stones were characteristically labeled as evidence that ancient pre-Israelite religion was animistic. Countless scholars have argued that ancient people worshiped standing stones because in doing so they worshiped the god who lived inside the stone. In the case of Israelite/Canaanite remains, Baal was typically suggested as the deity in question.[2]

While it is true that certain standing stones, such as the one installed on an elevated platform by the gate of Bethsaida, do appear to represent a deity resident in a shrine,[3] the presumption that all standing stones were viewed animistically blinds one to the possibility that other reconstructions of ancient religious practice are equally likely with regard to some stones. For example, a small shrine in Area C at Hazor, in which a statue of a seated god was uncovered sitting next to a row of small stelae, one of which bears a carving of hands raised as if in worship,[4] is more likely to represent a scene such as the one described in Exod 24:4, in which standing stones represent worshipers, not deities. Such stones

---

[2] For a summary of such opinions, see Elizabeth C. LaRocca-Pitts, *"Of Wood and Stone": The Significance of Israelite Cultic Items in the Bible and its Ancient Interpreters* (HSM 61; Winona Lake, Ind.: Eisenbrauns, 2001), 5–12.

[3] Monika Bernett and Othmar Keel, *Mond, Stier und Kult am Stadttor: Die Stele von Betsaida (et-Tell)* (OBO 161; Göttingen: Vandenhoeck & Ruprecht, 1998).

[4] Amihai Mazar, *Archaeology of the Land of the Bible: 10,000–586 B.C.E.* (ABRL; New York: Doubleday, 1990), 254, fig. 7.10.

might have been erected as a witness to the presence of worshipers, and thus they might serve to stand forever in the presence of the god in the worshipers' stead.

Another ubiquitous theoretical assumption about ancient Israelite religion was that it positioned itself in opposition to a thoroughgoing fertility cult practiced by the Canaanites. In such a reconstruction, Canaanite religion is interested in little else but issues related to sexuality and fertility. Thus, any pre-Israelite ritual objects uncovered would be linked somehow to a reconstruction of Canaanite religion focused solely on fertility issues. Any Israelite-era remains uncovered that had features that resembled those one expected to find in a fertility cult were labeled examples of unorthodox or syncretistic worship by errant Israelites.

The notion that Israelite religion positioned itself in opposition to a thoroughgoing fertility cult can generate several errors. The broader culture of ancient "Canaan" (which we are able to study from primary sources uncovered at Ras Shamra) continues to be reduced to the caricature of religion presented by the anti-Canaanite polemics in the biblical text. This projection of a fixation with fertility onto the Canaanites exclusively obscures the fact that ancient Israelites were also quite concerned with fertility issues. There are figurines (known as pillar figurines[5]) that appear to be images of Asherah, a mother goddess worshiped in both Israel and Canaan, found throughout the Iron Age strata of Israelite sites.[6]

How to Avoid Pitfall 1: Let the Artifacts Speak for Themselves without Undo Interpretation

Perhaps coming to the artifacts with a theory already in place was simply an accident of the fact that most biblical archaeologists began first as scholars of the text and became archaeologists later. As more and more scholars come to the archaeological data first and to theories about the nature of ancient religion second, we may be able to avoid this pitfall. This is not certain, however. Some scholars whose primary training is in archaeology are less critical than they might be of older scholarship on the phenomenology of religion and are currently resurrecting, perhaps unwittingly, certain of these same largely unsupportable theories for a new era

---

[5] Ibid., 500, fig. 11.25.

[6] Christoph Uehlinger, "Anthropomorphic Cult Statuary in Iron Age Palestine and the Search for Yahweh's Cult Images," in *The Image and the Book: Iconic Cults, Aniconism, and the Rise of Book Religion in Israel and the Ancient Near East* (ed. K. van der Toorn; Leuven: Peeters, 1997), 122.

of readers.[7] In virtually all cases it is best to keep an open mind about what the ancients may have thought their artifacts represented philosophically or theoretically.

PITFALL 2: NAIVE ACCEPTANCE OF MODERN HEBREW
USES OF ANCIENT HEBREW CULTIC TERMS

An unfortunate side effect of reawakening an ancient language for a modern era is that ancient words may be borrowed by modern speakers without a very careful definition governing that borrowing. For example, some archaeologists tend to use the term *bāmâ*, a biblical term of obscure semantic range, to cover a dizzying array of structures thought somehow to be cultic in nature. The term *bayit*, "temple," tends to be reserved for monumental structures with some cultic evidence about them, but the term *bāmâ*, "high place" in Modern Hebrew parlance, may be used to refer to small shrines of any type, whether enclosed or open to the air. One site so designated does not even have any structures at all! It is simply a large stone in an open field in the Samarian hill country at which a small statuette of a bull was found.[8] Another so called "high place" has been reconstructed at Hazor. It consists of a small divided room with a large stone in one chamber.[9]

One might ask: Why is this problematic? In the Bible large shrines were called temples, and small shrines were called *bāmôt*. Why shouldn't Modern Hebrew speakers use the term *bāmâ* to refer to a small shrine? The problem is one of perception. This use of a biblical term gives the impression that archaeologists know what biblical *bāmôt* looked like. It gives the impression that all of the installations that are today being called *bāmôt* would have been so called in ancient times. This is something we cannot know.

HOW TO AVOID PITFALL 2: NEVER ASSUME THAT A LABEL IS CORRECT

Unfortunately, most of us do not have the time to research every example that we wish to use in class. We depend on the labels that

---

[7] See, for example, Uzi Avner's animistic interpretations of rings of standing stones found in the Negev in "Ancient Agricultural Settlement and Religion in the Uvda Valley in Southern Israel," *BA* 53 (1990): 134–35.

[8] Amihai Mazar, "Bronze Bull Found in Israelite 'High Place' From the Time of the Judges," *BAR* 9/5 (1983): 34–40.

[9] Amnon Ben Tor, "Notes and News: Excavations and Surveys, Tel Hazor, 1996," *IEJ* 46 (1996): 262–69.

others attach to items and assume them to be true. In the case of objects known to be obscure in the text, one should assume that such obscurity still exists, even when scholars are positivistic in their use of technical terms. While it may be correct in our era to call any shrine that is smaller than a temple a *bāmâ,* we cannot assume that the ancients would agree. If there is any doubt that a term had a simple universal meaning in the Bible, there should be doubt that it can have a simple universal meaning today.

PITFALL 3: ASSUMING THAT AN ARTIFACT IS CULTIC WITHOUT SUFFICIENT EVIDENCE

This pitfall raises the basic question: How do we know a given item is actually cultic? It is often a challenge to tell the difference between cultic objects and mundane objects that are simply unusual looking. Often objects surface in excavations for which no mundane purpose can be imagined by the archaeologist, so frequently it is suggested that these strange objects must have had some religious function because they obviously had no mundane function.

This mistaken logic often occurs in contexts where we know virtually nothing about the culture from which the object emerged or in situations where an object is found in a larger archaeological context that cannot give any clues as to its original function. Using the criterion that an odd appearance indicates a cultic use for a given object causes many simply strange objects to be labeled cultic; unfortunately, once that label has entered the literature, it becomes difficult to remove.

One case in point is a Chalcolithic statuette from Gilat that appears to be a naked female figure, decorated with stripes of red paint, holding a milk churn on her head. Because the female figure is naked and oddly decorated, and perhaps because of the fact that she has an object related to a basic dietary staple on her head, countless archeologists describe the female figure represented in it as a fertility goddess. It is a fact, however, that we know little or nothing about the religious life of the Chalcolithic period, its deities, or its rituals. There is really nothing about this object by itself, apart from its odd appearance, that demands it to be viewed as anything more than a rather strange example of representational art.

Given the fact that this object was uncovered in a context that could be construed as a Chalcolithic cult site, it may well be a statuette of a "fertility goddess," but this is merely a hypothesis, not a fact. It might also be a representation of a human being engaged in some sort of ritual behavior or display. The figure is also holding what looks like a drum under one arm. The idea that this is a goddess precludes the idea that the figure might be a priestess or perhaps a musician, when any such theory has the same amount of evidence to support it, namely, only the statue itself. While it may be cultic, it may also be commemorative. We cannot know.[10]

Many other objects have been labeled as cultic that merely may be objects whose mundane function we have simply failed to understand. Among these are the objects known as kernos rings (hollow circular ceramic rings with sculpted animals or pomegranates attached to them[11]), zoomorphic vessels of various kinds,[12] and numerous examples of figurines of the "horse and rider" type modeled on those from Cypriot culture. Concerning pillar figurines, one scholar has gone so far as to suggest that for Israelites they may simply have been children's toys.[13] It is also possible that many so called "standing-stone shrines," essentially rooms with a large central pillar but without any other remains that would suggest a cultic use, may simply have been rooms that used a large stone pillar to support the roof.[14] In short, the sheer appearance of an object is insufficient to warrant it being labeled cultic.

How to Avoid Pitfall 3: Save the Label "Cultic" for Objects with Unambiguous Iconography or Ritual Contexts

There are many examples of archaeological finds that can be rightly labeled "cultic." Two good criteria for this are the presence of iconographic symbolism on the object or the location of the object in an unambiguous ritual context. Below are a few categories of ritual objects that are generally agreed upon as to their designation as cultic.

Standing stones. One recent find that meets both the iconographic symbolism and ritual context criteria suggested above is the installation in the gate of Bethsaida, mentioned above, which includes a small stepped platform containing offering vessels and an inscribed stela with identifiable

---

[10] For two treatments of this item, one that considers it a goddess, and one that reconsiders that hypothesis, see Ruth Amiran, "Some Observations on Chalcolithic and Early Bronze Age Sanctuaries and Religion," in *Temples and High Places in Biblical Times* (ed. A. Biran; Jerusalem: Hebrew Union College, 1981), 47–53; and Alexander H. Joffe, J. P. Dessel, and Rachel S. Hallote, "The 'Gilat Woman': Female Iconography, Chalcolithic Cult, and the End of Southern Levantine Prehistory," *NEA* 64 (2001): 8–23.

[11] Ruth Amiran, *Ancient Pottery of the Holy Land from Its Beginning in the Neolithic Period to the End of the Iron Age* (Rutgers, N.J.: Rutgers University Press, 1970), 306, photo 350. Amiran classifies kernos rings as cultic items, noting that they are known from the Mycenean/Minoan world from which they originated, but she goes on to state that it is only a surmise that they were used in religious rituals once they were borrowed by the Israelites (305).

[12] Mazar, *Archaeology of the Land of the Bible,* 325, fig. 8.18.

[13] Shmuel Yeivin, "On the Use and Misuse of Archaeology in Interpreting the Bible," *American Academy For Jewish Research Proceedings* 34 (1966): 151.

[14] Conversation, Shlomo Bunimovitz.

Baalistic iconography.[15] Other standing stones that can be rightly identified as cultic are the large monoliths commonly referred to as MacAlister's "High Place" at Gezer (some of which were situated over infant burials[16]), the small stelae collection from Hazor mentioned above, similar collections of small stelae found at Tel Dan,[17] and the large standing stone at Tel Balatah (biblical Shechem).[18] Again, however, one must decide what type of cultic use such stones may have had. Those at Tel Dan and Hazor appear to be assemblages that may represent worshipers rather than deities. Tel Balatah's stone and those at Gezer are uninscribed and so might present many plausible explanations as to their function.

Altars. Perhaps the most notable example of an Israelite altar is the large "horned altar" recovered from Beersheba.[19] A more ambiguous assortment of smaller horned altars was discovered at Tel Miqne-Ekron. What makes this collection curious is the context. Although some eighteen small horned altars were found at Tel Miqne-Ekron, some of them were found within an olive oil–producing factory, raising the question of whether their use here was industrial and not cultic.[20]

Ceramic incense burners and stands. Several different types of ceramic stands exist in the repertoire of Israelite pottery. Most notable of these may be the molded incense burning stands recovered from Taanach that contain iconographic symbolism sculpted onto them.[21] Other less-ornate examples of ceramic incense stands, some with figures and some with "windows" cut out (the so-called "fenestrated stands"), and chalice-shaped stands or burners have been found at various sites.[22] What the more plain of these stands lack in iconography, they make up for in ritual context.[23]

Statuary. There have been many examples of cast-metal statuary found in Israel and Canaan, the great majority of which can be identified by their iconography. Ora Negbi's famous catalogue *Canaanite Gods in Metal* provides a wealth of examples of the various types, many of which have been

---

[15] Bernett and Keel, *Mond, Stier und Kult.*

[16] William G. Dever, "Gezer," *OEANE* 2:398.

[17] Avraham Biran, "Sacred Spaces: Of Standing Stones, High Places and Cult Objects at Dan," *BAR* 24/5 (1998): 38–45, 70.

[18] Joe D. Seger, "Shechem," *OEANE* 5:20.

[19] Mazar, *Archaeology of the Land of the Bible,* 496, fig. 11.21.

[20] Trude Dothan and Seymour Gittin, "Miqneh, Tel," *OEANE* 4:33; Robert D. Haak, "Altars," *OEANE* 1:81.

[21] Ruth Hestrin, "Understanding Asherah: Exploring Semitic Iconography," *BAR* 17/5 (1991): 50–58.

[22] Amiran, *Ancient Pottery of the Holy Land,* 302–6.

[23] For a reconstruction of one such context, see Beth Alpert Nakhai, "What's a Bamah? How Sacred Space Functioned in Ancient Israel," *BAR* 20/3 (1994): 18–29.

recovered in Israel.[24] Several cast-metal bulls have been recovered, the most noted of which, perhaps, are those found at Ashkelon[25] and in the Samarian hill country.[26] Metal figures of Baal (with hand raised in the action of throwing a spear), and El (wearing a crown and sitting on a throne) have also been recovered.[27]

Ceramic statuary is also abundant. In addition to the pillar figurines noted above, there are various types of plaques (representations molded in the round on one side and flat on the back side) that depict an unknown goddess (possibly Astarte). These plaques show a female figure that is naked yet who also has some iconographic emblems, such as the characteristic "Hathor" hairstyle and lotuses or other emblems in her hands.[28] In addition to these more common Israelite types of statuary, the desert site of Qitmit unearthed statuary of such a radically different type than any found before that it has been theorized that this cult center was Edomite, not Israelite.[29]

Shrines. Architectural remains are perhaps the most difficult to identify correctly. If a building is empty, there can be little hard evidence to prove what its original function was, however monumental the structure itself may appear. Only if the remains of human activity are present can one be more or less assured of one's identification of a building's original purpose. However, there are several monumental structures whose content leaves little doubt as to their use as shrines.

Among these are the pre-Israelite shrine in Area H at Hazor, which contained altars, stelae, and other ritual equipment;[30] the pre-Israelite Fosse Temple at Lachish;[31] the Israelite shrine at Arad, which contained a raised platform as well as two stelae and an altar;[32] and the large ashlar building from Tel Dan, thought by many to be the state-sponsored shrine of the northern kingdom.[33] Another famous installation is the round stone

---

[24] Ora Negbi, *Canaanite Gods in Metal: An Archaeological Study of Ancient Syro-Palestinian Figurines* (Tel Aviv: Tel Aviv University Institute of Archaeology, 1976).

[25] Lawrence E. Stager, "When Canaanites and Philistines Ruled Ashkelon" *BAR* 7/2 (1990): 24–31, 35–37, 40–43.

[26] Amihai Mazar, "Bronze Bull Found in Israelite 'High Place' from the Time of the Judges," *BAR* 9/5 (1983): 34–40.

[27] Uehlinger, "Anthropomorphic Cult Statuary," 103–4.

[28] Miriam Tadmor, "Female Cult Figurines in Late Canaan and Early Israel: Archaeological Evidence," in *Studies in the Period of David and Solomon and Other Essays* (ed. T. Ishida; Winona Lake, Ind.: Eisenbrauns, 1982), 139–73.

[29] Itzhaq Beit-Arieh and Pirhiya Beck, *Edomite Shrine: Discoveries from Qitmit in the Negev* (Jerusalem: Israel Museum, 1987).

[30] Mazar, *Archaeology of the Land of the Bible*, 248–50.

[31] Ibid., 254–55.

[32] Ibid., 496–97.

[33] Nakhai, "What's a Bamah?" 18–19.

platform from the Canaanite strata of Megiddo. Although some have suggested that it might have been a platform for a silo or a granary, the fact that burned animal remains were found on the site suggest that it was, in fact, a large altar/shrine.[34] Also found at Megiddo was a smaller shrine containing a lovely assemblage of cultic items (stands, altars, offering vessels).[35]

Inscriptions. Written records are perhaps the most rare and valuable of finds when it comes to issues of ancient Israelite religion. Although, like iconographic symbolism, inscriptions may be interpreted in many ways, when a new inscription is found it tends to capture the imagination of scholars for years to come. Three such examples of inscribed materials include the inscriptions mentioning Asherah found at Qhirbet ʿEl Qom and at Kuntillet ʿAjrûd[36] and the small inscription found on an ivory pomegranate believed to be the only existing relic from Solomon's temple.[37]

PITFALL 4: FAILING TO TAKE CONTEXT INTO ACCOUNT WITH REGARD TO RELIGIOUS MEANING

In our world we can recognize that an object out of context changes meaning. A plastic statue of the Virgin Mary on the dashboard of a taxicab might have a very different meaning from one dangling from a teenager's earlobe. We would expect a large concrete version of the same image, tastefully displayed in a backyard garden, to receive perhaps less reverence than a similarly sized one painted and placed on a pedestal in a cathedral. One would not expect any reverence at all to be offered to such an icon if it were situated either on the factory floor with thousands of others or in an outdoor enclosure surrounded by cement St. Francises, lawn jockeys, purple cows, and frogs sitting in loveseats. Similarly, different levels of sanctity pertain to ancient iconographic objects as well.

For example, when the Bible describes the large golden calf statues that were supposed to stand in shrines at Dan and Bethel, one should not confuse this type of state-level religious iconography with the small metal bull statues found throughout the region. There is a difference between personal religion, which might involve small statuettes, amulets, or other iconographic material that might be kept in a home, and those larger executions

---

[34] Kathleen M. Kenyon, *Archaeology in the Holy Land* (4th ed.; London: Benn, 1979), fig. 41.

[35] David Ussiskin, "Megiddo," *OEANE,* 3:466.

[36] Andre LeMaire, "Who or What Was Yahweh's Asherah? Startling New Inscriptions from Two Different Sites Reopen the Debate about the Meaning of Asherah," *BAR* 10/6 (1984) 42–51.

[37] Nahman Avigad, "The Inscribed Pomegranate from the 'House of the Lord,'" in *Ancient Jerusalem Revealed* (ed. H. Geva; Jerusalem: Israel Exploration Society, 1994), 128–37.

of the same imagery one might expect to find in a state shrine. Thus, not every room that contains a statuette is a shrine.

How to Avoid Pitfall 4: Assume Ancient Society Was As Complex As Our Own

Not all iconography present in a modern home is tied to the religious behavior of the home's residents. I have in my living room a statue of the "Dancing Shiva" I acquired on a vacation to India. Possession of that object does not make me a Hindu. Similarly, iconography can cross the line out of religious symbolism and into the inert world of decorative motifs. In the Roman Period, for instance, oil lamps were mass produced, and many of them had mythological scenes on them.[38] Possession of such a lamp does not prove that the owner knew the myth in question or revered the characters depicted. They may simply have found the design beautiful.

Conclusions

The ancient world had the potential to be just as complex as our own with regard to human tastes and sensibilities, as well as human tendencies either to conform to or rebel against behavioral or religious norms. When teaching the biblical text one is confronted with a myriad of choices as to how the information contained in the text might be presented to students. What biblical archaeology offers to the teaching of ancient Israelite religion is an opportunity to augment the material students read and the lectures students hear with visual material they can see and possibly even actual artifacts they can touch. Making such graphic and tactile connections between the student, the text, and the ancient world can greatly enhance a student's experience of the material and increase the possibility that the information communicated will be retained.

Particularly with regard to Israel's religious life, the use of artifacts and visual information can make real an aspect of ancient Israelite life that has been expanded upon, enshrined, and otherwise abstracted by the descendent religions to which it gave birth. To return as often as possible to primary data is to restore the original face of Israel's religion, seen all too often today through the varied lenses of Judaism, Christianity, and Islam. Even though it is a difficult medium to master, archaeological data can provide for Israelite religion a large amount of such primary data. The use of this data, however, must begin with a dedication of letting the artifacts

---

[38] Renate Rosenthal and Renee Sivan, *Ancient Lamps in the Schloessinger Collection* (Qedem 8; Jerusalem: Hebrew University, Institute of Archaeology, 1978), 19–57.

speak without undo interpretation of either a religious or secular nature. Only then can these artifacts speak to their many possible interpretations without having many quite plausible ones filtered out by dominant ideological paradigms. After all, what often makes exploration of the ancient world interesting to students is the invitation to imagine and explore—to hunt for treasure and for magic. To let the artifacts inspire such imagination may give rise to a new generation of students for whom the Bible is an irresistible source of potential riches.

Suggested Texts and Resources

Coogan, Michael, ed. *The Oxford History of the Biblical World*. New York: Oxford University Press, 1998.

Mazar, Amihai. *Archaeology of the Land of the Bible: 10,000–586 B.C.E.* ABRL. New York: Doubleday, 1990.

Extensive slides and images on CD-ROM are available through the Biblical Archaeology Society; see further details in the annotated bibliography by Melissa Aubin in this volume or the BAS website: www.bib-arch .org/bswbMktSlide.html.

Extensive bibliography and links to images on the Internet can be found through ABZU (www.etana.org/abzu) and through the web site of the Oriental Institute of the University of Chicago (www-oi.uchicago.edu).

In Search of the Good Book: A Critical Survey of Handbooks on Biblical Archaeology

J. P. Dessel
University of Tennessee

Introduction

It is well recognized that the archaeology of the southern Levant is an essential component to the study of the Hebrew Bible, the New Testament, and the origins of Judaism and Christianity. However, due to the increasing degree of specialization in the field of biblical studies, it has become more difficult for many scholars competently to assess a larger and more diverse range of synthetic treatments of biblical or Syro-Palestinian archaeology.[1] These archaeological handbooks are not neutral vessels of raw data but rather espouse a range of interpretive biases and agendas that, at the very least, must be acknowledged if they are to be used properly. Of particular importance is how these volumes implicitly treat the relationship between scripture, history, and archaeology. Without some sense of the interplay between these three very disparate sources, an informed presentation of biblical history and archaeology is virtually impossible.

In order to facilitate a better appreciation of the variety of perspectives and orientations represented by these handbooks, a critical survey is sorely needed. This survey will include a history of such volumes beginning with the seminal work of William Foxwell Albright, *The Archaeology of Palestine*. Special attention will be given to the recent generation of synthetic handbooks as well as a consideration of some of the recent controversies in the archaeology of the southern Levant.[2] What exactly constitutes a handbook on biblical archaeology, as there is an ever-growing

---

[1] For an excellent consideration of these terms, see Ziony Zevit, "Three Debates about Bible and Archaeology," *Bib* 83 (2002): 1–27.

[2] This field is alternatively referred to as "biblical archaeology" and "Syro-Palestinian archaeology"; again, see Zevit, "Three Debates about Bible and Archaeology."

number of books dedicated to a broadly conceived vision of biblical history, which includes some archaeology? However, I will limit this
discussion to texts that are more or less dedicated to explicating the
archaeology and culture history of the southern Levant. The distinction
here is an explicit focus on the archaeology rather than the biblical history
or narratives. Of course, how one understands and defines biblical archaeology or an archaeological history of the southern Levant (modern Israel,
Jordan, and the Palestinian Authority) is dependent on when the volume
was written. The biblical world and its archaeological history of Albright,
writing in the 1940s or 1950s, is certainly not the biblical world and its
archaeology of the 1990s.

With these caveats in mind, the number of handbooks can be reduced
to a manageable handful of about twenty. While each of them share many
similarities, they also have some important differences, especially in regard
to their historiographic perspectives. When considered as a group, these
handbooks can be broadly organized into two approaches: the "biblical" or
"Albrightian" approach" and the "secular" approach."[3]

ALBRIGHT AND THE FIRST GENERATION OF BIBLICAL ARCHAEOLOGY HANDBOOKS

The roots of biblical archaeology go back to the middle of the nineteenth century and the early explorations of Palestine (understood as the
"Holy Land") by Edward Robinson.[4] Excavation began in earnest in the late
nineteenth century and greatly accelerated between 1925 and 1948, which
Moorey refers to as "the Golden Age" of biblical archaeology.[5] It is with
the conclusion of this period that the first "modern" synthetic study of the
archaeology of the southern Levant appeared, *The Archaeology of Palestine,* by William Foxwell Albright.[6] It should come as no surprise that the
author of this work was Albright, who almost single-handedly fashioned
the discipline of "biblical archaeology." This volume was somewhat of a

---

[3] See ibid.; and Leo Perdue, Lawrence E. Toombs, and Gary L. Johnson, eds., *Archaeology and Biblical Interpretation: Essays in Memory of D. Glenn Rose* (Atlanta: John Knox, 1987).

[4] For two excellent overviews of the history of biblical archaeology, see Philip J. King, *American Archaeology in the Mideast: A History of the American Schools of Oriental Research* (Philadelphia: American Schools of Oriental Research, 1983); and P. R. S. Moorey, *A Century of Biblical Archaeology* (Cambridge: Lutterworth, 1991).

[5] Moorey, *A Century of Biblical Archaeology,* 54–67.

[6] William F. Albright, *The Archaeology of Palestine* (rev. ed.; London: Penguin, 1954). It was originally published in 1949 (Harmondsworth Middlesex: Penguin) and then reprinted six times by two different publishers, the last of which was in 1971. Although Albright's is clearly the first modern attempt at this kind of study, see Zevit, "Three Debates about Bible and Archaeology," for a useful review of early biblical archaeology handbooks that preceded Albright's.

departure from Albright's earlier works, such as *Archaeology and the Religion of Israel* and *The Archaeology of Palestine and the Bible,* both of which focused more directly on religion, especially ancient Israelite religion and the development of Judaism and Christianity, as well as how the study of archaeology related to these developments.[7] While *Archaeology of Palestine* still integrated religion into the culture history, the organization of the book had an explicitly archaeological focus that worked to extend the temporal parameters of biblical Israel[8] from the earliest known prehistoric periods through the classical period. Albright succeeded in constructing a single historical narrative by wedding artifact and text, with the archaeological data used to support the historicity of the biblical narratives.

A careful perusal of the table of contents reveals a veritable "how-to guide" for the study of biblical archaeology, creating a basic pedagogical structure that endures to the present.[9] Albright begins with discrete chapters on "The Art of Excavating a Palestinian Mound" and "The Discovery of Ancient Palestine," providing wonderfully succinct excursuses into the history and practice of excavation methodology, as well as a history of the discipline.[10] Chapter 2 remains a useful précis on the Western explorations of biblical lands (beginning with the Crusades) and the religious interest in this part of the world. Most, if not all, of the major excavations up through the early 1950s are mentioned and given an intellectual and historical context. Additionally, the basic chronology of the area is

---

7 William F. Albright, *Archaeology and the Religion of Israel: The Ayer Lecture of the Colgate-Rochester Divinity School, 1941* (Baltimore: Johns Hopkins University Press, 1942); idem, *The Archaeology of Palestine and the Bible* (New York: Revell, 1932).

8 It is interesting to note the lengthy subheading below the title on the cover of the 1954 revised edition: "A survey of the ancient peoples and cultures of the Holy Land illustrated with photographs, diagrams, and line drawings." Already on the cover there is a clear indication of the two basic approaches to the study of the history and archaeology of ancient Israel: a more secular approach in which the area under consideration is referred to by its geographical designation, Palestine (as seen in the title), and a more clerical perspective in which the same area is referred to as "the Holy Land" (as seen in the subheading). It is the tension between these two perspectives that was, in part, the focus of the conference that produced this volume.

9 See, e.g., Amihai Mazar, *Archaeology of the Land of the Bible, 10,000–586 B.C.E.* (ABRL; New York: Doubleday, 1990); Walter E. Rast, *Through the Ages in Palestinian Archaeology: An Introductory Handbook* (Philadelphia: Trinity Press International, 1992); Volkmar Fritz, *An Introduction to Biblical Archaeology* (JSOTSup 172; Sheffield: JSOT Press, 1994); and John C. H. Laughlin, *Archaeology and the Bible* (London: Routledge, 2000).

10 Chapter 1 is filled with many interesting reflections as well as wonderful anecdotes that provide lively insights into the archaeology of the time. He discusses how to handle field teams, hire laborers, and organize surveys and sprinkles in definitions of important terms such as *loci, tell,* and *stratum.* In a postscript in the 1954 revised edition, he even discusses the newly discovered chronometric method of radiocarbon dating, 22.

presented, which became the basal level for all subsequent chronological refinements.

Albright covered the geological history of the region as well as the Paleolithic through the Neolithic periods. This chapter is a classic articulation of Albright's view of the all-encompassing nature of the "Biblical World," a secular archaeo-historical approach integrating prehistoric periods into a culture history squarely derived from and focused on the biblical narratives. Albright's "Biblical World" spanned prehistory and history and had an extremely wide geographic distribution, from southern Russia to Ethiopia, across North Africa and over to Iran.[11]

The archaeological core of the book is chapters 4–7, which cover the Chalcolithic through "Graeco-Roman" times, with the greatest emphasis on the Bronze and Iron Ages, the foundation of biblical history. Albright's inclusion of the later periods (especially the Roman period) is even more essential than his inclusion of the prehistoric periods, for these are the periods during which the events of the New Testament transpired.

The final chapters of the book are thematic in nature, discussing such topics as language, writing, literature, and daily life. The use of thematic chapters is another enduring legacy of Albright's landmark volume. Most interesting is chapter 9, "Daily Life in Ancient Palestine," which is divided into short accounts of selected periods designed to help illuminate key biblical figures. Here we see Albright's vision of the interplay between the biblical texts, archeology, and history, as well as his interest in the environment, technology, and social organization. He correlates the patriarchs to the Middle Bronze II and compares patriarchal society to the contemporary Arab bedouin and *fellahin* of the region. This is then woven into a more wide-ranging synthesis of the entire period, incorporating other data, such as the Middle Bronze Age archives from Mari and Alalakh, Egyptian tomb paintings, and population movements of the Indo-Europeans. Later periods are also considered, such as the Iron Age II, which is linked to Elijah.

The final three chapters return to the familiar themes that Albright treated more formally in his earlier books.[12] In these chapters we find a

---

[11] See G. Van Beek, "William Foxwell Albright: A Short Biography," in *The Scholarship of William Foxwell Albright: An Appraisal* (ed. G. Van Beek; HSS 33; Atlanta: Scholars Press, 1989), 7–15. For more on Albright's perspectives on field archaeology, see J. P. Dessel, "Reading between the Lines: William Foxwell Albright 'In' the Field and 'On' the Field," *NEA* 65 (2003):43–50, and especially the bibliography.

[12] See note 7 as well as William F. Albright, *From the Stone Age to Christianity* (Baltimore: Johns Hopkins University Press, 1940); and idem, *History, Archaeology, and Christian Humanism* (New York: McGraw-Hill, 1964). Albright's protégé G. Ernest Wright wrote a similarly styled biblical history, *Biblical Archaeology* (Philadelphia: Westminster, 1957), that is very reminiscent of Albright's *Archaeology of Palestine and the Bible*.

careful explication of many of the most important trends and controversies still extant in the discipline. Perhaps the most important issue is that of the influence of religious beliefs on interpretation, which Albright downplays.

> It is true that some archaeologists have been drawn to Palestine by their interest in the Bible, and that some of them had received their previous training mainly as biblical scholars. The writer has known many such scholars, but he recalls scarcely a single case where their religious views seriously influenced their results.... their archaeological conclusions were almost uniformly independent of their critical views.[13]

This optimistic conviction was appropriate for the time, especially as Albright himself saw great historical accuracy in the biblical texts. At the conclusion of this volume Albright clearly stated his view on the role and purpose of archaeology:

> Though archaeology and geography can thus clarify the history and geography of ancient Palestine, it cannot explain the basic miracle of Israel's faith, which remains a unique factor in the world history. But archaeology can help enormously in making the miracle rationally plausible to an intelligent person whose vision is not shortened by a materialistic world view. It can show the absurdity of extreme sectarian positions.... Against these and other modern forms of ancient magic, archaeology wages an unceasing war.[14]

The graphics in this volume are beautifully rendered, and through their presentation Albright successfully made available to the public images that were then hard to obtain. They include architectural and stratum plans, line drawings of artifacts (especially pottery from Tell Beit Mirsim), and thirty plates of wonderful black and white photographs of important artifacts and sites, such as Megiddo and Beth Shan as they appeared in the 1940s.

This volume reflects an exceptional clarity. It was the most significant formulation of a coherent culture history of the region yet produced, and it established a pedagogical framework for the study of this material that has lasted to the present.[15] Albright's attention to field methodology, the history of the discipline, and the more critical integration of the archaeological data, biblical texts, and extrabiblical Near Eastern documentary evidence

---

[13] Albright, *Archaeology of Palestine,* 219.

[14] Ibid., 256.

[15] Later biblical archaeology handbooks have continually updated Albright's basic structure, almost always focusing on the Bronze and Iron Ages. Even now we lack a good archaeological handbook for the classical periods in the southern Levant.

all became standard practice in other handbooks. Without understanding Albright and his organization of both the material and its presentation, it would be hard fully to appreciate later attempts at this same type of synthetic volume. In point of fact, *Archaeology of Palestine* remained useful well into the 1960s, when the preponderance of new data began to outstrip Albright's interpretations and, more important, his interpretative framework.

It was not until 1960 that a second major synthesis appeared, *Archaeology in the Holy Land* by Dame Kathleen Kenyon, a British archaeologist.[16] Kenyon, trained by Sir Mortimer Wheeler and with extensive excavation experience in Africa, the Near East, and Europe, represented a much different tradition of archaeology than did Albright.[17] Her interest in the southern Levant was less explicitly based on religion, and her broad range of experiences in prehistoric archaeology made her approach less an exercise in culture history and more an investigation into cultural processes and human behavior. She also viewed the entire Near East as an integrated whole into which her work in the southern Levant could be contextualized.

Kenyon directed the excavation at Jericho (Tell es-Sultan), one of the most important Neolithic and Early Bronze Age sites in the region.[18] While working at Jericho she greatly refined Near Eastern excavation methods, and it is in this area that Kenyon made her greatest and most lasting contribution to the discipline. Her refinements in stratigraphic excavation and her understanding of the formation of debris layers and the importance of baulks and section drawing were nothing short of revolutionary in the practice of biblical archaeology, and at Jericho she helped train an entire generation of archaeologists. She had a particularly powerful influence on younger American archaeologists working in Israel and Jordan, who adopted her methodological innovations with particular zeal.

Having excavated early in her career at Samaria and then directing the work at Jericho, it seemed only natural that Kenyon would turn these rich experiences into a synthetic archaeological history. Oddly, the resulting publication, which went through four editions from 1960 to 1979, was quite traditional, even Albrightian, in its outlook. As with Albright, Kenyon seemed most interested in illuminating the Bible, noting "that this book will be of interest to the wide general public which regards the Bible as the greatest literary document in the world, and which likes to be able to understand it as the record of an actual people against a factual

---

[16] Kathleen M. Kenyon, *Archaeology in the Holy Land* (London: Benn, 1960).

[17] See Moorey, *Century of Biblical Archaeology,* 94-98.

[18] Ironically, this site is of little importance to the Late Bronze Age or Iron Age I.

background."[19] In this same preface Holland adds his own *coda:* "Everyone interested in the Holy Land will find much food for thought in these pages which reflect the culmination of a lifetime devoted to a greater understanding of the Bible through archaeological excavation and research."[20] This historical, really biblical, approach to the archaeology of the southern Levant is somewhat at odds with Kenyon's predisposition toward prehistory and its interpretative framework. It is ironic that Kenyon, so influential in the development of excavation methodology, a methodology heartily embraced by the "New Archaeologists,"[21] produced a synthetic treatment that adopted a retrograde culture-historical approach. This was a real missed opportunity, especially since the volume itself underwent numerous extensive revisions up through 1979.[22] The result was that Kenyon's summary statement left almost no imprint on the discipline and was out of date, both in terms of the data and, more important, its theoretical perspective, shortly after its original publication and subsequent revisions.

It is interesting to note Kenyon's usage and placement of terms such as *Holy Land* and *Palestine*. In this case *Holy Land* appears in the title, whereas *Palestine* appears in the chapter headings. This is the reverse juxtaposition used by Albright (where *Holy Land* appeared in a subheading on the title page). It is hard to know precisely why these terms are used in particular places, but surely aspects of marketing must be suspected. In the case of Kenyon, her name and degree of recognition outside of England must have been limited, and the use of *Holy Land* in the title would have made the volume more broadly appealing. In the case of Albright, the circumstances are quite different. His name was quite well known throughout leading Protestant circles in America. He was closely associated with all aspects of biblical studies and especially with the area of ancient Israel and had no need to emphasize his clerical connections. He did, however, need forcefully to establish a certain secular legitimacy to his archaeological undertakings, and the use of the term *Palestine* in the title might well have helped. Of course, these musing are highly speculative, but, as we shall see, many terms are used for the southern Levant, each of which transmits subtle but important nuances and shadings.

---

[19] From the preface of the first edition of *Archaeology of the Holy Land* (1960), as quoted from T. A. Holland in the preface to the fourth edition of *Archaeology of the Holy Land* (London: Benn; New York: Norton, 1979), ix.

[20] Holland in Kenyon, *Archaeology of the Holy Land,* ix.

[21] See William G. Dever, "Impact of the 'New Archaeology,'" in *Benchmarks in Time and Culture: An Introduction to Palestinian Archaeology* (ed. J. F. Drinkard Jr., G. L. Mattingly, and J. M. Miller; SBLABS 1; Atlanta: Scholars Press, 1988), 337–352.

[22] For those interested in Kenyon's views, it is the fourth edition of *Archaeology of the Holy Land,* published in 1979, that is of greatest value, with significant updated revisions.

Kenyon's introductory comments about the history of the discipline and field methodology are quite brief, but she is much more expansive about the environment and the Paleolithic and Neolithic periods. Kenyon pays special attention to plant and animal domestication, which is not surprising, based on her work at Jericho. Though dated, Kenyon's coverage of the Natufian and the Neolithic periods is particularly strong, where she includes much of the entire Near East. Each major period is then covered on a chapter-by-chapter basis, concluding with the destruction of Jerusalem by the Babylonians and a few pages dedicated to the post-exilic period.

The number of diagrams and illustrations is limited, but they are usually well placed and useful.[23] More extensive are the ninety-six black and white photographs that present material from the Paleolithic through the Iron Age. Many of these come from Kenyon's own work at Samaria and Jericho. There is also an appendix of excavated sites and bibliography.

Unfortunately, in addition to being out of date, there are several real concerns with this volume. First, although Kenyon herself was very interested in prehistory,[24] the bulk of the volume is a culture history of ancient Israel with a strong biblical flavor, not Kenyon's strong suit. Kenyon, like Albright, also tends to view cultural change as the result of the arrival of new peoples, advancing an "invaders hypothesis" whenever possible (a perspective that fits nicely with the biblical narratives). For Kenyon, newcomers continually arrive into the southern Levant, bringing with them innovative technologies and new styles of material culture. This kind of perspective was already beginning to break down in the late 1960s, and to see it so forcefully presented as late as 1979 is vexing.

This is not to say that this model is not entirely without merit; after all, there were many significant movements of peoples throughout Near Eastern history. However, Kenyon tended to reduce many of the most significant changes in culture to outside invasions. She viewed destruction levels as indications of new peoples arriving, especially when accompanied by a change in the ceramic decorative style. For Kenyon, pots clearly equaled peoples, a proposition that was squarely challenged in an important article by Carol Kramer entitled "Pots and People."[25] This very traditional approach was used by Kenyon to understand the origins of the

---

[23] These consist mainly of line drawings of pottery and architectural plans.

[24] Kenyon made her most important scholarly contributions in the prehistoric periods, especially the Neolithic, the Early Bronze I, and the Early Bronze IV periods. See note 27 below on the issue of Early Bronze IV terminology.

[25] Carol Kramer, "Pots and People," in *Mountains and Lowlands: Essays in the Archaeology of Greater Mesopotamia* (ed. L. D. Levine and T. C. Young Jr.; BMes 6; Malibu: Undena, 1977), 99–112.

Neolithic, Early Bronze I (Kenyon's Proto-Urban period), Early Bronze IV,[26] Middle Bronze Age, and Iron Age. Certainly the archaeological and historical records abound with examples of the movements of social groups, but the relationship of these movements to actual changes in material culture or site-specific events is not axiomatic and must be carefully documented.

A final problem in *Archaeology in the Holy Land* is Kenyon's use of idiosyncratic chronological terminology; she referred to the Early Bronze I as the Proto-Urban period and the Early Bronze IV as the Intermediate Early Bronze–Middle Bronze Age.[27] In both cases, while the terminology might be apt, since they nicely describe the periods they name, they were never fully adopted in the literature.

The last of the founding generation of handbooks is *The Archaeology of the Land of Israel* by Yohanan Aharoni.[28] In the foreword, written by his wife Miriam, she notes that Aharoni quite consciously followed Albright's model used in the *Archaeology of Palestine,* published some thirty years earlier.[29] She then adds that *Archaeology of the Land of Israel* was necessitated by the need to update Albright's work both in terms of the data and "new concepts." Miriam Aharoni also noted that this work would reflect some of the controversial views her husband had held: "From the beginning of his career, however, it was always his practice to disregard the majority opinion when he [Y. Aharoni] believed in some new idea based on actual finds in the field."[30] Such candor regarding the interpretative process is refreshing.

Aharoni's handbook was not just an updated recapitulation of Albright but an opportunity to present an Israeli view of their own past.[31] The

---

[26] Albright had already suggested that the Early Bronze IV and its distinct material culture and the change in settlement patterns were indicative of the arrival of the Amorites.

[27] There is still some lingering ambiguity over Early Bronze IV (ca. 2200–2000 B.C.E.) terminology, which Albright (*Archaeology of Palestine,* 80) referred to as the Middle Bronze I. Some still refer to it as the Middle Bronze I or even the EB IV/MB I (e.g., Mazar, *Archaeology of the Land of the Bible* [see below]), somewhat preserving Kenyon's terminology. More commonly it is referred to as the Early Bronze IV. That being said, some Israeli archaeologists use the term Intermediate Bronze Age; for instance, R. Gophna in A. Ben-Tor's, *Archaeology of Ancient Israel.*

[28] Yohanan Aharoni, *The Archaeology of the Land of Israel: From the Prehistoric Beginnings to the End of the First Temple Period* (trans. A. F. Rainey; Philadelphia, Westminster, 1982). It was originally published in Hebrew in 1978 [*Ha-Archeologiyah Shel Eretz Yisrael* (Jerusalem: Shikmona Publishing Company)]. Both versions were published posthumously.

[29] Miriam Aharoni in Y. Aharoni, *Archaeology of the Land of Israel,* xv.

[30] Ibid., xvi.

[31] For an interesting review of archaeological schools of thought, see part 1 in Perdue, Toombs, and Johnson, *Archaeology and Biblical Interpretation,* on the roles of Albright and

American biblical archaeologists had had their opportunity, the British had theirs (though ultimately it looked a lot like the Americans), but Israelis, who were doing the bulk of the fieldwork, had not yet published a "modern" synthetic overview of the archaeology of their own country. This is an important cross-current in archaeology that underscores the potential of archaeological data and its interpretation to serve a variety of political, religious, nationalistic, and ethno-historical aims. This is why, for instance, in the case of the southern Levant the use of different names for the region can be so revealing. Whereas Albright and Kenyon referred to the southern Levant as either Palestine or the Holy Land, Aharoni used the term "Land of Israel" (translated from the Hebrew *eretz yisrael*), a term invoking both biblical and modern connotations.[32]

Aharoni had a great deal of interest in historical geography, and in many respects this volume on archaeology was a follow-up to his earlier volume, *The Land of the Bible: A Historical Geography.*[33] This volume was a straightforward historical geography of biblical Israel and was a significant contribution to the field of biblical studies. Without straying too far from its intended purpose of providing a detailed historical geography based on the biblical texts, its liberal admixture of environmental studies, history, and archaeology made it innovative and very useful. However, because it was strictly a historical geography, it avoided the kind of tension between biblical narratives and archaeological data commonly found in biblical archaeology handbooks.

Like Kenyon, Aharoni also toyed with chronological terminology. While Kenyon developed new terms that were meant to more appropriately describe periods just coming into focus, Aharoni seemed more intent on imbuing chronology with ethno-history, as opposed to technology. Thus he replaced "Bronze" with "Canaanite" and "Iron" with "Israelite." This type of terminology is extremely problematic for a number of reasons, not the least of which is that it assumes the primacy of singular ethnic identities as meaningful designators of chronological periods. Thankfully, this terminology never gained any traction in the field.

Wright, as well as how Israeli archaeology deals with the biblical texts and the impact of processual (or New) archaeology. See also part 1, "Archaeologists: The Practitioners," in Drinkard, Mattingly, and Miller, *Benchmarks in Time and Culture*. Part 1 covers American, British, French, German and Israeli archaeologists and their history, perspectives, methods, aims, and excavations as well as the institutions in which they work.

[32] See especially the comments of A. F. Rainey, the volume's translator, on the use of this term (Y. Aharoni, *The Archaeology of the Land of Israel*, xiii).

[33] Yohanan Aharoni, *The Land of the Bible: A Historical Geography* (trans. A. F. Rainey; London: Burns & Oates, 1967), which appeared originally in Hebrew in 1962.

Aharoni's keen interest in the environment and archaeological survey in some way presaged the development of processual archaeology in North America, as well as the approach Robert McC. Adams pioneered in Mesopotamia.[34] In fact, some of Aharoni's then-idiosyncratic views of topics such as the Israelite conquest and settlement were based on the results of survey work and not excavation itself.[35]

By the time Aharoni wrote his volume there was a great deal more raw data; however, the basic organization of that data remained the same. As with Albright and Kenyon, Aharoni also came to rely too heavily on the biblical texts. Aharoni's introductory chapter covers field methodology, environment, and history of the discipline, but more briefly than his predecessors. Most of the book is dedicated to the Bronze and Iron Ages, which Aharoni referred to as the Canaanite and Israelite periods (see above). Based on his own excavation interests, it is not at all surprising that his main thrust was on the Israelite period, or Iron Age, with an especial interest in "the period of the formation of the Israelite people in its land."[36] He devoted much less attention to the prehistoric periods from the Paleolithic through the Chalcolithic period, periods in which Aharoni himself was not deeply engaged.

Illustrative material is extensively used, including some eighty-eight figures, thirty-four plates, and fifty-five photographs. Most of the figures are individual architectural plans integrated into the text. Entire pages are dedicated to plates of either pottery or flint tools, and the photographs are grouped together at the back of the volume and cover a wide variety of subject matter. There is a great number of illustrations from Aharoni's excavations at Arad and Beersheba. Considering Aharoni's interest in settlement pattern and historical geography, both the quantity and quality of the maps are disappointing.

The Archaeology of the Land of Israel was never as influential or popular as Aharoni's *Land of the Bible*. However, as the first modern and explicitly archaeological example of an Israeli perspective on the culture history of the southern Levant, it is a landmark volume, and Aharoni was indeed a trailblazer. It is interesting to note that Aharoni's chief rival in

---

[34] See Robert McC. Adams, *Land behind Baghdad: A History of Settlement on the Diyala Plains* (Chicago: University of Chicago Press, 1965); idem, *Heartland of Cities: Surveys of Ancient Settlement and Land Use on the Central Floodplain of the Euphrates* (Chicago: University of Chicago Press, 1981); and Robert McC. Adams and Hans J. Nissen, *The Uruk Countryside: The Natural Setting of Urban Societies* (Chicago: University of Chicago Press, 1972).

[35] In this case, his own survey-work in the Upper Galilee and Negev Desert, areas which had been relatively ignored by archaeologists until then.

[36] M. Aharoni in Y. Aharoni, *The Archaeology of the Land of Israel*, xv–xvi.

the field, Yigal Yadin, never attempted to write this kind of synthetic overview.[37]

A last set of books must also be included within the "founding generation." Although they had little impact in the field, they appeared in a well-regarded series, Archaeologia mundi, published by Nagel. That Syria-Palestine[38] was included in such a popular series was a validation that this branch of Near Eastern archaeology had achieved a degree of acceptance in a wider world of a more anthropological-styled archaeology.

These volumes, *Syria-Palestine I* and *II*,[39] were not meant to be authoritative, but they are visually impressive; their real value lies in their extensive use of high-quality photographic reproduction, including extensive use of color (which is still unusual due to its high cost). These books provided some of the best available views of artifacts, buildings, and sites, and the use of color photographs made the archaeology truly come alive. While the text is long out of date and only served to identify and contextualize the photographs, it is still a pleasure to leisurely peruse their pages simply to get a better glimpse of some of the most spectacular artifacts from the region.

It is on these very solid foundations that all later handbooks are built. While this first generation of handbooks is by and large out of date, they maintain some relevancy in terms of how the discipline and its pedagogy has developed.

THE NEW CANON: BIBLICAL ARCHAEOLOGY HANDBOOKS COME OF AGE

In the early 1990s two very important new handbooks were published, *Archaeology of the Land of the Bible: 10,000–586 B.C.E.*, by Amihai Mazar, and *The Archaeology of Ancient Israel*, edited by Amnon Ben-Tor.[40]

---

[37] Yadin and Aharoni both started out at the Institute of Archaeology at Hebrew University. Yadin became the director of the Hebrew University program, while Aharoni went on to found a competing program and institute at the University of Tel Aviv.

[38] Note the use of the term Syria-Palestine rather than Palestine, the Holy Land, or the Land of Israel. This term was embraced by American self-styled "processual" archaeologists and strongly promoted by William G. Dever (see Zevit, "Three Debates about Bible and Archaeology"). While it suggests a larger region than just Palestine, in reality it includes at most coastal Syria (probably in order to include Ugarit, whose texts became well integrated into biblical studies).

[39] Jean Perrot, *Syria-Palestine I* (trans. J. Hogarth; Archaeologia mundi; Geneva: Nagel, 1979); Aharon Kempinski and Michael Avi-Yonah, *Syria-Palestine II* (trans. J. Hogarth; Archaeologia mundi; Geneva: Nagel, 1979).

[40] Amihai Mazar, *Archaeology of the Land of the Bible: 10,000–586 B.C.E.* (ABRL; New York: Doubleday, 1990); Amnon Ben-Tor, ed., *The Archaeology of Ancient Israel* (trans.

These two new offerings, while continuing the tradition established by Albright, have considerably revised the juxtaposition of text and artifact. For the first time we have an archaeologically based history in which the ties to the biblical texts have been considerably loosened. In this second generation, it is the Israelis who have taken a leadership role and produced both popular and scholarly synthetic handbooks that have become mainstays on college campuses.

Archaeology of the Land of the Bible by Amihai Mazar, first published in 1990 and soon thereafter reprinted in an affordable paperback version, is a marvel at concision and elegance. Finally there was an updated volume (at least through the 1980s) that constructed history from an explicitly archaeological perspective. Though it is filled with references to both the biblical and historical texts, Mazar's purpose, as stated in the preface, was "to present a comprehensive, updated and as objective as possible picture of the archaeological research of Palestine relating to the Old Testament period."[41] This book clearly expressed the view that Syro-Palestinian archaeology was an independent discipline, not inherently linked to the study of the biblical texts. In this publication, Mazar hoped "to narrow the growing fissure between archaeologists and other scholars of disciplines relating to biblical studies."[42] Mazar broke the tension between the archaeological and biblical source material without discounting the relevance of the texts.[43] However, for the first time, it was the archaeology that was given priority and not merely plugged into a biblically derived culture history and used to "illuminate" past historical events.

The result is a comprehensive volume that traces some 9,500 years of history, from the Neolithic period through the end of the Iron Age, in a succinct 572 pages. Needless to say, this is a much longer and more thorough presentation of a greatly expanded database than is found in the earlier works. It is also the first volume fully to digest the wealth of material culture produced in the 1970s and 1980s, one of the richest periods of excavation in the southern Levant. Mazar, a professor of archaeology at Hebrew University, was well positioned to essay this task, having extensive excavation experience in the Bronze and Iron Ages and, perhaps more

---

R. Greenberg; New Haven: Yale University Press; Tel Aviv: Open University of Israel, 1992), which appeared first in Hebrew in 1991 as *Mavo la-arkhe'ologyah shel Erets-Yisra'el bi-teku-fat ha-Mikra* (Tel Aviv: Open University of Israel, 1991).

[41] Mazar, *Archaeology of the Land of the Bible*, xv.

[42] Ibid., xvi.

[43] In his chapters on the Middle and Late Bronze Ages, as well as the Iron Age, all manner of textual and epigraphic data are considered, not only for their historical contents, but also for their archaeological contexts.

importantly, an exemplary record of publication.[44] The end result was a well-rendered archaeological history of the southern Levant. As a single author, Mazar's voice is unerringly clear, and the book has a high degree of internal consistency, making it eminently readable and very engaging.

The introductory chapter includes a thorough overview of the environment, site formation, history of the discipline, excavation methodology, terminology and chronology, publications, and nature of the interpretative process (with an important consideration of the role of ideology). It is in the chapters dedicated to specific time periods where we find real innovation. Interestingly, though the chapter headings themselves are traditional and often invoke biblical periodization, "The Days of the Judges" as opposed to the Iron Age I, there is no doubt as to the clear archaeological orientation of the volume.

Each period chapter is identically organized according to discrete topical units. Chapters begin with some introductory comments and in most cases a section devoted to the historical (and biblical) background, including its internal chronology. The settlement pattern and occupation histories are fully covered, and in most chapters there is a useful chart detailing the comparative stratigraphy of the major sites. Site planning and architecture, pottery, trade, metallurgy, burial customs, and all important forms of material culture, as well as period-specific topics (such as writing or sealing traditions), are all carefully reviewed. Examples of special period-specific topics include: Egypt in the Early Bronze I, international trade and the Egyptian presence in the Late Bronze Age, and the emergence of the Israelites in the Iron Age I.

Because each period chapter is arranged identically, it is relatively easy to access important information both synchronically and diachronically. This allows readers to follow the development of cultural processes and artifact categories across time and in this way gain a much better feel for how archaeologists themselves conceptualize research questions and organize their data. This arrangement underscores Mazar's concern with the importance of comparing underlying historical processes between different periods.

Period chapters begin with the Neolithic. However, close to half the book is dedicated to the Iron Age I and II, dating from 1200 to 586 B.C.E. This comes as no surprise, since the great wealth of archaeological data derives from Iron Age contexts. Separate chapters are dedicated to overall coverage of the Iron Age I, the Iron Age IIA (the united monarchy),[45] and

---

[44] Mazar is currently directing the excavation of Tel Rehov in the Jordan Valley.

[45] Obviously the use of this type of periodization reflects a culture history based on the biblical narratives. One could argue that it might be more accurate to present, say, the tenth-

the Iron Age II B–C (the divided monarchy). There are also more detailed chapters covering "General Aspects of the Israelite Material Culture" and "Israel's Neighbors and the Assyrian and Babylonian Dominations."

Because of its explicit emphasis on archaeological data, the volume is replete with illustrative material, all clearly paginated in a comprehensive list of maps and illustrations. Providing access to the illustrative material is an essential part of any good handbook. If the reader cannot easily locate charts, maps, tables, and figures, it detracts immeasurably from the volume. There are eight tables (mainly comparative stratigraphy charts), eleven maps (with a map of each period indicating the major sites), and an incredible 256 illustrations that include black and white photographs, line drawings, and architectural plans and reconstructions. This emphasis on graphics adds immeasurably to the volume. Each chapter has some citations, but unfortunately there is no extensive bibliography. There is also an appendix enumerating recent discoveries and studies, but this is rather brief and, by now, somewhat dated.

Recently a follow-up volume has appeared, *Archaeology of the Land of the Bible, Volume II: The Assyrian, Babylonian, and Persian Periods (732–332 BCE)*, by Ephraim Stern.[46] This second volume, which begins with the Assyrian conquest of the northern state of Israel and concludes with the Persian period, is modeled on Mazar's but unfortunately is not nearly as successful. Stern's volume is more a reference volume, comprising undigested raw data with little in the way of synthesis.[47] It is also poorly edited, with innumerable errors, and is not suggested as a handbook for undergraduate courses. This is a shame, since the Persian period is sorely neglected in the literature, and there is a tremendous need for just this type of book. Perhaps a second edition will undergo significant revisions.

The Archaeology of Ancient Israel, edited by Amnon Ben-Tor, appeared first in Hebrew, then shortly thereafter in English.[48] In many respects,

---

century B.C.E. material culture without necessarily embedding it within the biblical stories of David or Solomon (note that few, if any, archaeologists would directly relate any archaeological data to the reign of Saul). On this, see Israel Finkelstein and Neil A. Silberman, *The Bible Unearthed: Archaeology's New Vision of Ancient Israel and the Origin of Its Sacred Text* (New York: Free Press, 2002); and Lester Grabbe, ed., *Can A History of Israel Be Written?* (JSOTSup 245; Sheffield: Sheffield Academic Press, 1997). However, regardless of the historical connections Mazar makes, the actual presentation of the archaeological material he dates to a particular time period is on the whole very good.

[46] Ephraim Stern, *Archaeology of the Land of the Bible, Volume II: The Assyrian, Babylonian, and Persian Periods (732–332 BCE)* (ABRL; New York: Doubleday, 2001).

[47] See J. P. Dessel, review of Ephraim Stern, *Archaeology of the Land of the Bible, Volume II: The Assyrian, Babylonian, and Persian Periods (732–332 BCE)*, BAR 28/6 (2002): 58–59.

[48] See Amnon Ben-Tor, *Archaeology of Ancient Israel*, xix. The original Hebrew version was entitled *Mavo la-arkheʾologyah shel Erets-Yisraʾel bi-tekufat ha-Mikra*. Notice the use of

Archaeology of Ancient Israel is very similar to Mazar's volume. This is not unexpected, as Ben-Tor is a colleague of Mazar's at the Institute of Archaeology at Hebrew University, also with a tremendous amount of excavation experience.[49] Additionally, both books were published within two years of each other. In general, there is also a less overt emphasis on the biblical narratives in this volume as compared to Mazar; so, for instance, each chapter title is simply the name of the period, "The Iron Age I" or "The Iron Age II–III."

There is, however, one important difference, Ben-Tor's is an edited volume in which each chapter is written by an expert in that particular period. Though he models himself on Albright, Ben-Tor asserts the need for revision, noting that a single scholar can no longer handle the mass of material it takes to compose a handbook and thus the need for a "team approach."[50] The resulting volume indeed has some added advantage; each chapter reflects a fully developed and mature summary statement on a given period by an expert with direct experience in that period.[51]

However, the lack of a single voice and thus consistent narrative style is also a weakness. The contributors' methods of interpretation differ, especially in their handling of the interrelationship between biblical narratives, history, and archaeology. Usually, this unevenness affects only the style of presentation and not the quality of the content. Still, style or, more specifically, strength of narrative can be an important consideration in the selection of a textbook.

Ben-Tor's introductory chapter is much briefer than many other such chapters, but his musings over the name of the discipline and the traditions of archaeological research are important. Unfortunately, his coverage of the environment is weak, although some of this material is handled within the individual chapters. Because specialists are handling their own material, several chapters are particularly strong. Bar-Yosef's chapter on the Neolithic is perhaps the best general overview of this period in any of the texts under consideration. Other particularly strong contributions include Ben-Tor's on the Early Bronze Age and Kempinski's on the Middle Bronze Age.

As with Mazar, the quantity of illustrative material is exemplary, as is the quality of reproduction. There are eleven tables, most of which are on chronology, handled here in greater detail than in most any other

---

the term *eretz yisrael* for the region, whereas in the English version Ben-Tor adopted the term "Ancient Israel." Mazar, on the other hand, used "Land of the Bible."

[49] Ben-Tor is currently directing the excavation of Hazor.

[50] Ben-Tor, *Archaeology of Ancient Israel*, xix.

[51] Note that Mazar wrote the chapter on the Iron Age I, replicating the same chapter in his own book.

book.[52] There are twenty maps that include period maps of excavated sites and useful artifact distribution maps (e.g., obsidian trade in the Near East, distribution of Abydos ware in the Early Bronze Age, or Negev fortresses in the Iron Age). There are 268 illustrations, again comprised of line drawings and black and white photographs of most of the important artifacts, pottery assemblages, and architectural and stratum plans. Additionally, there are forty-seven color plates of particularly famous artifacts and site views that add greatly to the volume. The use of high-quality paper, even in the paperback edition, makes for high-quality graphic reproductions.

The Archaeology of Society in the Holy Land, edited by Thomas E. Levy, must also be included in the "new canon."[53] This is an unusual volume that does not really follow in the Albrightian tradition, perhaps because, unlike any of the other handbooks, Levy's is the published proceedings of a symposium held at the University of California, San Diego, entitled "The Archaeology of Society in the Holy Land—New Perspectives on the Past."[54] The unusual nature of the volume is made clear by the title, which juxtaposes *Archaeology of Society,* indicating an anthropological orientation, to *Holy Land,* which redirects the reader back to the parochial origins of biblical archaeology.[55] Levy, a prehistorian by training, never really explains why he opts for the term *Holy Land,* although in the preface he goes to great lengths to situate this volume squarely in the camp of anthropological archaeology and in direct opposition to biblical archaeology.[56] Another unusual characteristic, but also a real strength, is the extraordinary temporal coverage, from the Lower Paleolithic through the twentieth century C.E. This is unmatched by any other handbook and makes this volume very useful.

This is another example of an edited volume that intersperses a few thematic contributions into an overall chronological framework. As in Ben-Tor, the contributors are all experts in their field, an obvious strength when

---

[52] The emphasis on chronological and stratigraphic details probably reflects the nature of an edited volume, in which individual experts in specific periods have a greater mastery over and interest in the chronological minutia and its implications for synthetic overviews.

[53] Thomas E. Levy *The Archaeology of Society in the Holy Land* (New York: Facts on File, 1995).

[54] This symposium was sponsored by the Department of Anthropology and Judaic Studies Program at University of California, San Diego, in 1993.

[55] Between political, religious, cultural, and marketing agendas, as well as issues of sponsorship, it is becoming increasingly difficult to parse the precise intentions of these terms. In this case, the use of the term *Holy Land* is perplexing, as Levy assiduously tries to decouple the Bible from the archaeology. Additionally, for most of the periods covered, beginning with the Lower Paleolithic, it is not at all clear that the "land" under consideration is at all "holy."

[56] Levy, *Archaeology of Society in the Holy Land,* x. Levy is currently codirecting, with Dr. Russell Adams, the excavations at Jabal Hamrat Fidan in Jordan.

faced with such an ambitious temporal spread. However, because there are so many contributors (thirty in all) who work in several disparate fields, the flow of the text is somewhat stilted. While each contributor strives to adhere to Levy's "contextual archaeology" approach (stressing the role of the environment, interdisciplinary methodology, and an avoidance of historical particularism), there is a great deal of variability between chapters (unlike in Ben-Tor). There is no overall consistency in the organization of the data, the types of data presented, the theoretical orientations used, levels of sophistication, or the style of writing. This makes for a choppy and uneven volume, with some chapters geared toward the specialist and others more general. In this way the volume reflects its origins as a scholarly symposium, but this structure might not be as well suited for use as a handbook.

Unlike other handbooks, *Archaeology of Society in the Holy Land* covers most of the human history in the southern Levant. It is divided into six parts with a total of thirty-two chapters. The first part, entitled "Approaches to the Past," is a series of five introductory chapters covering some important themes alluded to, but never elaborated on, elsewhere. Three chapters alone are devoted to the natural environment and human population, by far the most developed presentation of this material available anywhere. "Power, Politics and the Past: The Social Construction of Antiquity in the Holy Land" is an excellent history of the discipline by Neil Asher Silberman, who has written extensively on the politics of archaeology in the Near East.[57] Levy himself, along with his long-time collaborator Augustin Holl, introduces the Annales School and the work of Fernand Braudel as a useful historical framework for better understanding the Levantine archaeological record.

Part 2 reaches back into deep time, covering the Lower Paleolithic up through the Epipaleolithic, with detailed coverage of the Natufian. Part 3, "Farmers, Priest, and Princes: The Rise of the First Complex Societies," covers the Neolithic through the Early Bronze III, with a thematic chapter dedicated to animal husbandry in the southern Levant. Part 4, "Canaan, Israel and the

---

[57] For another excellent overview of the archaeological institutions dedicated to the study of the southern Levant, see "Session I: Recollections of the Past," in *Biblical Archaeology Today, 1990: Proceedings of the Second International Congress on Biblical Archaeology, Jerusalem, June–July 1990* (ed. A. Biran and J. Aviram; Jerusalem: Israel Exploration Society and the Israel Academy of Sciences and Humanities, 1993). These "recollections" are charming and highly informative, written by scholars who are intimately involved with the following institutions: the Palestine Exploration Fund, the École Biblique, the American Schools of Oriental Research, the Deutsches Evangelisches Institut für Altertumswissenschft des Heiligen Landes, the Studium Biblicum Franciscanum, the British School of Archaeology in Jerusalem, the Israel Antiquities Authority, and the Israel Exploration Society.

Formation of the Biblical World" covers the Early Bronze IV through the Iron Age I, with specific chapters on the Philistines and the rise of territorial states. Part 5, "Local Kingdoms and World Empires," covers the Iron Age II through the Roman period, with specialized chapters devoted to Israel and Judah from 1000 to 750 B.C.E., the Transjordanian states from the Late Bronze Age to the Iron Age III, and Iron Age destructions in the region. Part 6, "The Rise of Christianity and Islam in the Holy Land," covers the Byzantine, Early Islamic, Crusader, medieval and Ottoman periods, along with a chapter on technology in nineteenth- and twentieth-century Palestine.

It is important to notice how Levy is clearly interested in creating new chronological frameworks based, presumably, on more meaningful socio-political categories. However, as with any attempt at giving greater meaning to chronological divisions, Levy's division is no less artificial than the one it replaces. So, for instance, should the Early Bronze IV be decoupled from the Early Bronze Age and connected to a section (part 4) dedicated to the formation of the biblical world from the Middle Bronze Age to the Iron Age I? Is the Early Bronze IV part of the biblical world? It was for Albright, but should we continue to link the patriarchal narratives to the Early Bronze IV, a form of historical reductionism usually avoided by anthropological archaeologists? Or do the Iron Ages I and II belong in different sections (parts 4 and 5), and should Palestine in the Persian, Hellenistic, and Roman periods be conceptualized in the same way as the Iron Age II? Lastly, should part 6, which considers the rise of Christianity, begin with a chapter that starts in the fourth century C.E.? While Levy's attempt to reorder the chronological units is novel, it is not necessarily any more meaningful than the preexisting system.

Even with these kind of organizational quirks, Levy's volume packs a wallop. It is filled with a tremendous amount of information, cutting, as mentioned, a wide temporal swath. Each period chapter has an excellent topographic map with the major sites indicated. Additionally, the shear volume of graphics, over two hundred in all, is extraordinary; there are countless black and white photographs, maps, line drawings, architectural plans and reconstructions, and even a few color plates. Unfortunately, there is no index or list of the illustrative material, making it hard to access. There are also "windows" at the end of each chapter: self-contained, one-page units illuminating a particular point raised in the chapter. This technique is regularly employed in most university textbooks. The book includes an excellent, comprehensive, and up-to-date bibliography, arranged by chapter.

While Levy's volume is weighty, it is probably too dense and overspecialized for most undergraduate courses. Additionally, quite a few of the articles are not well edited and are riddled with jargon. That said, it is really the only text available that includes periods before the Chalcolithic and after the end of the Iron Age, and in that way it fills a real niche.

Alongside the "new canon" are several very important multivolume encyclopedias that are fundamental reference works. These include the four-volume *New Encyclopedia of Archaeological Excavations in the Holy Land* (*NEAEHL*), edited by Ephraim Stern; the five-volume *Oxford Encyclopedia of Archaeology in the Near East* (*OEANE*), edited by Eric Meyers; and the four-volume *Civilizations of the Ancient Near East* (*CANE*), edited by Jack Sasson.[58] Each is absolutely essential as a starting point for undergraduate research.

NEAEHL is a completely revised and updated edition of the work that first appeared in English in 1978. It is an indispensable encyclopedia of all the excavated sites in modern Israel.[59] Each entry includes information about the site's identification, its history and exploration, excavations, stratum synopses, and a bibliography of the main publications. It is also filled with a tremendous amount of illustrative materials.

Unlike *NEAEHL*, *OEANE* has a wider geographic scope, the entire Near East, and includes many thematic entries. The entries tend to be shorter, with less in the way of graphics or bibliography, but the overall scope is much grander. The inclusion of a wide range of thematic entries (e.g., "building materials and techniques") makes these volumes invaluable.

CANE is organized in a much different fashion. It is comprised of four volumes divided into eleven thematic sections. Themes are wide ranging and include such topics as the environment, history and culture, technology and artistic production, and language, writing, and literature, to name but a few. Within each section are numerous essays that cover most areas of the Near East from Egypt to Iran and from prehistory through the Persian period. The essays are written by experts and provide an excellent introduction to particular topics. Essays tend to be longer and more wide ranging than in the *OEANE* and include a bibliography. There is less in the way of illustrative materials, but this does not diminish the overall high quality of the essays and thus the utility of *CANE*.

THE NEXT GENERATION: A SLIMMER, TRIMMER HANDBOOK

Beginning in the 1990s, the available number of handbooks greatly increased, though interestingly, they appear to be less comprehensive or

---

[58] Ephraim Stern, ed., *The New Encyclopedia of Archaeological Excavations in the Holy Land* (4 vols.; Jerusalem: Israel Exploration Society and Carta; New York: Simon & Schuster, 1993); Eric Meyers, ed., *The Oxford Encyclopedia of Archaeology in the Near East* (5 vols.; New York: Oxford University Press, 1997); and Jack M Sasson, ed., *Civilizations of the Ancient Near East* (4 vols.; New York: Scribner's, 1995).

[59] It includes sites within the projected Palestinian Authority.

authoritative. There is a clear trend here: as the scholarly literature has become more dense and complex, the handbooks have tended to become leaner, with far less actual data. Perhaps, then, these "next generation" handbooks are operating under reductionist pressures, the goal of which is to present simple and straightforward views of greater amounts of data, analyzed in more sophisticated ways.

Three of the best of this new generation are slender but well conceived: *Through the Ages in Palestinian Archaeology: An Introductory Handbook,* by Walter Rast;[60] *An Introduction to Biblical Archaeology,* by Volkmar Fritz;[61] and *Archaeology and the Bible,* by John Laughlin.[62] They all espouse a secular perspective and are explicitly archaeological in their outlook.

Though similar in orientation, all three use different terminology in their titles. Rast uses *Palestine* in the title, the traditional geographic term for the southern Levant, signaling his intent to stick to the archaeology, whereas Fritz uses *Biblical Archaeology.* For Fritz, this controversy over terminology is clearly not an issue.

> Recently there has been, particularly in America, a tendency to replace the term "biblical archaeology" with "Palestinian archaeology." This is directed mainly against too close a connection being made between archaeology and biblical studies, in particular a fundamentalist one. In Germany, the term "biblical archaeology" has never really been used so one-sidedly as a proof for the historical truth of biblical texts.... Biblical archaeology is, just as the archaeology of other regions, a science aimed at regaining, defining and explaining the heritage of peoples formerly inhabiting the land. Thus, biblical archaeology is a means of establishing the historical and cultural heritage of Palestine.[63]

Laughlin's title, *Archaeology and the Bible,* is one of the more innovative. By avoiding the use of any geographical terminology, Laughlin has also cleverly avoided the potential political or religious biases associated with these now "loaded" geographical terms.

Though short (none exceeds 223 pages), they are well written, easy to read, and provide a sound and balanced presentation of contemporary trends and the critical data in Syro-Palestinian archaeology. Their approach

---

[60] Walter Rast, *Through the Ages in Palestinian Archeology: An Introductory Handbook* (Philadelphia: Trinity Press International, 1992).

[61] Volkmar Fritz, *An Introduction to Biblical Archaeology* (JSOTSup 172; Sheffield: JSOT Press, 1994).

[62] Laughlin, *Archaeology and the Bible* (London: Routledge, 2000).

[63] Fritz, *Introduction to Biblical Archaeology,* 12. Fritz's use of the term *Palestine* is in its traditional geographic usage, roughly the area under the British Mandate from 1920 to 1948.

is summed up by Rast in his introduction: "In what follows, this broad picture will be traced in one area only, that of ancient Palestine. We will not pretend to cover everything.... the objective should be to obtain something of an integrated understanding rather than a barrage of factual data that may seem diffuse and unrelated."[64]

However, can less be more? Because these handbooks do not go into detail, they lack a certain gravity, and some of their conclusions are reached after a much too abbreviated presentation of data. In many respects, then, they are abridged versions of Mazar or Ben-Tor, which raises the question, How much data needs to be presented in order adequately to support a systematic overview?

That being said, there is much to commend in these short handbooks, or even better, primers. Rast's volume covers a great deal of ground, from the Paleolithic through the Islamic period, in addition to three introductory chapters that discuss field methodology, archaeological theory, the environment and geography, historical geography, and chronology. Rast, who has a tremendous amount of field experience, writes in an engaging and lively fashion and manages to squeeze many of the most important controversies and ideas into his text. While Rast does include a few observations on biblical history, overall the volume is a straightforward presentation of the archaeological history without any overt reliance on the biblical texts. Each period chapter has a small chronological chart and a highlighted topical "window." However, due to the volume's slender nature, there are few illustrations, photographs, charts, or maps, and the quality of the graphics is lacking. It concludes with a list of selected readings (now out of date) arranged by chapter.

Fritz's volume is limited to the Neolithic through the Iron Age, with a short chapter on the Hellenistic and Roman periods, unfortunately ignoring the Persian period. This is too bad, since the Persian period is increasingly recognized as of particular importance in understanding the cultural context of the period in which Israelite religion and culture transformed itself into Judaism and the Hebrew Bible underwent the process of final editing and canonization.[65]

Chapter 1 is a useful meditation on the interrelationship between biblical studies and archaeology, the "task" of biblical archaeology, the geographical terminology for the region, and the nature of culture-historical studies in the region. Chapter 2 is dedicated to a careful explication of the historical and biblical names used for the southern Levant since the second

---

[64] Rast, *Through the Ages in Palestinian Archaeology*, xii.

[65] See especially Shaye J. D. Cohen, *The Beginnings of Jewishness* (Berkeley and Los Angeles: University of California Press, 1993).

millennium B.C.E., as well as historical geography. The environment is also considered in a brief but remarkably thorough fashion, including a discussion of the topography, climate, and geology, with several useful maps and charts. Chapter 3 is yet another brief but thorough history of the discipline, discussing both the exploration of the region and the development of archaeological research and methodology, including an extremely useful discussion of survey work. Fritz also mentions the most prominent excavation projects, their dates, excavators, and methodology. Chapter 4 is a more detailed look at excavation methodology, explaining about routine field observations, excavation techniques, the process of field documentation, and the variety of scientific analyses (e.g., animal bones, plant remains, pottery, and metal) that are common on most projects. Lastly, Fritz discusses the publication process and an extremely useful how-to guide for reading site reports. The final introductory chapter reviews the chronology of the southern Levant, Egypt, and Mesopotamia. Included are some useful chronology charts, with one comparing the schemes of Fritz, Kenyon, G. E. Wright, and the *Encyclopedia of Excavations*.[66] It is a shame Fritz did not select more current and frequently used chronological schemes, such as those found in Mazar, Ben-Tor, or Levy.[67]

At the core of the book are period chapters. Some of the periods have been combined: the Neolithic and Chalcolithic, and the Middle and Late Bronze Ages. The Iron Age is presented in two chapters, with coverage divided geographically between Israel and Judah in one and Israel's neighbors in another. After an awkward gap, there is a final chapter on the Hellenistic and Roman periods. Obviously, due to their lengths these chapters can cover only so much material. That being said, Fritz is judicious in his selection of material and nicely presents the nuts and bolts of the archaeology, while touching on both the historical and biblical contexts. There is also a postscript entitled "Biblical Archaeology and Biblical Studies," which nicely summarizes Fritz's thinking regarding the secular/biblical split in the discipline.

This book has an impressive amount of illustrative material: forty-two figures comprised of maps, line drawings of artifacts and pottery, architectural plans, and charts; and sixteen plates of black and white photographs of sites, artifacts, and ceramic assemblages. Of special note

---

[66] The sources for these dating schemes are not specifically cited, though Fritz does include a bibliography at the end of the chapter. Presumably the sources are: G. Ernest Wright, *The Pottery of Palestine from the Earliest Times to the End of the Early Bronze Age* (New Haven: American Schools of Oriental Research, 1937); Kenyon, *Archaeology in the Holy Land*; and Stern, *NEAEHL*.

[67] Mazar, *Archaeology of the Land of the Bible*; Ben-Tor, *Archaeology of Ancient Israel*; Levy, *Archaeology of Society in the Holy Land*.

are the striking renderings of artifacts that add immeasurably to the volume. At the end of each chapter is a bibliography, often subdivided by topic.[68] These bibliographies are quite helpful and cite either timeless chestnuts or, as of 1994, up-to-date books and articles. Fritz has done an excellent job in covering a wide range of important topics and intelligently discussing the most important material.

The last, and most recent, of this group is *Archaeology and the Bible* by John Laughlin, published in 2000. Laughlin has benefited by carefully reviewing earlier attempts at this exercise, resulting in a volume similar to Fritz's. Laughlin's intent is clear: "This book is concerned with field archaeology as it is practiced in the Near East, particularly in the modern state of Israel, and its implications for reading and understanding the Bible. It is not intended for archaeologists and/or biblical specialists. It is written for those who are only beginning a serious study of this complex issue."[69] He continues: "My main concern will be with the question of how best to interrelate the data now known through archaeological discovery with the world and text of the Hebrew Bible, commonly called the Old Testament."[70] While this might sound more like a prolegomena to a "biblical" approach, Laughlin makes it clear that he understands "biblical archaeology" as an independent discipline linked to, but in no way dependent on, biblical studies.

The three introductory chapters cover the history of the discipline, the ongoing debate over the relationship between archaeology and the Bible, and field methodology. The description of the various positions in the biblical archaeology "debate" is a helpful précis. A great deal of attention is given to American contributions and especially the position of William G. Dever, who strongly advocated for the term "Syro-Palestinian archaeology."[71] It is a nicely balanced and reasonable introduction to this thorny and probably unresolvable issue.

The chapter on field methodology introduces a number of terms and ideas, such as *stratigraphy, locus,* and *section,* that are important in understanding how the data are obtained. Chronology is covered more specifically in each period chapter (see below), but there is a handy chart

---

[68] So, for instance, at the end of ch. 7, "The Early Bronze Age," topics include urbanization, Narmer, and cylinder seal impressions. For ch. 9, "The Iron Age" topics include the temples of Arad and Jerusalem, fortresses, tombs, Assyrian reliefs, and weights.

[69] Laughlin, *Archaeology and the Bible,* 1.

[70] Ibid., 2.

[71] William G. Dever, "Retrospects and Prospects in Biblical and Syro-Palestinian Archaeology," *BA* 45 (1982): 103–7. See also idem, *What Did the Biblical Writers Know and When Did They Know It? What the Archaeology Can Tell Us about the Reality of Ancient Israel* (Grand Rapids: Eerdmans, 2001), for a much fuller discussion of this issue. See also Zevit, "Three Debates about Bible and Archaeology."

that presents the periodization as found in *OEANE* and the *NEAEHL*.[72] This chapter is based to a large degree on Laughlin's experiences at the site of Banias, which adds to its readability and makes the book accessible to the desired audience.

The heart of the book comprises five chapters devoted to specific periods, with the greatest attention devoted to the Middle Bronze Age through the Iron Age II. Prehistory is given short shrift, packing the Neolithic through the Early Bronze Age, some 6,500 years, into one short chapter, too short really to be of any use. On the other hand, the Iron Age gets two chapters (the Iron Age I and II). In all cases, these chapters are divided by topic, denoted by the judicious use of subheadings. In most cases the topics include an introduction to the period(s), chronology, settlement pattern and population, architecture, material culture (often divided into pottery and other common artifact categories), burial practices, historical and/or biblical texts and contexts, and a useful consideration of how the period ended. Specific issues are given their own subheadings; in this way Egyptian connections in the Early Bronze I, the Hyksos in the Middle Bronze Age, the Amarna Age and the "problem of the 'exodus' out of Egypt" for the Late Bronze Age, the emergence of the Israelites in the Iron Age I, and inscriptional material in the Iron Age II receive special attention.

Of course, the inclusion of topics such as the historical accuracy of the exodus is extremely problematic for an archaeology handbook, although it is a legitimate topic for biblical history. While this issue has become quite popular, there is absolutely no independent archaeological or historical data to substantiate the story of the Israelite exodus from Egypt.[73] The inclusion of this as a topic more usually indicates a "biblical-Albrightian" orientation rather than a "secular" one, so, for instance, Fritz does not even raise this issue in his book. However, as I note below, Laughlin's book is in many ways a very personal exploration, and obviously this is an issue in which he is invested. The topic of the emergence of the Israelites is a bit different from that of the "exodus" and does require more serious attention. With the appearance of the term *Israel* in the Merneptah Stela and the need to explain a variety of changes in the Iron Age I settlement pattern, there are real archaeological and historical problems that need to be

---

[72] Meyers, *Oxford Encyclopedia of Archaeology*; Stern, *New Encyclopedia of Archaeological Excavations in the Holy Land.*

[73] See especially Ernest Frerichs and Leon Lesko, eds., *Exodus: The Egyptian Evidence* (Winona Lake, Ind.: Eisenbrauns, 1997); Finkelstein and Silberman, *The Bible Unearthed;* for a more literal interpretation, see James K. Hoffmeier, *Israel in Egypt* (New York: Oxford University Press, 1997).

tackled. However, whether this issue would be constructed in the same way if there were no biblical texts is important to consider.

The bibliography is cumulative, making it harder to use for the beginner interested in finding topical readings. There are also endnotes for each chapter that are often quite illuminating, touching on some of the most current finds and controversies. There are only twenty-four illustrations, including charts, site plans, photographs, and line drawings of artifacts, architecture, pottery, and reliefs. Interestingly, Laughlin includes a number of architectural reconstructions, which can be helpful for illuminating static architectural plans but are also very problematic if not handled properly. Many of the black and white photographs were taken by Laughlin himself, and while some are acceptable, quite a few are found lacking.

Laughlin's book is unusually engaging; the use of the first person, drawing on his own excavation experiences, the inclusion of his own photographs, and his personal perspective on understanding the material at hand makes for a very lively and agreeable book. There is a sense of a shared journey (a term Laughlin uses freely), and one gets a real feeling of just how hard Laughlin is working to comprehend this diverse body of material and its purported biblical context. In this regard, it is more of a personal and experiential account than the others. While this might not be the best approach for a handbook, one cannot help but admire and enjoy Laughlin's very readable account of one scholar's trek through the trials and tribulations of archaeology in the "Holy Land."

Several handbooks reflect a higher degree of biblical literalism, including *Archaeology and the Old Testament,* by Alfred Hoerth;[74] *Biblical Archaeology: The World, the Mediterranean, the Bible,* by Henry O. Thompson;[75] and *Doing Archaeology in the Land of the Bible,* by John Currid.[76] Each of these scholars appears to accept the basic historicity of the biblical narratives and uses archaeology for support. The inability of these handbooks critically to examine the biblical narratives makes their attempts at integrating text with archaeology problematic. Hoerth may be the most doctrinaire of the three. He flatly asserts that "Abraham was born shortly after 2000."[77] Another example of this kind of inappropriate mixing and matching of archaeology with what Hoerth might consider "tradition" is "Predynastic Egypt: Egypt before Joseph."[78] For most every historian and

---

[74] Alfred Hoerth, *Archaeology and the Old Testament* (Grand Rapids: Baker, 1998).

[75] Henry O. Thompson, *Biblical Archaeology: The World, the Mediterranean, the Bible* (New York: Paragon House, 1987).

76 John Currid, *Doing Archaeology in the Land of the Bible* (Grand Rapids: Baker, 1999).

77 Hoerth, *Archaeology and the Old Testament,* 60. Note that there is no indication of whether this date is B.C.E. or C.E.

78 Ibid., 128.

archaeologist working in the Near East, any consideration of Joseph in Egyptian history is deeply troubling.[79] Simply put, these are not the kinds of assertions that belong in an archaeology handbook, since there are no textual or archaeological data to corroborate them. It is this overwhelming desire to "prove" the validity of the biblical narratives that completely undermines the integrity of Hoerth's volume. Currid's and Thompson's books falls into the same category and are iterations of the same basic material from the same basic perspective.

ARCHAEOLOGY AND A NEW GENERATION OF BIBLICAL HISTORY BOOKS

There is a new generation of biblical history books that also deserve some attention within the context of this survey. They are clearly historical in their orientation and methodology but rely heavily on archaeological data in their interpretation. The most significant of these include *The Israelites,* by B. S. J. Isserlin; *The History of Ancient Palestine,* by Gösta Ahlström; *The Oxford History of the Biblical World,* edited by Michael D. Coogan; and *Ancient Israel, From Abraham to the Roman Destruction of the Temple,* edited by Herschel Shanks.[80] While these are biblical histories in the style of John Bright,[81] they have a sophisticated appreciation and utilization of the archaeological data. In this regard, they follow more closely in the tradition established by J. Maxwell Miller and John Hayes in their *History of Ancient Israel and Judah.*[82]

As the name implies, *The Israelites* is a thorough study of Israelite society and culture, seamlessly interweaving the archaeological, historical, and biblical sources, though its structure is comparable to archaeology handbooks. The introductory chapters undertake a discussion of the archaeological and biblical sources along with a consideration of the origins of the Israelites, a crucial subject for any biblical history. This is followed by an excellent overview of the environmental and human geography, complete with maps. There is also a brief history of the Israelites and a description of their political organization based on the biblical texts.

---

[79] See note 73.

[80] B. S. J. Isserlin, *The Israelites* (London: Thames & Hudson, 1998); Gösta Ahlström, *The History of Ancient Palestine* (ed. Diana Edelman; Minneapolis: Fortress, 1994); Michael D. Coogan, ed., *The Oxford History of the Biblical World,* (rev. ed.; New York: Oxford University Press, 2001); and Herschel Shanks, ed., *Ancient Israel: From Abraham to the Roman Destruction of the Temple* (rev. ed.; Washington, D.C.: Biblical Archaeology Society, 1999).

[81] John Bright, *A History of Israel* (3d ed.; Philadelphia: Westminster, 1981).

[82] J. Maxwell Miller and John H. Hayes, *A History of Ancient Israel* (Philadelphia: Westminster, 1986).

The Israelites is particularly focused on the Iron Age II to illustrate topics such as town and village planning and architecture, agriculture, crafts and industry, trade, warfare, language, religion, and art. Although the use of artifacts to "illustrate" biblical history is traditional, the topical arrangement can be helpful from a student's perspective. In this way it is a nice complementary volume to a more biblical/historical-based approach, also emphasizing the Iron Age. There is a rich array of illustrative materials, including eighty-five high-quality black and white photographs and seventy-four line drawings and illustrations, including maps, architectural plans and reconstructions, and most forms of material culture, even a musical score.

Unfortunately, there is no list of plates and illustrations, making them difficult to access. The bibliography is also not user-friendly, especially for a book designed for a popular audience. However, the biggest drawback to this book is assuming that the author is correct in correlating aspects of Israelite society with exemplars chosen from the archaeological record. So, for example, connections drawn between a biblical description of civil engineering and an architectural feature are by no means direct. This is, of course, the main problem in the general application of archaeology to biblical texts and what distinguishes the archaeologically oriented handbooks (e.g., Mazar, Ben-Tor, or Fritz) from biblical history books.

Ahlström's, Coogan's, and Shanks's volumes are designed as biblical history texts. However, each author or editor went out of his way to include scholars who are either archaeologists themselves or have a great deal of archaeological experience.[83]

Ahlström's *History of Ancient Palestine* deserves special attention. Ahlström clearly understood the problems associated with "doing history" by relying on the biblical texts, in short, that scholars who reconstructed the history of ancient Israel worked in a different way from those reconstructing the history of Mari, Ugarit, or Mesopotamia. He was clearly troubled by the influence of the biblical texts (and their historical limitations), and this was Ahlström's attempt to write a history of the southern Levant in the same way ancient historians routinely do for the rest of the ancient Near East. This synthetic overview, published posthumously, of the history of the Bronze and Iron Ages had a single goal.

---

[83] In Shanks, *Ancient Israel*, Callaway, Miller, Horn, E. Meyers, and Levine are all archaeologists. In Coogan, *Oxford History of the Biblical World*, the archaeologists who contributed include Redmount, Stager, C. Meyers, and Campbell. Ahlström's chapter on prehistoric times (ch. 2 covering the Paleolithic through the Chalcolithic) was written by Gary O. Rollefson, an archaeologist who directed the excavation of 'Ain Ghazal.

The existing handbooks about the history of Israel and Judah all have their limitations. Their main concern has been a presentation of the peoples of Israel and Judah, and too often they merely accept the views of the biblical writers as reliable reflections of past events and their causal relationships. Throughout my years of teaching Syro-Palestinian history I have felt the need to try to present the history of the peoples of Palestine through the millennia in a form freed from the bias of the biblical writers.[84]

Ahlström saw this effort as a complement to Helga Weippert's study of the archaeology of the southern Levant.[85] Both studies are quite dense, detailed, and lengthy; *History of Ancient Palestine* alone is over nine hundred pages and represents Alhström's life's work. One of the most important aspects of it is Ahlström's approach toward the source material (biblical texts, extrabiblical texts, and archaeological data) for writing this history. Consider his views on writing a history of the united monarchy, now a flash point in the controversy between biblical maximalist, minimalist, and self-styled centrist positions:[86]

A period completely unknown in Near Eastern texts except from the Hebrew Bible is that of the so-called united monarchy. No kingdom called Israel or Judah, much less an Israelite empire, is anywhere attested in the

---

[84] Ahlström, *History of Ancient Palestine*, 10.

[85] Helga Weippert, *Palästina in vorhellenistischer Zeit* (Munich: Beck, 1988). This text has been omitted from this overview for several reasons. While it is a comprehensive, thorough, and well regarded work, it is also dense and hard to use. Though Weippert presents an extremely large amount of data, she is less interested in fully digesting it. For these reasons, it is not particularly effective for undergraduate use. It is, however, an excellent reference volume.

[86] There is an ever-growing body of literature on the minimalist/maximalist controversy regarding the historicity of the biblical texts (see especially Zevit, "Three Debates about Bible and Archaeology"). It is increasingly difficult to ignore this topic, in addition to the issue of Iron Age chronology, that is, whether the archaeological strata traditionally dated to the tenth century B.C.E. and thought to be evidence of a united Israel under David and Solomon should be dated to the tenth century B.C.E. (the traditional position increasingly seen as a maximalist) or rather up to a century later, thus reflecting the period of the divided kingdoms of Israel and Judah. For an overview of this complicated and increasingly polemical set of issues, see Finkelstein and Silberman, *The Bible Unearthed;* Dever, *What Did the Biblical Writers Know,* and the bibliographies within. Briefly, the minimalists see no evidence for a united monarchy and have a dubious view even of the period of the divided monarchies (for the minimalists, see Grabbe, *Can a "History of Israel" Be Written?*). Minimalists tend to see the Hebrew Bible as a very late document edited, if not written, in the Hellenistic period and the product of Hasmonean political ambitions. Within this controversy Finkelstein styles himself a centrist, viewing the united monarchy as greatly exaggerated in the Hebrew Bible but endorsing a historical reality for the monarchies of ancient Israel and Judah in the ninth century B.C.E. and fully supporting the "low chronology."

records of the non-Palestinian countries. A presentation of the history of this period, as of any other period in the history of Palestine which lacks external evidence, will therefore be tentative. This is not to deny that there is any reliable information in the biblical texts, but, without the corroboration of external source material, the picture that can be presented from   Judges, Samuel and 1 Kings will be no more of a discussion of what could have been possible. However, when supplemented with the archaeological remains, the plausibility of a kingdom in the hills has to be acknowledged.[87]

Ahlström clearly understands the difficulty in working with the biblical narratives, and though he relies on them for much of his historical interpretation, he struggles with the entire enterprise. For Ahlström, archaeology as well as extrabiblical texts are indispensable for the purposes of historical reconstruction; thus, he has rejected the traditional hierarchical ordering of the sources, with the biblical narratives at the top.

The Coogan and Shanks volumes are useful in that they cover the time periods encompassed by both the Hebrew Bible and New Testament, from the Bronze Ages (understood as the "patriarchal period") to the Roman-Byzantine period, in a relatively thorough fashion. Books that cover this entire time spread are not all that easy to find, though courses often aspire to cover these disparate periods. Shanks's volume is traditional, with individual chapters dedicated to specific biblical periods, such as the patriarchal age or the Roman domination, into which the significant archaeological and historical data are appropriately melded. There are a considerable number of illustrations (thirty-four in all), line drawings, and site plans along with seventeen maps and ten color plates. The color plates include photographs of regions, sites, and artifacts. Though a great deal of archaeological material is responsibly presented, this is first and foremost a history book.

Coogan's volume, which was reissued in paperback in 2001, is also a history book but is constructed in a slightly different fashion. Because this is not wholly devised as an archaeology text, the amount of illustrative material is severely limited; there are only twenty-four maps and eight plates of photographs. The first two chapters cover the Neolithic through the Middle Bronze Age, clearly pre- and protohistoric periods in the southern Levant with little direct connections to the biblical narratives. However, the authors use their treatments to sketch out the setting into which the biblical narratives are embedded from a variety of perspectives: the physical setting, social organization, Near Eastern mythology, and historical

---

87 Ahlström *History of Ancient Palestine,* 35-36.

contexts, as well as the biblical narratives themselves. In later chapters biblical topics and themes are used as points of departure to elucidate the overall history and archaeology. So, for instance, Carol Redmount uses the exodus story to eventually discuss the Late Bronze Age from a more strictly historical and archaeological perspective.[88] In chapter 5, Carol Meyers uses the theme of kingship and kinship in the Iron Age II to elucidate a clear discussion of both the construction of monarchy as found in the biblical narratives and a more archaeological understanding of state formation.[89]

One of the most unusual but successful books in this category is *Life in Biblical Israel* by Philip King and Lawrence Stager, a critical melding of biblical history and archaeology.[90] This is a wonderful volume that uses archaeology to explore everyday life in biblical times. The topics themselves are gleaned from the biblical narratives and represent the most important aspects of biblical society and culture. Douglas Knight, the general editor of the series in which this book appears, The Library of Ancient Israel, clearly states the unambiguous goal of the volume: "The present volume is devoted to precisely that level of social existence that was scarcely known to students of the Bible until the advent of archaeology. In fact, only in recent decades have archaeologists trained their sights on this most fundamental aspect in the history of antiquity—the everyday life of Israelites."[91] The authors themselves see their task as "Utilizing an array of texts and artifacts ... to outline the main features of life in the biblical world. While focusing on the Iron Age, in order to contextualize a vast amount of material, we also called upon the ambient cultures of the ancient Near East."[92]

Is this a return to an Albrightian-styled biblical archeology, or is it more of an attempt to marshal a tremendous amount of new data and apply them to the texts in an appropriate and sensitive fashion? The authors clearly recognize the issues involved with integrating archaeology and scripture, but because their goals are so clearly stated and discrete, the text is allowed to breathe freely, without pressure from unstated theoretical agendas. King and Stager understand the context of the Bible as belonging to the Iron Age and go on intelligently to utilize the vast amount of new Iron Age archaeological data. The life ways King and Stager consider

---

[88] Carol A. Redmount, "Bitter Lives: Israel in and out of Egypt," in Coogan, *Oxford History of the Biblical World,* 58–89.

[89] Carol Meyers, "Kinship and Kingship: The Early Monarchy," in Coogan, *Oxford History of the Biblical World,* 165–205.

[90] Philip J. King and Lawrence E. Stager, *Life in Biblical Israel* (Louisville: Westminster John Knox, 2001).

[91] Douglas A. Knight, "Foreword," in King and Stager, *Life in Biblical Israel,* xviii.

[92] King and Stager, *Life in Biblical Israel,* xix.

include the material and social constructions of "the Israelite house and gousehold," "the means of existence," "the patrimonial kingdom," "culture and the expressive life," and "religious institutions."

Life in Biblical Israel is very well written and organized, and in this way it is more of a reference volume than a handbook. However, the book's lavish production makes it truly stand out. The illustrative materials are simply fabulous; there are over 228 high-quality illustrations reproduced on high-quality paper. They include a wide range of line drawings and black and white photographs, but what is especially noteworthy is the prevalence of color photographs, maps, architectural plans, and site reconstructions. Simply put, this is a beautiful volume that truly makes the material come alive. While it cannot be used alone, it would be an exceptional complement to an appropriate archaeological or historical handbook.

BIBLICAL ARCHAEOLOGY IN TEXT AND IMAGE: TO INFINITY AND BEYOND

The tradition of biblical archaeology handbooks can be traced back to Albright and his powerfully succinct *Archaeology of Palestine,* first published in 1949. The original canon of Albright, Kenyon, and Aharoni took this tradition up through the 1970s, when the discipline underwent tremendous growth in terms of its theoretical underpinnings, methodological practice, and sheer quantity of data. From the growth spurts of the 1970s and 1980s came a new canon: Mazar, Ben-Tor, and Levy. The highly commendable efforts of Mazar and Ben-Tor, in particular, continue to be of great pedagogical importance. Easy to read, well produced, and reflecting a high level of scholarship, they are probably the best overall handbooks on the archaeology of the southern Levant.

That said, they are also a little over ten years old, closer to fifteen if dated to their points of origin. Since then the amount of data has continued to grow, as has the complexity of interpretive frameworks. New controversies abound, especially regarding the Iron Age chronology,[93] and some important old ones have never quite been resolved, especially regarding the historicity of the biblical texts and the relationship between text and artifact. It would be a real service if both Mazar and Ben-Tor were revised and thoroughly updated; regardless, their influence will be felt for a very long time.

---

[93] It would interesting to see how Mazar and Ben-Tor would handle this issue; both are "traditionalists" when it comes to the tenth century B.C.E. and interpretations of the united monarchy. Mazar in particular has been quite involved in Iron Age chronology, as C-14 dates from his site of Rehov are of great importance vis-à-vis the redating efforts of Finkelstein (see in general Finkelstein and Silberman, *The Bible Unearthed,* and bibliography). Regardless of where the dates finally settle out, Finkelstein has raised important issues in Syro-Palestinian archaeology that cannot be ignored.

WHY DECLARE THE THINGS FORBIDDEN? CLASSROOM INTEGRATION OF ANCIENT NEAR EASTERN ARCHAEOLOGY WITH BIBLICAL STUDIES IN THEOLOGICAL CONTEXT

Scott R. A. Starbuck
Gonzaga University and Whitworth College

Whether deliberately added as multimedia to a biblical studies curricula or simply included as illustrations in an introductory text, the pedagogical impression left by archaeological remains, even when used simply as "visual aids," can hardly be overstated. The integration of ancient Near Eastern archaeology with biblical studies in theological contexts, however, is another matter. This article offers empathetic and practical reflection for biblical studies instructors who recognize the integral relationship between theological reflection and the assessment of archaeological realia but are perplexed if not beleaguered by student resistance to the task. To this end, the article begins with an elucidation of the epistemological culture that is often implicit in the biblical studies classroom. Second, a particular theological hermeneutic is offered as a working example of one sustainable approach to a theological integration of text and artifact. Finally, the article offers a test case through an examination of the material remains of Kuntillet ʿAjrûd (Horvat Teiman).

THE CHALLENGE OF INTEGRATION

It is important for me to clarify that I write from the theological perspective of a Christian biblical scholar. In doing so I am reminded of Moshe H. Goshen-Gottstein's comment that "Jewish scholars instinctively shrink back from the very mention of 'theology' in the context of biblical studies."[1] Perhaps excusably, then, the "theological context" I know and,

---

[1] Moshe Henry Goshen-Gottstein, "Tanakh Theology: The Religion of the Old Testament and the Place of Jewish Biblical Theology," in *Ancient Israelite Religion: Essays in Honor of Frank Moore Cross* (ed. P. D. Miller Jr., P. D. Hanson, and S. D. McBride; Philadelphia: Fortress, 1987), 618.

hence, have in mind throughout this article is a seminary or a church-related liberal arts college or university. My assumption is that these theological contexts have an interested stake in biblical theology as well as doctrinal and systematic theology. Although the relationship between archaeological reconstruction and biblical historiography is complex, multifaceted, and controversial, the aim here is to provide hermeneutical sophistication for the integration of Near Eastern archaeological theory and biblical theological reflection. For the sake of this essay, all of these terms must be held rather loosely. Suffice it to say that biblical theology, at least in the view of this essay, is not synonymous with a history of Israelite religion but inclusive of it.

There are different ways to quantify the outcomes of integration of Near Eastern archaeology and biblical studies.[2] For the purposes of this essay, I will isolate four primary outcomes:

Outcome 1: Archaeological findings hold essential continuity with the biblical text.
Outcome 2: Archaeological findings provide additional information beyond what is provided in the biblical text.
Outcome 3: Archaeological findings conflict with and/or correct the biblical text.
Outcome 4: Archaeological findings conflict with assumed dogmatic perspectives, necessitating a new understanding of the text and its theological claims.

Outcome 1 examples would include findings such as the "House of David" inscription found at Tel Dan. A broad listing of data would fit under outcome 2, much of which has profitably been implemented in classroom settings as "visual aids" that illumine the cultural and ideological milieu. Iconographic representation of a cherub throne on the Meggido Ivories, for example, expands a student's understanding by analogy to the Jerusalem temple throne. Likewise, the discovery of a first-century "fishing vessel" in the mud of the Sea of Galilee can help students envision, at least partially, the plight of fisherman at the time of Jesus.[3] At the same time, it must be admitted that the archaeological data unearthed thus far has rendered, practically without exception, outcome 3, with regard to the narratives of

---

[2] For a recent example, see Janice Catron, "Digging for Truth: Archeological Studies Are Shedding New Light on Biblical Accounts," *Presbyterians Today* (April 2002): 10–15.

[3] James H. Charlesworth, "Archaeology, Jesus, and Christian Faith," *What Has Archaeology to Do With Faith?* (ed. J. H. Charlesworth and W. P. Weaver; Faith and Scholarship Colloquies; Philadelphia: Trinity Press International, 1992), 10.

Joshua and Judges. Finally, the epigraphic finds at Kuntillet ʿAjrûd that make mention of "Yahweh and his Asherah" have provided additional insight into the struggle within Israel between polytheism and monolatry, not to mention monotheism. When students are presented with these finds, their often-inherited assumptions around the perspicuity of monotheism in ancient Israel is challenged, often in such a way as to call into question their own theological beliefs.

Among students in the biblical studies classroom in theological contexts, outcomes 1–2 are generally given enthusiastic welcome. However, when the instructor presents data or interpretations that lead to outcomes 3–4, many students will, at a minimum, experience significant cognitive dissonance. For the instructor, this means that, in addition to the challenges inherent in working with archaeologically diverse material, evolving concepts, and competing scholarly positions outside one's expertise, one must also spend significant energy on helping students through their anxiety, doubts, and confusions, while at the same time mitigating a regressive drive to prejudge all archaeological data by whether or not they confirm normative belief (outcome 1). This regressive drive, of course, is far from a ridiculous or completely misguided assumption on the part of the students, considering not only the complexity of archaeological presentation but especially given the tendency of religious leaders to use archaeological findings rather simplistically to bolster and illustrate the biblical narrative. Moreover, it has not been simply the proclivity of religious leaders. "Conservative scholars in particular, but liberal scholars as well," reminds Ziony Zevit, "assumed that if archaeology could demonstrate that something might have occurred, that was proof sufficient that it had occurred if the Bible so indicated."[4]

Indeed, in theological settings the classroom experience can be confusing for teacher and student alike. All too often when archaeological datum is presented that disconfirms or contradicts the presumed historicity of the biblical account, passions flair and insecurities circle. From a student perspective, things "fascinating" quickly turn to things "forbidden," especially when the class is unprepared to process unanticipated or competing truth claims. Many an instructor has found herself echoing Robert Frost's wonderment: "But why declare the things forbidden that while the Customs slept I have crossed to Safety with?" Poetry aside, the question becomes: How does the instructor integrate archaeological findings implying an array of outcomes (1–4) and that, having safely survived centuries, now press themselves upon biblical as well as "normative" belief developed through traditional theological discussion and practice over centuries? It is seldom an easy or simple task.

---

[4] Ziony Zevit, "Three Debates about Bible and Archaeology," *Bib* 83 (2002): 7.

In some contexts matters are complicated further by a reluctance to allow the discipline of ancient Near Eastern archaeology an independent voice in biblical discussions. Again, this tendency, though regrettable, is understandable. Over the last decade my observation has been that student loyalties are more naturally given to scriptural tradition than to distinct fields of academic inquiry. Many students who enter the biblical studies classroom from a theological perspective hold tight to positivistic assumptions that archaeological data will, eventually, confirm the "truth" of the bible (outcome 1). Even more, for students the "truth" of the Bible encompasses more than historical accuracy and includes an assumption of normative religious practice in biblical times. Although I run into few students who are willing to dismiss archaeological data out of hand, throughout each semester I am ever aware that many, if not most, students emotionally cling to a positivistic perspective something like: "When *all* of the evidence is in, and has been *properly* understood, archaeology will confirm what the Bible has already stated to be true."[5]

Whereas one can hold to the *logical possibility* of such ultimate corroboration, to honor such a perspective as a *necessary* solution among students could be considered a form of theological dysfunction. If all *proper* archaeological interpretation must ultimately confirm biblical "truth," then the field of archaeology itself is wrested from its status as an independent discipline and becomes the "yes-person" of biblical theology. In other words, a form of theological enmeshment manifests where the archaeological discipline is engulfed, distorted, and abused.

It is the instructor's task, then, to provide students with a hermeneutical sophistication that will allow them properly to integrate the fields of biblical studies and archaeology as well as to allow these disciplines to inform, challenge, mature, and broaden confessional faith perspectives already held. At the core, it is the broad and multifaceted task of relating science and religion, the possibilities of which Ian Barbour has characterized as conflict, independence, dialogue, and integration.[6] The first step is to allow both disciplines their own integrity.

METHODOLOGICAL DIFFERENTIATION

To those working in theological contexts, it may seem counterintuitive to stress a healthy differentiation between biblical studies and ancient Near

---

[5] Randall Price, *The Stones Cry Out: What Archaeology Reveals about the Truth of the Bible* (Eugene, Ore.: Harvest House, 1997), 344.

[6] Ian G. Barbour, *Religion and Science: Historical and Contemporary Issues* (New York: HarperCollins, 1997), 77–105.

Eastern archaeology. For much of the last century archaeology has been viewed as an aide-de-camp for biblical studies. The Biblical Theology movement in particular looked to the discipline of archaeology to confirm the likelihood of segments of the biblical record. Archaeological possibility turned, as a matter of course, to theological probability. Remains of the earth provided intellectual bedrock for biblical theological discourse in a positivistic climate.

Understandably, when William Dever proposed in the 1970s that the rubric known as "biblical archaeology" should be corrected to "Syro-Palestinian archaeology," a firestorm of controversy erupted. At heart, as Zevit observes, was the struggle over interpretation of archaeological data and its relation, if any, to theological context:

> There are many more teachers of the Bible in the world than there are archeologists working in the Iron Age period, and the overwhelming majority of these teachers work in denominational settings which are explicit and implicit theological programs that are *a priori* to whatever archeologists might discover. The call for a change in terminology was intended to sever the connection between the archeological and the theological, to disallow any claims that archeology of the physical had implications for the metaphysical, and to delegitimize any interpretive authority that theologically driven Biblicists might claim over archeological data.[7]

Despite initial rejections, Dever's call for a distinction between the disciplines of archaeology and biblical studies won the day. The modifying adjective "biblical" increasingly was shown to be illusive. Not only was archaeological praxis far-extended beyond Syro-Palestine, but the practitioners themselves were experts in excavating, cataloguing, and proffering interpretation, but not necessarily in the disciplines of biblical scholarship. Notably, in its sixty-first year of publication (1998), the American Schools of Oriental Research renamed its flagship journal, *Biblical Archaeologist,* as *Near Eastern Archaeology.* The change in masthead is significant not only in terms of scope but even more in demarcating a separation of methodologies.

The insistence upon methodological differentiation by archaeologists has, unfortunately, encouraged biblical theologians to read the Bible synchronically as nonhistoric literature. This is hardly a satisfactory pedagogy within the biblical studies classroom in theological contexts, particularly given the reasonable expectation among most students that the God of the biblical text would be reflected in actual history. The question is not

---

[7] Zevit, " Three Debates about Bible and Archaeology," 8.

whether an integration of the two fields is needed, but if and how it can
be done.

AN INTEGRATIVE THEOLOGICAL HERMENEUTIC

Allowing each field of study given voice in the biblical studies classroom to have its own methodological integrity is not only desirable but a
necessity, if any genuine integration can take place. At the same time, an
integration of archaeological studies and biblical studies in theological context must rest on an epistemological verification other than historical
positivism. Within the theological context that I work and teach, I have
found a Barthian "incarnational" hermeneutic to offer a useful epistemological paradigm shift that equips students with a nonpositivistic model by
which to hold the two scholarly methodologies together without fragmentation or dilution. It is intelligible to students because the model itself
derives from a central theological perspective. It is rhetorically persuasive
in and as much as its implications can be anticipated analogously from the
discipline of pastoral counseling (a discipline with which most students
have a working awareness).

Of course, an "incarnational" hermeneutic is hardly a novel suggestion.
A decade ago W. Waite Willis Jr. suggested a similar epistemological
schematic. Seeking to avoid a positivistic approach that rejects a priori any
archaeological result that questions the historical accuracy of the Bible, or
its converse, a positivistic approach that blindly accepts archaeological
theory by dismissing biblical accounts out of hand, Willis posits an "open-
ness" to the Christian understanding of God's incarnation in Jesus Christ so
that the incarnation itself is considered an open and ongoing event. As
such, the incarnation

> reveals the way in which God has always acted and continues to act in
> and through history. This incarnational event is open towards the past as it
> perceives God's work in and indentification with ancient Israel as narrated
> in the Hebrew Bible, not merely in the so-called great acts but primarily in
> God's indwelling with the people. This incarnational event is open to the
> future as well. God continues to work in the Spirit in history.[8]

Willis holds that the cooperation between the human, which is historical
and fallible, and the divine, which is guided by the Spirit, can adequately
explain how, on the one hand, the biblical texts can be shown to be at

---

[8] W. Waite Willis Jr., "The Archaeology of Palestine and the Archaeology of Faith:
Between a Rock and a Hard Place," in Charlesworth and Weaver, *What Has Archaeology to Do
with Faith,* 102.

times historically inaccurate in comparison to archaeological reconstruction and, at the same time, remain divinely intended and hence theologically essential. This, according to Willis, alleviates the cognitive dissonance experienced by religious students per outcomes 3–4. In other words, the Bible may not always be historically factual (according to archaeological reconstruction), but it may be nevertheless "true" theologically.

In my view, Willis outlined the beginnings of a penetrating theological hermeneutic, but he did not develop it thoroughly enough to be serviceable for students. That is to say that, although such an incarnational understanding of scripture is an accurate hermeneutic in Christian theological contexts, it does not provide enough guidance for the classroom in which an interdisciplinary approach is desired. Willis has circumscribed the theological ontology of the text. How, then, should its students approach interpretation?

Practically, the discipline of pastoral counseling offers heuristic guidance by way of analogy. Often feeling a hybrid of sorts, pastoral counselors are trained in two distinct (and often competing) disciplines: theology and psychotherapy. The key methodological question in "treating" a patient for the pastoral counselor is, "how can pastoral counseling be at the same time an authentically theological and a scientifically psychological discipline?"[9] One could well restate this question in terms of the use of archaeological data in the theological contexts: How can biblical studies be at the same time an authentically theological and a scientifically historical-archaeological discipline?

Deborah van Deusen Hunsinger answers this dilemma with the application of a hermeneutical approach resident in Karl Barth's *Dogmatics,* referred to in her proposal as the "Chalcedonian Pattern."[10] This nomenclature is a direct reference to the Council of Chalcedon, which in 451 C.E. explicated the incarnational nature of Jesus Christ who was at once and the same time "fully God and fully human." For students, it is often more helpful to refer to it in terms of an interpretive lens.

For Barth, the lens or pattern held together the "indissoluble differentiation," the "inseparable unity," and the "indestructible order" of two integrated but distinct concepts.[11] Obviously applicable to the concept of God's incarnation in Jesus Christ, it is essential to note that for Barth the hermeneutical lens or pattern was applicable to concepts beyond particular

---

[9] Charles V. Gerkin, *The Living Human Document: Re-visioning Pastoral Counseling in a Hermeneutical Mode* (Nashville: Abingdon, 1984), 11.

[10] Deborah van Deusen Hunsinger, *Theology and Pastoral Counseling: A New Interdisciplinary Approach* (Grand Rapids: Eerdmans, 1995).

[11] Ibid., 65.

manifestation of the "divine" and the "human" in Christ. For example, Barth used the pattern to explicate the integration of body and soul as well as the paradoxical continuities between, and yet distinctiveness of, grace and human gratitude, God's command and human obedience, and God's promises and human faith.

As Hunsinger aptly demonstrates, the Chalcedonian hermeneutic provides the integrative model by which to relate to separate disciplines of theology and psychology. While avoiding simplistic reductionism, where terms from one field are understood as mere translations of terms from the other field (such as forgiveness = healing), the pastoral counselor is to be competently bilingual,

> as one who speaks not only the language of depth psychology but also the language of faith.... The pastoral counselor uses two distinctively different frames of reference for interpreting the counselee's material without confusing them with each other. At the same time the pastoral counselor recognizes the inseparability of theological and psychological materials in the life events of the counselee and in psychological constructs, such as the God representation.[12]

In other words, the disciplines of theology and psychology must be kept distinct and unconfused in the mind of the pastoral counselor while he treats a complex but unified human being.

This is particularly important because, at the most basic level, the two disciplines privilege different epistemologies. As a scientific discipline, psychology is based on empirical data. Theology, on the other hand, is most commonly grounded in authoritative textual tradition. Inevitably the two epistemologies will conflict, appearing on the surface to be mutually exclusive. In such cases it is incumbent upon the pastoral counselor to hold the perspectives of the two disciplines in tension as dual interpretive strategies rather than to seek a superficial resolution and to consider it a viable integration. The human being is too complex and the individual disciplines are each too limited for hasty generalization. At the same time, it is obvious that the two disciplines are unified in and as much as they center on the exposition and interpretation of an individual's being. In this way, the disciplines remain wholly separate with individual integrity yet, at the same time, are mutually influential. Interdisciplinary integration, then, is rather pragmatic. It is manifest throughout the pastoral counseling process as both disciplines are set to the task, and their unique perspectives are adjudicated by the counselor and patient alike as to their suitability for cogent explication.

---

[12] Ibid., 213.

What happens, though, when each discipline held in its own distinctiveness, conflicts with the other? Both psychology and theology have a good deal to say about sexuality, for example. Which perspective, according to the Chalcedonian hermeneutic, should hold sway? The Chalcedonian hermeneutical lens affirms not only the indissoluble differentiation and the inseparable unity but also the *indestructible order* of two integrated but distinct concepts. For Barth this meant that there was a logical precedence of one concept over the other: the divine over the human. Hunsinger describes this in terms of asymmetry in relationship. Simply put, and according to the internal logic of the ordering of Chalcedonian language itself, "fully God and fully human," an asymmetrical logical priority is to be given to theology over psychology.

> When these principles are applied to pastoral counseling, one would say that theology depends on psychology to operate competently in its own sphere, to give us reliable knowledge of human psychological functioning. However, a knowledge of psychology, no matter how profound, cannot provide us with what we believe about God and the world and our place in it. What we believe about the deep purposes of human life, and the particular human life that is ours to live, can only be addressed from the standpoint of faith.[13]

Such asymmetrical logical priority should be viewed more in terms of a final arbitrating perspective rather than a first voice in dialogue. In other words, the empirical science (psychology) is limited to a description of how things "are," whereas theology seeks to describe what things are "intended to be."

By analogy, in the biblical studies classroom one might well envision the scriptural text as the "patient" and the distinct fields of biblical theology and ancient Near Eastern archaeology as interpretive strategies for understanding and explicating the "patient." If so, the Chalcedonian hermeneutic becomes vital.

In theological contexts, an authoritarian epistemology that renders a canon of hallowed texts must be given full and distinct voice. At the same time, the fact that the God of the canonical text is portrayed being intrusive to the physical world in actual historical settings, necessitates, on the other hand, the full voice of the archaeological discipline. Since the epistemological foundation of archaeology is empiricism and not authoritarianism,[14] students should be instructed to anticipate periodic epistemological conflict (i.e., outcomes 3–4). According to the Chalcedonian pattern, biblical theology and ancient Near Eastern archaeology should be approached in the

---

[13] Ibid., 22.
[14] Lewis R. Binford, *An Archaeological Perspective* (New York: Academic Press, 1972), 5–32.

biblical studies classroom as "indissoluble in differentiation," hence wholly distinct and separate. In other words, when archaeological and theological epistemologies stand in conflict, it is a confirmation that they have been allowed the unique integrity of their perspective. At the same time, students should be able to experience the "inseparable unity" of the two disciplines as each is used to explicate the ancient historical world of biblical times. Note that according to this hermeneutical paradigm, both disciplines are integrated in as much as they explicate the ancient historical context. They *do not* explicate each other.

The fact that the disciplines of biblical theology and ancient Near Eastern archaeology are integrated *in the process* of explicating the ancient historical context affirms the third aspect of the Chalcedonian hermeneutic: *indestructible order.* Archaeologists set their sights on the historical and cultural reconstruction of a given site. The biblical theologian's aim is different. The biblical theologian attempts to explicate the meaning of a text that is tempered and grounded in a particular historical and cultural matrix. For each, the drive toward an accurate explication of the ancient historical context is of extreme importance. However, the discipline of biblical theology goes beyond the limits of ancient Near Eastern archaeology. Biblical theology seeks to exegete meaning that ultimately, though rooted within, transcends the particularity of the original historical context. "[Archaeology] does, however, have its limits," reminds Dever. "[A]rchaeology illuminates, but cannot confirm; it brings understanding, but not necessarily belief."[15]

A TEST CASE: KUNTILLET ʿAJRÛD (HORVAT TEIMAN)

Although it was published in 1978, the epigraphic and nonepigraphic remains found at Kuntillet ʿAjrûd continue to excite, boggle, and distress biblical studies students in theological contexts. It is a particularly interesting archaeological site for a test case of the Chalcedonian hermeneutic, since its data render each of the four outcomes.

Excavations at Kuntillet ʿAjrûd, approximately fifty kilometers south of Kadesh-barnea, revealed two buildings, wells, several plaster inscriptions, inscribed stone bowls, and inscribed pithoi. Located atop a prominently rising mound in the northeast Sinai Desert, the larger of the two buildings contains a small courtyard and a large bench room. On the basis of paleography as well as an internal analysis of the inscriptions, P. Kyle McCarter Jr. dates the realia to the beginning of the eighth century

---

[15] William G. Dever, "Biblical Archaeology," *OEANE* 1:318–19.

B.C.E. (138).[16] Pottery samples confirm an Iron II date, and Ze'ev Meshel reports that Neutron Activation Analysis locates their origin in the vicinity of Jerusalem.[17]

Three plaster inscriptions attest Hebrew language written in Phoenician script. Two additional plaster inscriptions attest Hebrew written in Hebrew letters. One of the inscriptions, apparently a ritual liturgy, twice makes reference to "Yahweh of Teman and his Asherah." The most extensive plaster inscription attests the language of theophany of El. Here, too, a blessing is recorded: "bless Baal in (the) day of war ... the name of El in (the) day of war."[18]

Similarly, an inscription written in red ink on one of the large pithoi records a priestlike blessing by a certain "Amaryo" through the invocation of "Yahweh of Teman [Edom] and his Asherah." In addition, a second blessing can be discerned that reads: "Yahweh of Shomron [Samaria] and his Asherah" from a certain "A[shyo m[lk]." Meshel suggests this to be a reference to Joash, the king of northern Israel who ruled from approximately 802–786 B.C.E.[19] Curiously, this inscription is written above two artistic representations of the Egyptian deity Bes. Additional figures, namely, a seated harp-playing figure that is probably an Asherah representation, the tree of life, and various animals, decorate the storage jar as well. On the other pithos, five or six human supplicants are painted in procession. The relationship between the inscriptions and artwork is not immediately evident, though it appears that the scribe and artist comprise two different people.[20]

Four inscriptions were found on the rims of the stone bowls, the most well preserved of which read, "Belonging to Obadiah son of Adnah. Blessed be he to Yahw[eh]."[21] Presumably the bowls were dedicated by supplicants seeking divine blessing.

Meshel provided his overall assessment in 1997:

> The subject matters of the inscriptions, the references to various deities, and the presence of dedicated vessels all suggest that Kuntillet ʿAjrud was not a temple but a kind of religious center. Given its location (it may have been associated with journeys of the Israelites to Eilat and to Ezion-Geber and perhaps with those of pilgrims to southern Sinai), the absence of

---

[16] P. Kyle McCarter Jr., "Aspects of the Religion of the Israelite Monarchy: Biblical and Epigraphic Data," in Miller, Hanson, and McBride *Ancient Israelite Religion,* 138.

[17] Ze'ev Meshel, "Kuntillet ʿAjrud," *OEANE* 3:311.

[18] Ibid.

[19] Ibid., 3:312.

[20] Pirhiya Beck, "The Drawings from Horvat Teirman (Kuntillet ʿAjrud)," *TA* 9 (1982): 3–68.

[21] McCarter, "Aspects of the Religion," 150.

ritual appurtenances usually associated with cult or sacrifices (e.g. altars), as well as its architectural plan, it may have been a wayside shrine. A journey south along the Darb Ghazza from Qadesh-Barnea might have included stopping at this well side station to make dedications to Israel's god in the bench room of the main building.[22]

Amihai Mazar notes that the site attests ties to both northern Israel and southern Judah.[23] On the one hand, the large pithoi are typically Judean (which corresponds to the neutron activation analysis). On the other hand, the inscribed names, mention of "Yahweh of Samaria," and Phoenician motifs all suggest ties to northern Israel. From the lack of Negevite (local) pottery, one might infer that relations with local nomads were underdeveloped or avoided.

Consistent with the Chalcedonian hermeneutic, the summary of realia at Kuntillet ʿAjrûd was reported without reference to the biblical text, biblical studies, or theological reflection. The archaeological discipline has been allowed to stand on its own. As such, the data are suggestive. At this eighth-century B.C.E. wayside shrine, Yahweh, El, Baal, Yahweh's Asherah, and possibly the god Bes were worshiped. Worshipers most likely included Israelites and Judeans (and perhaps Edomites). Some of the Yahweh worshipers also worshiped "his Asherah," the exact identification of which remains debated. For the purposes of this essay, we will assume that "his Asherah" refers to a divine consort. Apparently Baal and El were also venerated by some in tandem. Most important is the constellation of the worship of all these deities under the same roof. By analogy and extrapolation, one might posit that Kuntillet ʿAjrûd presents a window into popular worship within Israel and Judah in the eighth and seventh centuries B.C.E.

When brought into comparison with the biblical text, the archaeological realia of Kuntillet ʿAjrûd render each of the four outcomes. According to 2 Kgs 23:4–6 (NRSV),

> [Josiah] commanded the high priest Hilkiah, the priests of the second order, and the guardians of the threshold, to bring out of the temple of the LORD all the vessels made for Baal, for Asherah, and for all the host of heaven; he burned them outside Jerusalem in the fields of the Kidron, and carried their ashes to Bethel. He deposed the idolatrous priests whom the kings of Judah had ordained to make offerings in the high places at the cities of Judah and around Jerusalem; those also who made offerings to Baal, to the sun, the moon, the constellations, and all the

---

22 Meshel, "Kuntillet ʿAjrud," 3:312.

23 Amihai Mazar, *Archaeology of the Land of the Bible, 10,000–586 B.C.E* (ABRL; New York: Doubleday, 1990), 449.

host of the heavens. He brought out the image of Asherah from the house of the LORD, outside Jerusalem, to the Wadi Kidron, burned it at the Wadi Kidron, beat it to dust and threw the dust of it upon the graves of the common people.

Although referring to the temple in Jerusalem and the high places around Judah, Josiah's cleansing is predicated on the actual worship of Baal, Asherah, and the host of heaven within Judah. Likewise, in 1 Kgs 18:19–20, Elijah summons 450 prophets of Baal and 400 prophets of Asherah to Mount Carmel. The vast number of prophets itself signals the popularity of Baal and Asherah worship in northern Israel. That fact that Baal and Asherah were worshiped at Kuntillet ʿAjrûd, a wayside shrine for Israel and Judah, renders outcome 1, essentially confirming the historical and cultural understanding present in the biblical text.

Outcome 2 (archaeological findings provide additional information beyond what is provided in the biblical text) is rendered by a contrast between the force of archaeological data and the relative silence of the biblical text. As P. Kyle McCarter points out, "Most often the religion supported by those in power in Jerusalem and Samaria was a kind of Yahwism different from that represented by the Bible, and it seems impossible to determine the full character of this religion on the basis of the study of the Bible alone."[24] By examining building structure, artistic representations, inscriptional prayer and invocation, students are able vastly to supplement their perception of popular worship in ancient Israel and Judah. According to this facet of interpretation, archaeological data confirms and supplements the biblical text.

It is with outcome 3 that the need for the Chalcedonian hermeneutic becomes more desirous in theological contexts. If "his Asherah" is to be understood as Yahweh's consort, then we have direct evidence that a female deity was venerated in conjunction with Yahweh in popular worship. The rub is *in conjunction with Yahweh.* It is one thing for students to imagine the worship of gods other than Yahweh and to consider such worship to be tantamount to idolatry and/or human projection. The augmented worship of Yahweh with his Asherah seems, perhaps illogically, another matter altogether. It is almost as if students of faith experience an empathy or kinship with the worshipers of Yahweh. So in this case, where there is an archaeological epigraphic record of worshipers of Yahweh and a consort, the students feel confronted with competing truth claims in ways that create much more cognitive dissonance than being confronted with worshipers of El or Baal or Molech. If the students

---

[24] McCarter, "Aspects of the Religion," 138.

are informed of other similar epigraphic finds, then they will be undoubt-edly left with the strong impression that Yahweh together with Asherah were widely and popularly worshiped in the eighth and seventh centuries B.C.E. (Halpern),[25] a matter relegated to virtual silence in the biblical text.

According to the Chalcedonian hermeneutic, the cognitive dissonance experienced between the archaeological record of how things were and the theological normative view of how things should have been (and should be), is resolved, and thus integrated, by the principle of indestructi-ble order. Although there is empirical proof that Yahweh and his Asherah were venerated at Kuntillet ʿAjrûd, the authoritative and normative theo-logical text, which holds initial position in the two discipline's indestructible order, continues to provide the perspective on how things should have been. In other words, despite its historical manifestation, Asherah worship is theologically disallowed.

Finally, pertaining to outcome 4 (archaeological findings conflict with assumed dogmatic perspectives), the findings at Kuntillet ʿAjrûd require students to reassess their understanding of monotheistic faith and its devel-opment in ancient Israel. Many students enter the biblical studies classroom assuming that Israel was essentially monotheistic from its wilder-ness wanderings. In light of the Kuntillet ʿAjrûd materials, students will struggle to reassess their dogmatic assumptions. For some, that fact that Israel developed (on a common level) from polytheism to monolatry to monotheism will lay some doubt on their own monotheistic beliefs. Here, again, the Chalcedonian hermeneutical principle of *indestructible order* proves useful. Although Israelites commonly worshiped Yahweh in con-junction with other deities, including even and especially his Asherah, theologically speaking there is no deep reality behind such a historical occurrence. Nevertheless, monotheism is neither obvious nor easy, as the historical archaeological record indicates. Hopefully students will gain more nuance, empathy, and insight into the human dynamics that lead to worship projections such as Asherah as well as discard any naïveté regard-ing the unfolding of biblical faith.

FINAL REFLECTIONS

The Chalcedonian hermeneutic is helpful in as much as it holds together (and distinguishes) epistemologies of divine revelation and natu-ral revelation and as such is, in fact, an "incarnational" hermeneutic. After

---

[25] Baruch Halpern, "The Baal (and the Asherah?) in Seventh-Century Judah: Yhwh's Retainers Retired," in *Konsequente Traditionsgeschichte: Festschrift für Klaus Baltzer zum 65. Geburtstag* (ed. R. Bartelmus; Göttingen: Vandenhoeck & Ruprecht, 1993), 115–54.

all, ancient Near Eastern archaeology is not the only scientific discipline applied to the scriptural text that unearths epistemic conflict. Higher and lower criticisms raise many of the same questions as to the historical accuracy of the biblical text, not to mention the reliability of the textual tradition itself. Like the discipline of archaeology, these disciplines are founded upon an empirical epistemology. The Chalcedonian hermeneutic can be applied to a range of disciplines founded on empirical epistemologies (and hence mutually conversant and hierarchically dependent) and disciplines based on authoritarian epistemology.

At the same time, the Chalcedonian hermeneutic is but one of a variety of ways of relating religion and science, theology and archaeology. Any genuinely integrative attempt will, of course, require much of its practitioners. However, to dismiss either voice (or for that matter, any voice) to obscurity or mute silence is to allow *conceptual* realia to remain hidden, an untenable prospect for archaeologist and theologian alike. Increased dialogue along such lines will benefit not only classroom practitioners but within the biblical and archaeological fields as well. For theological contexts, such dialogue remains a courageous *desideratum*.

On The Convergence of Texts and Artifacts: Using Archaeology to Teach the Hebrew Bible

John C. H. Laughlin
Averett University

Introduction

The history of archaeology in its relationship to biblical studies stretches back into the nineteenth century c.e.[1] From the very beginning there emerged the notion that archaeological data could be directly related to stories in the Bible. This was especially true of the excavations of imposing tells identified with major biblical cities. The discoveries at sites such as Jericho, Megiddo, Shechem, Samaria, Jerusalem, Gezer, and Tell Beit Mirsim (this site's identification with ancient Debir is uncertain) were quickly related to biblical events. For example, the archaeological evidence of the violent destruction of some LBA/Iron I sites such as Bethel and Lachish was used to support the biblical model of a military invasion of Canaan by nomadic Israelites swarming into the country from the Transjordan. (Garstang's interpretations of his discoveries at Jericho in the 1930s made headline news.) The notion that archaeological data could corroborate, if not outright "prove" the truth of, the biblical stories was prevalent in many circles, including academic, during the first seven decades or so of the twentieth century. In America this view was encouraged, wittingly or not, by the late William F. Albright (1891–1971) and some of his students (particularly John Bright and G. Ernest Wright). This perception of how archaeological discoveries relate to the Bible is still popular in conservative circles and still makes its voice heard in various ways, including programs on the Discovery Channel.

In recent years the optimism of Albright and others concerning the role that archaeology can and/or should play in biblical studies has all but

---

[1] For a convenient summary of this history, see Peter R. S. Moorey, *A Century of Biblical Archaeology* (Louisville: Westminster John Knox, 1991).

disappeared among practicing field archaeologists and biblical historians. What follows is the briefest of summaries of these developments.[2]

In the New World, dissatisfaction with the more traditional archaeological methods led to a revolution of sorts made popular by Lewis Binford and his disciples in the 1960s. Dubbed the "New Archaeology" or "processual archaeology," this approach sought to provide universal explanations for the archaeological record and to shun history writing based upon archaeological data. To achieve this goal, methods were borrowed from other disciplines, especially anthropology. Furthermore, in addition to this paradigm shift, newer field techniques were developed (e.g., ground radar, infra-red photography, paleobotany), and multidisciplinary staffs began to be introduced into fieldwork. The rationale and method behind this New Archaeology began to be introduced into discussions on Near Eastern archaeology primarily through the publications of William G. Dever.[3] While the influence of the New or processual archaeology cannot be denied, it too has been challenged recently by such people as Ian Hodder in Great Britain and even by Dever in America.[4] For these scholars, we have entered a "postprocessual" era that recognizes that archaeological data do allow for historical reconstructions of ancient societies, at least on a broad scale. However, as Dever has pointed out, this postprocessual agenda has not yet been widely adopted by those who engage in Near Eastern archaeology. If he, Hodder, and others in the field are right, then not only does archaeology hold great potential for understanding the history of ancient Israel, but it may also be our only reliable source given the debate over the "nonhistoricity" of the biblical texts.

Regardless of the outcome of these sometimes tedious, albeit important, theoretical methodological discussions, a historical description only of the changes (especially political) seen in the archaeological record of prominent tells, measured by both stratigraphical profiles and ceramic analysis, can no longer suffice. Contemporary archaeologists and historians now attempt to provide a more holistic *explanation* of past societies that includes not only political but also environmental, social, economic, religious and

---

[2] For a helpful perspective on this history, see Colin Renfrew and Paul Bahn, *Archaeology: Theories Methods and Practice* (3d ed.; London: Thames & Hudson 2000), 38–44.

[3] William G. Dever, "Impact of the 'New Archaeology,'" in *Benchmarks in Time and Culture: An Introduction to Palestinian Archaeology Dedicated to Joseph A. Callaway* (ed. J. F. Drinkard Jr., G. L. Matthingly, and J. M. Miller; SBLABS 1; Atlanta: Scholars Press, 1988), 337–52.

[4] See Ian Hodder, *Reading the Past: Current Approaches to Interpretation in Archaeology* (Cambridge: Cambridge University Press, 1986); William G. Dever, *What Did the Biblical Writers Know and When Did They Know It? What Archaeology Can Tell Us about the Reality of Ancient Israel* (Grand Rapids: Eerdmans, 2001), 53–58.

cross-cultural anthropological theorizing. Regional surveys have also helped to take away the earlier concentration on major tells identified with biblical cities and have provided a much broader perspective within which historians/archaeologists are now attempting to understand the history of ancient "Israel." These changes have resulted in a more "secular" approach to what for a long time was termed "biblical archaeology."[5] Building on the terminology of Dever, we may express the goal of archaeology simply as the attempt "to explain what happened in the past as well as to describe it."[6]

At the same time that archaeological field methods, paradigms, models, and the like are being refined, critical theorizing about the biblical texts has also continued unabated. Newer developments in Hebrew Bible studies include such things as reader-response criticism and deconstruction as well as literary analyses from feminist, psychoanalytic, and materialist perspectives.[7] As if this were not enough to weary the modern mind interested in such stuff, there has also appeared during the past twenty years or so biblical scholars who have been dubbed the "minimalists" (as well as a few other choice words), who essentially deny any historicity to the Bible.

Furthermore, the popular pendulum vis-à-vis archaeology and the Bible is, in some instances, beginning to swing in the opposite direction from the heyday of the "biblical archaeologists." If too much was assumed for archaeology's support of the historical veracity of the Bible in a previous generation, is too little being assumed now?[8] Given these rapid and, some would say, revolutionary, developments in both disciplines (archaeology and the Bible) over the past few years, what if anything can archaeology hope to contribute to the study of the Hebrew Bible beyond "illustrating" the cultural/historical background of the biblical world in general and/or some physical part of that world in particular (e.g., a cooking pot, a building, a sword blade, a water system)?

The issue here is a valid methodological procedure that honestly and fairly assesses and interprets *both* the biblical and archaeological data. Perhaps the question can be rephrased: Since archaeologists recover the *material* remains left by real people (as well as by the environment) who

---

[5] Space does not allow a discussion of the history of this movement, but see Moorey, *A Century of Biblical Archaeology;* and the discussion most recently with bibliography by Dever, *What Did the Biblical Writers Know.*

[6] Renfrew and Bahn, *Archaeology,* 39.

[7] See J. Cheryl Exum and David J. A. Clines, eds., *The New Literary Criticism and the Hebrew Bible* (Valley Forge, Pa.: Trinity Press International, 1993).

[8] See most recently Daniel Lazare, "False Testament: Archaeology Refutes the Bible's Claim to History," *Harper's Magazine* (March 2002): 39–47.

lived in a real, empirical world, does this world and the world of the text, or at least the world behind the text, of the Hebrew Bible ever intersect? Or again, when the biblical textual record and the archaeological material record are both properly interpreted and understood, can they illuminate or "speak" to each other? This begs the question of what "properly interpreted and understood" means, yet my point is that both texts and artifacts are objective data that contemporary readers interpret subjectively.

Furthermore, in this day of proliferating specialized studies in both disciplines, it is extremely unlikely that any of us has the time or expertise to become competent in both fields of study. Consequently, the archaeologist will have to depend on the competency of the textual scholar and vice versa. Otherwise, both disciplines run the risk of continuing on parallel courses that never shall meet. While it is not my intention to try to denigrate the use of biblical texts to try to recover some "history" of ancient Israel, I think Dever was correct when he argued that archaeological data are often primary and even superior to the biblical and other ancient texts when undertaking this task of history writing.[9] If Dever is correct, archaeology should play a pivotal role in any attempt to reconstruct the history of ancient Israel. What follows are simply suggestions for trying to integrate some of what is now known archaeologically from Israel and elsewhere into introduction courses to the Hebrew Bible. These are only suggestions, and only tentative ones at that. Hopefully there will be enough latitude so anyone interested in trying to do this will be able to adapt/adopt this material in ways compatible to his or her own purposes. Furthermore, although frequent references will be made to the biblical text, my perspective will be that of the excavator, not that of the exegete. Obviously the character of the biblical text must be determined independently of the archaeological record. Are the two subjects even speaking about the same reality? Most of the exegesis I must leave up to the reader. My central question is: Can what is known archaeologically about Israel (I use this term simply to refer to a particular geographical location, not a political one) as well as surrounding Middle Eastern sites be used in a positive way if one's primary goal is to understand the Hebrew Scriptures?

ASSUMPTIONS UNDERLYING INTEGRATING ARCHAEOLOGY AND THE HEBREW BIBLE

While it is to state the obvious to say that all thinking is based on assumptions, oftentimes one's assumptions stay hidden, particularly from the one holding them. Thus I wish to express mine as clearly as possible. The issues involved in this brief essay can be intimidating and overwhelming,

---

[9] Dever, *What Did the Biblical Writers Know*, 89–90.

even to one who is no stranger to the discussion. That other scholars in the field might, and probably do, have a different set of operating assumptions is both recognized and appreciated. Nevertheless, the following minimal observations will underlie what follows. It is my hope that the implications of these assumptions will lead to a conscious and responsible attempt to make use of current archaeological data/methods in teaching the Hebrew Bible.[10]

1. Your students are probably as woefully ignorant of all of this discussion as are mine.
2. Your primary emphasis is going to be on the *biblical texts* and not on archaeology.
3. Your approach to teaching the Hebrew Bible will be thoroughly grounded in historical-critical assumptions/methodologies regardless of your own predilections and idiosyncrasies.
4. You may have limited time and/or interest to deal directly with archaeological issues.
5. You will have limited visual resources (but a picture really is worth a lot of words—especially in the case of archaeology).
6. There is little if any recoverable "history" from the stories making up what is now called the Pentateuch. I realize that there are still attempts among certain conservative scholars to show that the patriarchs really lived and that Moses really did bring *millions* of people out of Egypt, but I have never seen the objective (read: archaeological) evidence to support such conclusions. Consequently, I will not deal with these stories. That they, as well as other stories in this mass of material, may have profound moral and/or theological meanings is not the issue here.[11]
7. There is little or no direct archaeological data for the Psalms, wisdom literature, and other books constituting the Writings. Consequently, these sections of the Bible will also be ignored for our purposes.
8. If archaeological data and biblical texts can "talk" to each other, our best hope is in those stories making up what is commonly known as the Deuteronomic History of Israel (hereafter DH), found basically in the biblical books of Joshua, Judges, Samuel, and Kings. The question here is not the final dating

---

[10] See ibid., 97–157.

[11] For a brief but important discussion of the biblical story of the "exodus" from the perspective of Egyptian history and archaeology, see Ernest S. Frerichs and Leonard H. Lesko, eds., *Exodus: The Egyptian Evidence* (Winona Lake, Ind.: Eisenbrauns, 1997).

and authorship of these stories but whether or not the stories can be used at all for history writing. In this regard I am also going to operate on two other basic presuppositions: that the DH is a complex, layered literary production whose final form does not antedate the seventh century B.C.E.; and that regardless of the history or nonhistory of the stories in this work, they have been placed by the author(s) in what is called archaeologically Iron Age I (ca. 1200–1000 B.C.E.) and Iron Age II (ca. 1000–587/540 B.C.E.). In any case, the major emphasis will be on the archaeological data known from these two periods.

9.   The same kinds of archaeological/historical questions can be asked for the prophetic material found in the books of the so-called three major prophets (Isaiah, Jeremiah, Ezekiel) and the twelve minor. I am not referring here to the possibility of "proving archaeologically" that an Isaiah or an Amos lived as persons in a certain time and place. Rather, do we have archaeological data that reflect the social, economic, political, and religious conditions discussed by these books' authors, whoever they may turn out to have been and from whatever date they may have been composed? I raise the issue without expecting to have the space to deal with each prophet, but what, for example, would be required to see if the archaeological data now known from eighth century B.C.E. northern Israel reflect the cultural situation as presented in the book of Amos? Can "Amos" be excavated from the ruins of Samaria? (I am indebted to Dominic Crossan for phrasing the question this way.)

TOPICS FOR DISCUSSION IN ARCHAEOLOGY AND THE HEBREW BIBLE

I do not know of just one way to do any of this, and the topics that could be chosen are many. The following proposals are simply suggestions that can enable a teacher to introduce to students of the Hebrew Bible the difficulties and, one would hope, the value(s) of using archaeology as a critical tool for helping one to become a more responsible interpreter of the Bible (or at least parts of it).

The questions and problems surrounding the emergence of ancient Israel (Late Bronze Age/Iron Age I) is a good place to begin. There is currently a lively controversy among scholars over the particulars of the history of the appearance of "ancient Israel." From where did the people who should be included in this group come? When was there an Israel? What counts for ethnic markers in Israel's case? Was there an exodus of any biblical proportion? a conquest? Who where the people who settled the central hill country of Canaan during Iron Age I? How are these people to be related to preceding Late Bronze Age? How are they related to the following periods? Out of a daunting bibliography related to these and other questions, the following authors are highly recommended for background information and orientation: William G. Dever, Israel Finkelstein, and Nadav Na'aman.[12]

A second topic regards the major controversy that now exists over whether or not there ever was a Davidic-Solomonic monarchy. Involved in this question is the argument for and against a Solomonic temple. The major voices here are once more Israel Finkelstein, who continues to argue against a Solomonic state, and Dever, who argues the opposite.[13]

Perhaps a third topic—somewhat less controversial for integrating archaeology and texts—relates to issues about what is usually referred to as Iron Age II B, C (roughly 926–587/586 B.C.E.). There is an enormous amount of archaeological data from these periods that hold out the possibility for being used responsibly for understanding biblical texts. One could, for example, make use of inscriptional, ceramic, regional surveys, and other artifactual evidence to delineate the outlines of statehood for Israel and Judah during the first part of this period.

Another topic for which there is an ever-increasing amount of important data is the question of popular religious practices during these periods. The inscriptions from Kuntillet ʿAjrûd and Khirbet el-Qom, female figurines, and cultic material from Arad, Tel Dan (especially the sets of *massebot* recently discovered by Avraham Biran), and elsewhere all raise serious questions concerning the "monotheistic" lens through which the DH seems to have been written.

Still other problems that could be archaeologically elucidated are the political disasters of 722 and 586 B.C.E. and their impact on local populations, as well as economic and social structures. There is considerable archaeological evidence for the physical destruction of many sites during these conflicts that might profitably be integrated with the biblical texts.

---

[12] William G. Dever, *Recent Archaeological Discoveries and Biblical Research* (Seattle: University of Washington Press, 1990); idem, "Archaeology, Syro-Palestinian and Biblical," *ABD* 1:354–67; idem, "Israel, History of (Archaeology and the 'Conquest')," *ABD* 3:545–58; Israel Finkelstein, *The Archaeology of the Israelite Settlement*. (Jerusalem: Israel Exploration Society, 1988); Israel Finkelstein and Nadav Na'aman, eds., *From Nomadism to Monarchy: Archaeological and Historical Aspects of Early Israel* (Jerusalem: Israel Exploration Society. 1994).

[13] While both scholars have published voluminously on this topic, see most recently, Israel Finkelstein and Neil A. Silberman, *The Bible Unearthed: Archaeology's New Vision of Ancient Israel and the Origin of Its Sacred Texts* (New York: Free Press, 2001); and Dever, *What Did the Biblical Writers Know*.

CASE STUDIES FOR INTEGRATING ARCHAEOLOGY AND THE HEBREW BIBLE

It is impossible here to present in any detail the possibilities that one might be interested in for using archaeology in Hebrew Bible courses. The following examples are intended as illustrations only and have been chosen because, for me, they represent some of the more exciting and challenging questions now being faced by archaeologists and biblical historians alike. These issues also afford a real opportunity for the teacher to alert students to the fact that final answers to many of these questions have not been forthcoming. To live with a certain amount of ambiguity is not only humbling but also necessary if one is to think critically and honestly in this field. I will limit myself to the following questions:

1. What do we know about the place that would be called "Israel" in the Bible from the archaeological data dating to the Late Bronze Age/Iron Age I? Do these data shed any light on the origin/culture of a people the Bible calls "Israelites"? Can the archaeological and biblical data tell us anything historically concerning the origin of Israel and its appearance in the land of Canaan? (Among other questions, I am interested here in what in the past has been referred to as "conquest" stories found primarily in the books of Joshua and Judges.)
2. Is there any history in the stories in Samuel and Kings concerning a David and a Solomon and the creation of a Hebrew monarchy?
3. Can the known archaeological data elucidate at all the biblical texts describing a split monarchy (Israel and Judah) beginning around the ninth century B.C.E.?
4. How does archaeological data compare and/or contrast with the biblical data concerning the rise and nature of Israelite religion during the Iron II (ca. 1000–587 B.C.E.)?

A very good test case for what archaeology can or cannot do for biblical historical study is the story (or stories) regarding the way in which "Israel" occupied the land that would later bear its name. If there is any history to these stories of violent conquest, surely there would be traces of such destructions left in the archaeological record, *provided archaeologists can determine when and where such supposed violence took place.* For my purposes I am going to assume that, if there is any historicity to these stories, it happened sometime during the end of the Late Bronze Age (thirteenth century B.C.E.). What is known archaeologically from this time vis-à-vis the sites that have been identified and excavated should provide some indication of what did or did not take place—at least at this or that specific place. Put this way, what is now known archaeologically poses some very real problems for those who would still take the biblical stories at face value. These problems demonstrate how archaeology can, at times, serve as a control on what can be asserted or, more importantly in this case, what cannot be asserted historically about a particular biblical event. It is impossible in such a short essay to discuss adequately all the textual/ archaeological data relevant to every site mentioned in the Hebrew Bible. Thus, I will reserve my comments for two of the more dramatic stories encountered: Jericho and 'Ai.

JERICHO AND 'AI AS CASE STUDIES

The city of Jericho is mentioned over fifty times in the Hebrew Bible. In almost 50 percent of these (twenty-six times), the reference to the site is for geographical location/orientation. Thus, the expression "across the Jordan from Jericho" often occurs (e.g., Num 22:1; 26:3, 63; 31:12; 33:48). Sometimes the expression is to the "plains of Jericho," as in Jer 39:5 and 52:8. Ten times "Jericho" appears in reference to its king: Josh 2:2, 3; 6:2; 8:2; 10:1, 28, 30; 12:9. To complicate matters just a little, there seem to be two different versions of the "battle" for Jericho by the "Israelites." The more famous one, with the tumbling walls, is found in Josh 6, but there are not a few curiosities to this story. After mentioning the city by name in the opening two verses of the chapter, Jericho is never mentioned again until verse 25. There is no mention of any king and, perhaps even more puzzling, no mention of any resistance on the part of the city's inhabitants.[14]

The story in Josh 24:11, however, is a much more cryptic account that links the defeat of Jericho with that of other peoples, including the Amorites and Canaanites. In addition, we are specifically told in this summary passage that the "citizens of Jericho fought against" Israel (24:11b). Conspicuously absent, however, is any mention of marching around, trumpet blowing, walls falling flat, harlot rescuing, or the imposing of the "ban" (6:17). Stuck in the larger Shechem renewal speech by the biblical editor(s), this version of the capture/destruction of Jericho seems to come from a very different source than that preserved in Josh 6.

When the archaeological data for Jericho are examined, both stories— whatever their ultimate origin—seem to be literary creations of their author(s). All archaeological discussion of this site must now deal with the

---

[14] Cf. Michael D. Coogan, "Archaeology and Biblical Studies: The Book of Joshua," in *The Hebrew Bible and Its Interpreters* (ed. W. H. Propp, B. Halpern, and D. N. Freedman; Biblical and Judaic Studies from the University of California, San Diego, 1; Winona Lake, Ind.: Eisenbrauns, 1990), 19–32.

work of the late Kathleen M. Kenyon, who showed that, although some tenth-century B.C.E. sherds were found in a tomb, the site of ancient Jericho, modern Tel es-Sultan, was abandoned from the Late Bronze Age I period (fourteenth century B.C.E.) to Iron Age II (seventh century B.C.E.). Furthermore, even what few remains she found that can with confidence be dated to LB I hardly indicate a city of biblical proportions.[15] The efforts by some to skirt this problem by suggesting that Tel es-Sultan is not the site of Jericho or that the LB city has "eroded" are not convincing and amount to what one archaeologist has called "wishful thinking."

When the biblical story of 'Ai (Josh 7:2–8:29) and its archaeological data are added to the discussion, the case for the nonhistory of the biblical conquest is only strengthened. 'Ai is located about one mile east of the site of ancient Bethel. Two major excavations have been carried out on the site. The first was directed by Judith Krause in the 1930s, the second by Joseph Callaway in the 1960s and 1970s. Both excavators concluded that 'Ai was violently destroyed around 2400 B.C.E. and was not occupied again until Iron Age I (ca. 1150 B.C.E.).[16] The site lay in ruins (hence its name 'Ai, which means "heap" or "ruin") throughout the Middle and Late Bronze ages. There is no way to harmonize the written account of the Israelite destruction of biblical 'Ai with the archaeological record.[17]

When the archaeological data from many other sites mentioned in the Bible are added to that from Jericho and 'Ai, the conclusion seems fairly obvious: the stories in Joshua concerning a pan-Canaanite conquest by Israelite nomadic warriors storming in from the eastern desert are a biblical fiction. While these stories may carry the theological and moral concerns of their author(s)/editor(s), their historical value is minimal at best. One might do well to remember here that the word *history* is not a biblical term. As one well-known archaeologist (Dever) put it, the biblical writers told the story the way it would have happened if they had been in charge!

The point to all of this is that the biblical exegete needs the archaeologist and the archaeologist needs the biblical exegete. Each needs to do her work independently of the other and then compare notes. Here I am concerned primarily with what can be said if one simply looks in the ground. Forget the Bible for the moment. If one had only the known archaeological data, what reasonable conclusions could one draw? This approach is especially useful in the next consideration: the controversy over whether or not there was ever a Davidic/Solomonic monarchy.

---

[15] See Kathleen M. Kenyon, "Jericho," *NEAEHL* 2:674–81; Thomas Holland, "Jericho," *OEANE* 3:220–24.

[16] See Joseph A. Callaway, "'Ai," *NEAEHL* 1:39–45; Robert E. Cooley, "'Ai," *OEANE* 1:32–33.

[17] See Dever, *Recent Archaeological Discoveries,* 37–84.

READING SUGGESTIONS AND TOPICS:
ISRAEL IN THE IRON AGE I (CA. 1200–1000 B.C.E.)

In what follows I outline the key primary and secondary literature for classroom discussions of the archaeology of the Iron Age I. Texts from the Bible that should be required reading prior to the discussion of Israel in the Iron Age I are Num 13–36; Josh 1–23; and Judg 1:1–2:6.

The best secondary literature available for students on the topic of the Iron I is listed below.

1. Elizabeth Block-Smith and Beth Alpert Nakhai's, "A Landscape Comes to Life: The Iron I Period,"[18] provides an excellent overview of the period and is essential reading that should be required. Like the work of Israel Finkelstein (see below), the authors consider settlement patterns in Canaan from the end of LBA through Iron Age I, including regional differences and the nature and complexity of the Iron Age sites.

2. The first two chapters of *Archaeology and Biblical Interpretation,* one by John Bartlett and the other by Dever, are especially useful for providing background perspectives for beginning students. Both essays also contain useful bibliographies of earlier sources.[19]

3. In my opinion, Dever represents the best effort by a contemporary American archaeologist to argue critically and positively what archaeology can do for biblical studies. Students should certainly be introduced to him and his publications, of which there are many. His *Recent Archaeological Discoveries and Biblical Research* contains several lectures given by the author at the University of Washington in 1985 and is highly recommended. Shorter articles that have been published in the *Anchor Bible Dictionary* and *OEANE* are also good starting points for classroom discussions.[20]

4. Israel Finkelstein is a leading Israeli archaeologist who provides a critical alternative to Dever's perspectives on some basic questions. Students should also be made aware of him and his many publications. A section from Finkelstein's *The Archaeology*

---

[18] Elizabeth Block-Smith and Beth-Alpert Nakhai, "A Landscape Comes to Life: The Iron I Period," *NEA* 62 (1999): 62–92, 101–27.

[19] John Bartlett, ed., *Archaeology and Biblical Interpretation* (London: Routledge, 1997).

[20] William G. Dever, "Archaeology, Syro-Palestinian and Biblical"; idem, "Israel, History of (Archaeology and the 'Conquest')"; idem, "Biblical Archaeology," *OEANE* 1:315–19.

of the Israelite Settlement (293–356) is a good beginning point. Additionally, reference should be made to his 1995 article, "The Great Transformation: The 'Conquest' of the Highlands Frontiers and the Rise of the Territorial States."[21]

5.   Israel Finkelstein and Nadav Na'aman's edited volume, *From Nomadism to Monarchy: Archaeological and Historical Aspects of Early Israel,* contains fourteen essays dealing specifically with the theme of the emergence of early Israel. The essays combine textual and archaeological as well as anthropological sources. Written entirely by Israeli scholars, this volume offers a valuable synthesis of problems, sources, and critically suggested solutions to the vexing question of the emergence of ancient Israel.

6.   Philip King and Larry Stager's *Life in Biblical Israel* is the first comprehensive effort, to my knowledge, by a skilled exegete (King) and a seasoned field archaeologist (Stager) to present a highly creative and informative synthesis of daily life in ancient Israel as reflected in both the material realia and biblical traditions.[22] Its rich illustrations and multiplicity of topics make it a valuable resource for both teachers and students. It is highly recommended.

7.   Many if not most students will not have heard of, much less read, ancient literary sources that bear on the subject at hand. Some of the more frequently discussed ones are listed below. All except the Papyrus Harris I are conveniently located in *ANET.*[23] Papyrus Harris I, according to Kyle P. McCarter, is "the longest and best preserved papyrus to survive from ancient Egypt."[24] This papyrus was discovered in 1855 and purchased by A. C. Harris (thus its name) and taken to the British Museum. Among other things, the papyrus describes Ramesses III's victory over the Sea Peoples, including the Philistines. The primary texts from this period that should be assigned include the

---

[21] Israel Finkelstein, *The Archaeology of the Israelite Settlement* (Jerusalem: Israel Exploration Society), 1988; idem, "The Great Transformation: The 'Conquest' of the Highlands Frontiers and the Rise of the Territorial States," in *The Archaeology of Society in the Holy Land* (ed. T. E. Levy; New York: Facts on File, 1995), 349–365.

[22] Philip J. King and Lawrence E. Stager, *Life in Biblical Israel* (Louisville: Westminster John Knox, 2001).

[23] James B. Pritchard, ed., *Ancient Near Eastern Texts Relating to the Old Testament* (3d ed.; Princeton: Princeton University Press, 1969).

[24] P. Kyle McCarter Jr., *Ancient Inscriptions: Voices from the Biblical World* (Washington, D.C.: Biblical Archaeology Society, 1996), 54.

Amarna letters, Papyrus Anastasi I, the Merneptah Stela, and Papyrus Harris I.[25]

8. Regarding the architectural trends of the Iron Age I and its relevance to the biblical material, reference should be made to Lawrence Stager's 1985 article, "The Archaeology of the Family in Ancient Israel."[26]

9. The archaeological evidence for religious practices during the LBA/Iron I horizon is very meager. For a brief discussion of cult sites from the Iron Age I, including the Mount Ebal "altar" and the "bull site" from northern Manasseh, reference can be made to Amihai Mazar's *Archaeology of the Land of the Bible 10,000–586 B.C.E.*[27]

10. Finally, a discussion of ceramics, particularly the "collared rim" store jar is recommended.[28] This particular ceramic form is singled out because of the discussion it has evoked going all the way back to the days of Albright. Including it in the discussion can provide the teacher an entry point to introduce his or her students to the important if complex issue of ceramics in general.

READING SUGGESTIONS AND TOPICS: THE QUESTION OF A CENTRALIZED GOVERNMENT/STATE IN THE TENTH CENTURY B.C.E.

There is no current issue more controversial among archeologists and biblical historians than that of the question of a united monarchy under David and Solomon during the tenth century B.C.E. Is there any history behind the biblical stories found primarily in 2 Samuel–1 Kgs 11? The literary and/or other functions of these stories I leave to you, the exegete. Here I am only concerned with what is now known from looking in the ground. If there was a state during the tenth century B.C.E. in Palestine, what material remains would indicate this?[29]

---

[25] Ibid., 54.

[26] Lawrence E. Stager, "The Archaeology of the Family in Ancient Israel," *BASOR* 260 (1985): 1–35.

[27] Amihai Mazar, *Archaeology of the Land of the Bible 10,000–586 B.C.E.* (ABRL; New York: Doubleday, 1990), esp. 348–52.

[28] On the collared-rim store jar, see the essays by Avraham Biran (71–96) and Joseph Yellin and Jan Gunneweg (133–41) in Seymour Gitin and William G. Dever, eds., *Recent Excavations in Israel: Studies in Iron Age Archaeology* (AASOR 49 (Winona Lake, Ind.: Eisenbrauns, 1989).

[29] For a chart suggesting archaeological remains indicative of state-formation processes, see John S. Holladay Jr., "The Kingdoms of Israel and Judah: Political and Economic

In July of 1993 a fragment of a stela inscribed in Aramaic was discovered in the gate complex at Tel Dan. Though dating to the ninth century B.C.E., this important inscription for the first time provides solid archaeological evidence that a king named David did in fact exist. Though dating later than the date given to a united monarchy, this literary evidence has very real historical implications denied by the so-called "minimalist school." That this David did and said what is recorded in the Bible is, however, an entirely different issue. When this inscription is added to others mentioning kings, such as the Mesha Stela's reference to Omri, a major criterion for state formation, namely, the existence of kings or centralized leaders/rulers of some sort, seems firmly established.

Dozens of sites in Israel containing tenth-century B.C.E. remains have now been identified.[30] Some of the most important, if not controversial, include Hazor, Megiddo, Gezer, Lachish, Samaria, Dan, and Tel Rehov in the Jordan Valley. The crucial issue here is the date of some of these remains. While most archaeologists who have cared enough to voice an opinion (Dever, Stager, Mazar, Holladay, among them) date these remains to the tenth century, others, notably Finkelstein, have argued for a ninth-century date for much of the controversial material. This material includes massive architectural fortification remains at Gezer, Lachish, Megiddo, and Hazor. Other remains include what have been described as "palaces" at such sites as Megiddo and Lachish. If these remains do turn out to be tenth century in date, they will offer strong archaeological evidence for some type of centralized/administrative organization during this period. Much of this material—especially the gate remains—is very similar, constituting what archaeologists call "monumental architecture."[31] Without any texts, the material remains would suggest that such massive constructions found all up and down the country from the same time period would have required resources, cooperation, and organization normally associated with some form of statehood. In other words, if David and Solomon were not known from the biblical texts, some one like them would have to be invented.

Crucial to this debate is a type of ceramic remains called "hand-burnished" pottery. Ceramic analyses are complicated affairs that only experts are competent to discuss. Suffice it to say here that this pottery is often found in the destruction debris of the monumental buildings referred

---

Centralization in the Iron II A–B (ca. 1000–750 B.C.E.)," in Levy, *Archaeology of Society,* 373, table 1.

[30] See especially Larry G. Herr, "The Iron II Period: Emerging Nations," *BA* 60 (1997): 114–83.

[31] See especially Dever, *Recent Archaeological Discoveries,* 124–57.

to above. The destruction of these sites has been attributed to Shishak of Egypt and dated to 925 B.C.E.[32] If indeed this hand-burnished material can be associated with the remains of these massive structures and stratigraphically located below the destruction level created by Shishak's raids, then a solid *terminus ante quem* (the latest date allowed by archaeological evidence) can be established for their usage. That is, the floors, walls, and/or other architectural remains associated with this pottery could not have been put underneath the pottery once the latter was fixed by the destruction. If the pottery is tenth century, then so are the material remains found with it. Whether these buildings were constructed under the orders of someone named Solomon or someone else, the archaeological evidence cannot decide, but whoever was responsible for the tradition in 1 Kgs 9:15–25 may have been in touch with a legitimate historical tradition.

It is common knowledge that so far not any physical, archaeological remains of the so-called Solomonic or First Temple have ever been discovered.[33] Does this mean, as some have claimed, that the description of this structure in 1 Kgs 6–8 was simply made up late in the postexilic period, or does the Kings' account rest on legitimate historical memory? While archaeologists are lacking totally any physical evidence of such a structure from tenth-century B.C.E. Jerusalem, the same is not true of many other sites containing such "temple" remains. In fact, the existence of so many Canaanite-Phoenician temple remains dating from the Middle Bronze Age to Iron Age II led Dever to conclude that "*every single detail* of the Bible's complicated description of the Jerusalem temple can now be corroborated by archaeological examples from the Late Bronze and Iron Ages. There is nothing 'fanciful' about 1 Kgs. 6–8."[34]

In conclusion, it can be asked, if we set aside the biblical and other texts (although the Tel Dan inscription, due to its date, counts almost as a contemporary witness) and look simply at material realia dated by many archaeologists to the tenth century B.C.E., what can we see? We can see monumental architectural remains composed of massive fortification

---

[32] For an estimation of the importance of Shishak's raid on Israel, see Holladay, "Kingdoms of Israel and Judah," 372–75; cf. 1 Kgs 11:40.

[33] See Dever, *What Did the Biblical Writers Know*, 144–57; John Monson, "The New 'Ain Dara Temple: Closest Solomonic Parallel," *BAR* 26/3 (2000): 20–35, 67.

[34] Dever, *What Did the Biblical Writers Know*, 155; emphasis original. Space considerations do not allow a detailed discussion of the many remains identified as temples now known from many sites. Articles in the *NEAEHL* and the *OEANE* on sites such as Hazor, Megiddo, Shechem, Tell Tayinat, and particularly 'Ain Dara will orient the interested reader. On the magnificently preserved remains at 'Ain Dora, see Monson, "New 'Ain Dara Temple." For the historical implications of the 'Ain Dora remains for the Solomonic temple, see Dever, *What Did the Biblical Writers Know*, 144–57.

systems (gates and walls), remains of buildings identified as palaces, and hand-burnished ceramic forms found in destruction debris dated to the time of Shishak (Sheshonq).[35] If we extend the time range to a few centuries before the tenth century and down to the mid-eighth century B.C.E., we can add the impressive remains of tripartite temples, especially the one now known from 'Ain Dara. All of these data, plus others, would seem to point to some type of centralized organization during this period. What this means for the exegesis of biblical texts remains for the reader to say.

IRON AGE IIB, C (LATE TENTH–SIXTH CENTURIES B.C.E.)

If there is an archaeological time period to which the expression "biblical archaeology" may be an appropriate rubric, it is Iron Age IIB, C. If there is any history at all in the biblical accounts of the kings of Israel and Judah, the classical prophets, the priesthood, the political disasters of 722 and 587/586 B.C.E., and the fully developed Israelite cult, it is during this archaeological time period. It should come as no surprise that Iron II B, C has been intensively studied and that the amount of secondary scholarly publications on this period are immense. As more and more relevant discoveries from this period are made, this literature can only be expected to increase.

The amount and kinds of archaeological realia available for study are varied and plentiful. They include everything from massive architectural remains (e.g., walls, defensive towers, gates, palaces, domestic buildings, "storerooms"), ingenious water systems (e.g., at Jerusalem, Megiddo, Hazor, Gibeon), tombs (from many sites), ceramics, jewelry, cultic remains (e.g., Tel Arad, Tel Dan), and innumerable small finds. In addition, there are now hundreds if not thousands of inscriptions known from this period. They include inscribed potsherds (ostraca) from such places as Arad, Samaria, and Lachish, jars with inscriptions (e.g., Kuntillet ʿAjrûd), seals, scarabs, and bullae. Some have particular historical significance, such as the Siloam Tunnel inscription in Jerusalem, the Tel Dan Stela, and the so-called "Moabite Stone." Thus the possibilities for integrating archaeological data from these periods into Hebrew Bible studies are rich indeed.

However, this does not mean that the relevant biblical texts from the DH can now be taken at face value. The temptation to "illustrate" this period with archaeological material while giving a "historical paraphrase" of the biblical material is probably not the best way to proceed. Nevertheless, despite

---

[35] Suggested readings about the archaeology of this period include, Dever, *Recent Archaeological Discoveries,* 124–57; Holladay, "Kingdoms of Israel and Judah," 368–98; and Herr, "Iron II Period."

the risks involved, we have an enormous about of material that should, and can, corroborate and elucidate the world behind the biblical text.

One example of this is Dever's treatment of the archaeological data vis-à-vis the text in 2 Kgs 23 in an article entitled, "The Silence of the Text: An Archaeological Commentary of 2 Kings 23."[36] After a brief but helpful discussion of his methodology, Dever uses what is known from Iron IIC archaeology to illuminate and corroborate the picture we get from 2 Kgs 23 concerning the reforms accredited to King Josiah by the DH.

Settlement patterns and architectural developments during the Iron II are other issues that could be addressed using archaeological data. This should include a discussion of the large urban centers of Jerusalem, Lachish, Ramat Rahel, Samaria, and Megiddo, with attention to the royal and domestic architecture at those sites. Additionally, students could be introduced to the archaeology of several provincial towns, including Beth-shemesh, Gibeon, Tell Beit Mirsim, and many small villages that have been surveyed by Zvi Gal.[37] Finally, several settlements in the Negev and Jordan Desert (e.g., Ein Gedi) could be introduced.

Israelite religion, burial customs,[38] and socioeconomic factors[39] are other areas with many avenues for exploration. Regarding religion in Israelite culture, the archaeological evidence now available points to a popular religion among the people of Israel and Judah that was not what the biblical writers wished it had been. On archaeology and religion in the Iron II, students should find the essay by Larry Herr on this period ("The Iron II Period: Emerging Nations"), and chapter 6 in King and Stager's *Life in Biblical Israel* particularly helpful.[40] Herr's summary of the Iron Age IIB, C periods is a helpful place for beginning students to start to obtain an overview of the major issues at stake during this time frame. Included in his essay are lists of known archaeological sites from these periods. Additionally, regarding religion in the Iron II, specific items and sites of interest include: (1) the Ta'anach cult stand;[41] (2) the *massebot* from Tel Dan;[42] (3) the inscriptions from Kuntillet ʿAjrûd and Khirbet el-Qom; (4) clay female

---

[36] William G. Dever, "The Silence of the Text: An Archaeological Commentary of 2 Kings 23," in *Scripture and Other Artifacts: Essays on the Bible and Archaeology in Honor of Philip J. King* (ed. M. D. Coogan, J. C. Exum, and L. E. Stager; Louisville: John Knox, 1994), 143–68.

[37] Zvi Gal, *Lower Galilee during the Iron Age* (Winona Lake, Ind.: Eisenbrauns, 1992).

[38] See King and Stager, *Life in Biblical Israel*, 363–81.

[39] A particular socioeconomic factor of great interest is the agriculture surpluses indicative of trade evidenced at Tel Miqne/Ekron vis-à-vis the olive-oil industry.

[40] See also the essays by Scott R. A. Starbuck and Elizabeth LaRocca-Pitts in this volume.

[41] See King and Stager, *Life in Biblical Israel*, 340–44.

[42] See Avraham Biran, "Sacred Spaces: Of Standing Stones, High Places and Cult Objects at Dan," *BAR* 24/5 (1998): 38–45, 70.

and other cult figurines; and (5) writing materials, including ostraca, seals, and inscriptions.[43]

CONCLUSION

Although trying to integrate archaeology into more traditional literary approaches to the Hebrew Bible may require a considerable amount of time and effort, the results can be satisfying to both teacher and student. In my own experience, I have discovered that, for many students, just "seeing" what some of this ancient world looked like (and still looks like!) is an educational experience in and of itself. Furthermore, for students who learn better through "visual" stimulation, such an approach can be quite beneficial.[44]

Furthermore, given the now fairly well accepted scholarly consensus concerning the history and production of the DH, the archaeological evidence is the only contemporary material we have of the issues under discussion. This fact in itself should warrant its use in every legitimate way possible by those who claim to be serious students of the Hebrew Bible. As Dever concluded in his "archaeological commentary" on 2 Kgs 23: "The past was always more complex, more intractable than we think; let it speak for itself, if possible."[45]

---

[43] Especially useful here is McCarter, *Ancient Inscriptions,* 102–21.

[44] While there is danger in using slides or other visual aids in this context (napping students, for one!), to the archaeologically challenged a picture really can be worth a lot of words. While one's own personal archives may provide sufficient resources, I am going to assume that not everyone has had the opportunity to travel throughout the Middle East, particularly Israel, to produce a private collection of usable material. Consequently, it is highly recommended that professionally produced resources be used. Readily available are slide sets from The Biblical Archaeology Society. Particularly useful are the slide sets entitled "Biblical Archaeology," "Archaeology and Religion," "Jerusalem Archaeology," and "Ancient Near Eastern Inscriptions." (Most of these slide sets are now available on a cd-rom from the Biblical Archaeology Society.) For a bird's-eye view of many of the famous sites (and maybe not so famous), R. Cleave's aerial set is well worth the investment.

[45] Dever, "The Silence of the Text," 161.

Archaeology in New Testament Courses

Milton C. Moreland
Rhodes College

Introduction: Why Integrate Archaeology into New Testament Courses?

In the past decade there have been so many significant developments in the reconstruction of the Early Roman period in Galilee and Judea—primarily based on recent archaeological excavations—that it should be self-evident how important it is to introduce students to the material culture of the region. Yet textbooks and key secondary reading for classroom use often do not reflect the advances in our knowledge of the setting of Jesus and his first followers. Students often only hear references to "archaeological material" when it is relegated to the role of a classroom visual aid that is used to illustrate a literary text. For example, a picture of the extant Herodian stones in the Temple Mount or an architect's drawing of Robinson's Arch might be shown as a way to illustrate the story of Jesus entering the temple. A photo of the extant Capernaum synagogue, postdating Jesus by hundreds of years, might be shown during a discussion of a passage from the Gospels in which Jesus is said to have preached in Galilean synagogues. While it is common to teach courses on the Gospels or the historical Jesus that only reference archaeology as illustrations, there are great rewards in using archaeology to unlock new aspects of the private and public life of Early Roman Palestine. In this essay I explore the benefits of using studies that incorporate recent archaeological discoveries, as well as suggest several practical ways of integrating this material into courses that typically are already overburdened.

The need for more emphasis on nonliterary evidence in New Testament courses arises anew each time I teach an introductory course on the subject. Over the past few years in my Introduction to the New Testament courses, I have begun the semester with a reflection paper on the Gospel of Mark. I ask the students to read the Gospel and discuss the socioeconomic and political settings that are revealed in the narrative. I also ask them to reflect on how Jesus fits into the narrative settings. The responses

I receive are not surprising. The first observation students commonly make is that the Pharisees appear to be the dominant force in this socioeconomic world. I ask them how many Pharisees they think lived in Galilee at the time of Jesus, and they do not hesitate to answer that the Pharisees must have numbered in the hundreds or even thousands. They appear on every corner, they watch where Jesus eats, they meddle in the fields, and they observe Jesus in almost every setting in Mark's story. This (mis)conception of the role of the Pharisees in the early first century in Galilee is something that is seemingly easy to counter. It provides an opportunity to examine the "story world" or narrative flow that Mark used in writing his Gospel. It allows the professor quickly to point out the ability of the author of Mark to set up an antagonist in the narrative that would drive the plot from beginning to end. Mark selected the Pharisees as the antagonists because this was the group that did have a competitive role with Christianity in the last third of the first century, forty to fifty years after Jesus lived in Galilee. In light of this, I can point the students to a variety of studies of the narrative of Mark that well illustrate the juxtaposition of Jesus and the "Jewish authorities" in the story and explain why the author of Mark and his early Christian community might have been interested in this portrayal of these Jewish groups.[1]

I also ask the students to study the geography of the Galilee through an examination of the travels of Jesus: Where did he go, and how long did the trip take, according to Mark? This is, of course, another attempt to help students understand the narrative context, in distinction from what we know about the actual geography of the Galilee and the surrounding regions and what archaeology has taught us about the ancient road systems in the area. I am then able to draw their attention to the work of several scholars who have shown how Mark has given us a travel narrative that does not necessarily make sense as a historical itinerary, although it functions well as a narrative tool.[2]

Turning their attention to the textbook I have assigned, the students are provided with little positive analysis of what it might actually have been like to live and travel in the Galilee during the first century. The textbook's chapter on the "Historical Setting of Jesus" focuses on a full

---

[1] For examples, see David Rhoads, Joanna Dewey, and Donald Michie, *Mark As Story: An Introduction to the Narrative of a Gospel* (2d ed.; Minneapolis: Fortress, 1999), chs. 5 and 6; and Elizabeth Struthers Malbon, *In the Company of Jesus: Characters in Mark's Gospel* (Louisville: Westminster John Knox, 2000), ch. 5.

[2] The argument was first elaborated in Karl Ludwig Schmidt, *Der Rahmen der Geschichte Jesu: Literarkritische Untersuchungen zur ältesten Jesusüberlieferung* (Berlin: Trowitzsch, 1919). More recently, see Sean Freyne, *Galilee, Jesus and the Gospels: Literary Approaches and Historical Investigations* (Philadelphia: Fortress, 1988), 33–68.

description of the Pharisees and several other small Jewish elite groups rather than a socioeconomic description of how the other 95 to 99 percent of the population lived. In summary, there are few classroom resources that are not beholden to Mark's narrative framework.

As the semester progresses and we pick up the Gospels of Matthew, Luke, and John for our consideration, we find little help in the presentation of the Galilean setting. Clearly all of the Gospel authors were influenced by their preconceived notions of who Jesus was and their attempts to provide a "theological" explanation for their early Christian communities; their interest in the socioeconomic setting of Galilee was only as a service to their theological aims.

In light of this, I can illustrate to the students the narrative attempts by the authors of Luke and John to establish a connection between Jesus and Jerusalem. Both authors connected Jesus to Jerusalem in a consistent pattern. I can point out the likely theological motivations each author had, and I can suggest what Jerusalem represented to the authors as they wrote their stories at the end of the first century. Having critically evaluated Luke and John's story world, I am left with little in the reading material that I can point to in order to show the students what the relationship between Galilee and Jerusalem may have actually been. Since it is no longer possible to accept that Luke's idea of large groups of pilgrims traveling to Jerusalem for holy days or John's idea that Jesus often traversed the roads between Galilee and Jerusalem are relevant to historical reconstructions of the first-century contacts between the two regions, we need the help of archaeology to complete the historical reconstruction. Unfortunately, the textbooks do not provide an alternative reconstruction of the socioeconomic setting that deals with the historical issue.

So, to state the problem even more bluntly, professors of introductory courses in the New Testament (or even courses on the historical Jesus) have very few resources when it comes to reconstructing the historical contexts and socioeconomic situations out of which arose the early Jesus movements and Christianity. The textbooks do a fine job of revealing the narrative context, but there still remains a lack of information that could be gleaned from the field of archaeology. When reconstructions of the socioeconomic settings are attempted, they are often created within the framework or thought worlds of the narrative Gospels. Thus, there is a basic assumption that even though we know that Mark developed the Pharisees as the antagonists in his story world, we should still begin our reconstruction of life in first-century Galilee by analyzing the role of the Pharisees. Reconstructions of the setting of Jesus that are based primarily on the literary sources not only neglect a major aspect of scholarship but also perpetuate a misleading, theologically predetermined picture of the setting of Jesus that does not account for the complex social world of Early Roman Palestine.

In what follows I will propose an integration of archaeological data into New Testament courses that will lead to more interdisciplinary reconstructions of the setting of earliest Christianity in Palestine. When it comes to developing a setting for the historical Jesus and his first communities of followers, it is now possible to introduce significant material from recent archaeological excavations, while still pursuing a critical assessment of the narratives of the Gospels. As an example of what might happen when we integrate archaeology and New Testament studies, I will examine methods and secondary sources that can be used to develop a socioeconomic setting in the Galilee at the time of Jesus.

ARCHAEOLOGY AND NEW TESTAMENT COURSES: THE KEY ISSUES

When attempting to integrate archaeology into courses on the New Testament, an interest in questions related to the larger cultural context of earliest Christianity is more important than simply trying to find "direct evidence" of a historical Jesus or his early followers. As Jonathan Reed has illustrated, references to the Pilate inscription that was found at Caesarea Maritima in 1962 or interest in a site mentioned in the Gospels, such as the potential site of the house of Peter or the place where a miracle is said to have occurred, may be intriguing to modern Christians, but it minimizes or even detracts from the real contribution that modern archaeology can make in New Testament studies.[3] Using archaeology as a way to "prove" the veracity of New Testament stories can quickly lead to a "show-and-tell" approach that values a defense of the literary material over attempts to critically examine the origins of Christianity. As Sean Freyne aptly states, "mention of archaeology together with Jesus conjures up images of the empty tomb, Peter's house and the Capernaum synagogue, topics best left to pious pilgrims."[4] Thus, rather than thinking of relevant archaeological data in terms of how the material might prove the existence of characters mentioned in the New Testament, this essay encourages more detailed analysis of three key socioeconomic and cultural issues that recent archaeological excavations in Galilee have clarified.

The first issue considered in this essay is the relationship between the urban and rural contexts in Galilee and the resulting impact on Jesus and his first followers. What possible effects did the Herodian building projects of the cities of Sepphoris and Tiberias have on Christian origins? The

---

[3] Jonathan L. Reed, *Archaeology and the Galilean Jesus: A Re-examination of the Evidence* (Harrisburg, Pa.: Trinity Press International, 2000), 18.

[4] Sean V. Freyne, "Archaeology and the Historical Jesus," in *Archaeology and Biblical Interpretation* (ed. J. R. Bartlett; London: Routledge, 1997), 118.

second issue regards the religious and cultural influences in Galilee in the first century. To what extent was the environment of Palestine Jewish? Was Galilee "Hellenized"? How has recent archaeology helped to define the types of religions in the context of Galilee? The third issue is the relationship between Galilee and Jerusalem. What role did the Jerusalem authorities have in Galilee, and to what extent was the Galilee influenced by the Pharisees? Although the archaeological data provide us with no enchanted realm of knowledge where all our questions are suddenly and conclusively answered, when appropriately used the data can recommend an autonomous explanation of the period that often fills in the gaps.

URBAN AND RURAL SETTINGS IN GALILEE

Since the first archeological investigations in Palestine in the nineteenth century, there has been a tendency to excavate cities that were directly referenced in the Bible. Therefore, it might seem odd that one of the most important excavations for students of Christian origins is the Roman city of Sepphoris, a site not mentioned in the Bible. Although Sepphoris was located only a few miles north of Nazareth and was clearly visible from the Nazareth Ridge, the Gospel authors never mention Jesus in this major Herodian administrative center. Similarly, the city of Tiberias is not mentioned in the Gospels even though the city was established in the life of Jesus just a few miles to the south of Capernaum. Although not yet as thoroughly excavated, there should be no doubt that Tiberias had a major impact on the inhabitants around the Sea of Galilee (Lake Kinneret), where Jesus is said to have spent much of his time. I have found that many fruitful discussions have been launched by asking students why the authors of the Gospels do not mention these cities. The question not only provides an opportunity to discuss the reasons why the Gospels were written—why certain information was included and other material left out—but it also suggests an interesting dilemma in the quest for the historical Jesus. Did Jesus visit these cities? If so, why are they not mentioned? If not, what are the possible reasons? Were the cities intentionally avoided, unsupportive of Jesus and his followers, or simply not on their itinerary? Although no definitive answers can be supplied for these questions, in what follows I will attempt to clarify what we can know about the impact of these cities on earliest Christianity.[5]

The extent to which the Herodian cities of Sepphoris and Tiberias shifted the economic and political environment of Galilee is still debated

---

[5] A useful summary of significant scholarly reflections on this subject is found in ibid., 127–32.

by archaeologists and biblical scholars. It is now common to think that the growth of these cities would have gradually shifted the economic focus in Galilee away from an agrarian society with a network of small markets in the villages to a system that was characterized by the relationship of the villages to the large urban and commercial centers. There is no doubt that the village network remained a significant and, by and large, unchanged part of Roman Galilee; however, there are several reasons to think that the socioeconomic shifts in the region were impossible for any socially conscious group (such as the followers of Jesus) to ignore.

An article by Mark Chancey and Adam Porter in *Near Eastern Archaeology* provides an excellent summary of the Herodian building projects and illustrates the extensive development of urban centers by Herod and his sons.[6] Additionally, students interested in the extent to which Herod shifted the economic conditions of his day and the consequences for the rise of Christianity should be referred to Peter Richardson's study of the life of Herod.[7] Richardson's summary is balanced and more positive than is typical of much New Testament scholarship. For example, he concludes that "Herod was not a monster; he had the good of his people at heart, just as he had the best interests of Rome in view."[8] Richardson's approach to the influence of Herod convincingly illustrates the positive impact that his building projects had on the local economy. He concludes, "The projects during this period [after 30 B.C.E.] were broadly conceived (military settlements, new cities, trade facilities, religious buildings, personal comfort projects...), but the overall strategy seems to have been aimed to stimulate the economy of Judea, enhance its trade position, and secure full employment."[9] However, it is also clear that the rural, agrarian-based population in Galilee did not benefit economically from the rapid expansion in the surrounding regions. Several recent studies (surveyed below) have argued that the peasants of the region were negatively affected by the Herodian policies and that many of the teachings of Jesus can be understood as responses to the economic conditions of the day.

There are many useful resources that introduce the material related to the Herodian building projects in Galilee and their socioeconomic functions and impact. It is difficult to overestimate the worth of the new archaeological finds for the study of the Gospels and the historical Jesus.

---

[6] Mark Chancey and Adam Porter, "The Archaeology of Roman Palestine," *NEA* 64 (2001): 164–203.

[7] Peter Richardson, *Herod: King of the Jews and Friend of the Romans* (Minneapolis: Fortress, 1999).

[8] Ibid., 314.

[9] Ibid., 194.

Information that is enhancing our understanding of the private lives of the ancient Galileans has never been as available as it is today. For example, an article by Mark Chancey and Eric Meyers provides a valuable overview of the archaeology and history of Sepphoris as well as a credible argument about the residents of the city being Jewish (a point discussed in more detail below).[10] In their richly illustrated presentation, Chancey and Meyers relate the development of the city from a small settlement in the Iron Age to a small Jewish community and military outpost during the Hasmonean period, emerging into the capital of Galilee during the reign of Herod. Significant in the archaeological material is the fact that the site did not become a well-populated city until the early first century. Only with the building projects of Herod and especially his son Herod Antipas (beginning in 4 B.C.E. and continuing throughout the first century C.E.) do we see the dramatic expansion of Sepphoris in the heart of Galilee. In the time of Jesus, Sepphoris had grown to a city of ten to fifteen thousand people. Sepphoris, as the capital of Galilee, was located in a prime administrative position; it overlooked one of the most fertile agricultural regions in all of Palestine, with easy access to the east-west corridors crossing the valley from the lake to the Mediterranean that linked Galilee to the rest of the world.

In the case of Tiberias, we find a similar development. John Dominic Crossan and Jonathan Reed's overview of the city, along with the drawings that were commissioned for their book, *Excavating Jesus: Beneath the Stones, Behind the Texts,* offers a useful starting point for classroom discussions.[11] The building of the city was initiated by Herod Antipas around 17–23 C.E. and continued into the middle of the first century. Tiberias, named after the emperor Tiberius, was positioned in an area that allowed for administrative control over trade passing through the region along the lakeshore road and dominance over the lively fishing industry found in almost all the villages scattered around the lake.[12] While most of the Herodian city is unexcavated, a small section of a Roman theater, a gate complex, and a paved Roman road have been found. The discovery of two Early Roman lead weights from Tiberias that use the term *agoranomoi* (market officials) is intriguing due to the mention of the city's *agora* and

---

[10] Mark Chancey and Eric M. Meyers, "How Jewish Was Sepphoris in Jesus' Time?" *BAR* 26 (2000): 18–33, 61.

[11] John Dominic Crossan and Jonathan Reed, *Excavating Jesus: Beneath the Stones, Behind the Texts* (San Francisco: HarperSanFrancisco, 2001), 62–71.

[12] A detailed analysis of the fishing industry in Galilee, with implications for Jesus and his followers, is found in K. C. Hanson, "The Galilean Fishing Economy and the Jesus Tradition," *BTB* 27 (1997): 99–111.

the fact that the Greek language is used in this context.[13] Excavations of parts of the ancient city are now beginning that will provide many more details about the site. From what we have discovered thus far about the typical Greco-Roman urban features, and in light of the location of Tiberias, it is clear that Herod Antipas was interested in developing and controlling the lake region to a greater extent than his predecessors. The conclusion of Marianne Sawicki may be overly confident, but in the following statement she provides a provocative rationale for why Antipas built Tiberias and how the city affected the lake region.

> In effect, when Antipas built Tiberias as a port of welcome to the land of Israel, he "italianized" the Lake and the lower Jordan. The need to transport elite international travelers over the Kinneret, and to entertain them while they rested at Tiberias, invited the establishment of a new kind of industry: imperial tourism. This may well have brought material disruptions of the fishing businesses; it certainly changed the perceived character of the water.[14]

Additionally, regarding the purpose of these new cities, Crossan and Reed observe that Herod Antipas was following in his father's footsteps when it came to the reason for promoting urbanization in the region. "[Antipas] covered Sepphoris and Tiberias with a Greco-Roman architectural veneer, which made them not only the first large cities in Galilee, but complete novelties in their style, in which traces of the same aesthetic-architectural themes found at Caesarea are apparent."[15] James Strange concluded, "This rebuilding [of Sepphoris by Herod Antipas] was his opportunity to redefine Sepphoris as a Roman city for his patrons, the Romans, and thereby absorb Sepphoris into the Roman urban overlay. In other words, now Antipas had the chance to achieve a classic Roman synthesis of foreign innovations and local tradition."[16] After examining the major references in the Gospels to urban imagery and metaphors and comparing those images to what could have been know in the milieu of Early Roman Galilee, Strange notes that "we do not need a Paul to urbanize and

---

[13] Shraga Qedar, "Two Lead Weights of Herod Antipas and Agrippa II and the Early History of Tiberias," *Israel Numismatic Journal* 9 (1989): 66–75. Similarly, see the lead weight from Sepphoris inscribed with the same Greek term twice (*agoranomoi*) in Eric Meyers, "Sepphoris, The Ornament of all Galilee," *BA* 49 (1986): 4–19.

[14] Marianne Sawicki, *Crossing Galilee: Architectures of Contact in the Occupied Land of Jesus* (Harrisburg, Pa.: Trinity Press International, 2000), 30.

[15] Crossan and Reed, *Excavating Jesus*, 65.

[16] James F. Strange, "Some Implications of Archaeology for New Testament Studies," in *What Has Archaeology to Do with Faith?* (ed. J. H. Charlesworth and W. P. Weaver; Philadelphia: Trinity Press International, 1992), 35.

universalize the Christian movement; it was at least partially so from the beginning."[17] As scholars of Christian origins have increasingly become aware of the cultural shifts that occur in a region when an urban site is established, the need to understand the relationship between the inhabitants of the new cities and the surrounding villages has been more acute.

One of the key elements in the discussion of the relationship between these new urban centers and the traditional village context has been the potential increase in peasant hardship and exploitation due to the new administrative structures. Reed, Douglas Edwards, Richard Horsley, and William Arnal have provided interesting analyses regarding various aspects of the potential increases in taxation, administrative structures, absentee landlordism, monetization of the economy, and shifts in the traditional forms of peasant farming (introduction of new crops and technology) that typically occur when a colonial power establishes an urban site in an agrarian setting. Each author provides a reconstruction of aspects of life in ancient Galilee and considers how this setting may have directly affected Jesus or his early followers. I have used selected readings from the following publications in undergraduate courses on the historical Jesus in order to illustrate the key socioeconomic conditions during the time of Jesus. While these scholars disagree about the degree to which the traditional life of the village inhabitants was changed by the new urban centers, they all agree that archaeology provides a major key in any plausible reconstruction of Early Roman Galilee.

Reed's analysis of the size and cultural impact of both the Herodian cities and several Galilean villages is accessible for undergraduate students.[18] He combines an expertise in archaeology (currently the Co-Director of the Sepphoris Acropolis Excavations) and New Testament literature in order to provide a well-argued reconstruction of the socioeconomic conditions of Galilee and a detailed consideration of the implications for studying the historical Jesus. Reed concludes that the Herodian building projects "placed an economic strain on Galilean peasants, added stress to families and challenged current values, and created new rural-urban dynamics. Each of these factors is reflected in the Gospels."[19] He also provides careful analyses of the population numbers for the villages and cities in Galilee that have become standard figures used by historians of ancient Galilee.

Furthermore, by observing that many of the sayings of Jesus reflect unease with the issues of debt, land division, tenancy, and the monetization of the economy, Reed illustrates how recent archaeological studies of

---

[17] Ibid., 47.

[18] Reed, *Archaeology and the Galilean Jesus,* 62–99.

[19] Ibid., 96.

the urban settings in Galilee can add to our understanding of Christian origins. In this regard he examines the Lord's Prayer, the parable of the Tenants, the parable of the Laborers in the Vineyard, and other sayings in which Jesus is said to have referenced the economic conditions of his day. By examining the language of Jesus that suggests a familiarity with the urban context, Reed notes that "urban-rural contacts were not uncommon, which raises the question of whether Jesus can be placed in an exclusively village context, first around Nazareth and then around Capernaum, or whether he did, in fact, visit Tiberias or Sepphoris."[20]

Several articles by Douglas Edwards, the Director of the Cana Excavations in Galilee, offer another noteworthy avenue for exploration.[21] Edwards is interested in the economic impact of the new urban centers on the residents of the many agrarian-based villages in the area. Using the analysis of pottery distribution in Early Roman Galilee completed by David Adan-Bayewitz as his starting point, Edwards provides evidence for a reasonably amenable relationship between urban and rural inhabitants in the time of Jesus.[22] Since the residents of a small Galilean village such as Kefar Hananya (25 km from Sepphoris) were able to produce pottery that was distributed over much of Galilee, including supplying over 50 percent of the kitchenware in Sepphoris, Edwards argues that at least some of the rural inhabitants were able to use the building of the urban centers as an opportunity for employment and economic gain. Rather than understanding the new Herodian cities as negatively affecting the village inhabitants, thus leading to animosity between the urban and rural settings, he suggests more collaboration than animosity was involved in the relationship. Regarding the potential impact on the early followers of Jesus, he concludes,

> it would be a mistake to assume that the [Jesus] movement operated in cultural, political or economic isolation from major urban areas. Villages mentioned in the tradition were near (Capernaum, Bethsaida) or connected to (Nazareth, Caesarea Philippi, region of Tyre and Sidon) urban areas and linked to a vibrant regional market network. Nor does an innate

---

[20] Ibid., 99.

[21] Douglas Edwards, "First Century Urban/Rural Relations in Lower Galilee: Exploring the Archaeological and Literary Evidence," *SBL Seminar Papers, 1988* (ed. D. Lull; SBLSP 27; Atlanta: Scholars Press, 1988), 169–82; idem, "The Socio-economic and Cultural Ethos of Lower Galilee in the First Century: Implications for the Nascent Jesus Movement," in *The Galilee in Late Antiquity* (ed. L. I. Levine; New York: Jewish Theological Seminary, 1992), 53–73.

[22] David Adan-Bayewitz, *Common Pottery in Roman Galilee: A Study of Local Trade* (Ramat-Gan, Israel: Bar-Ilan University Press, 1993).

rural hostility toward urban areas appear to have existed in the move-ment. Indeed, the audience could have been and probably was urban—as well as village centered.[23]

In support of Edwards's position, it should be noted that in the face of the rapid shifts brought on by these Herodian building projects, a substan-tial amount of stability prevailed in the region, at least from the late 20s to the late 50s C.E. For instance, no major military fortresses are known to have been founded in the region by the Herodian administration.[24] Thus, unlike the surrounding regions of Herod's empire, central Galilee was negligibly populated by military personnel or fortress structures.[25] Seppho-ris and Tiberias were not fortresses in the Early Roman period, even though the cities were well-positioned administrative centers responsible for tax collection. Even the Hasmonean "castra" or military outpost on the site of Sepphoris was no longer being used as a fortress in the first century, and it was completely destroyed prior to 66 C.E. Rather than a military fortress, part of the building had evidently been converted into an indus-trial space where a substantial area of bone-tool production for use in weaving was found in one of the large rooms.[26]

Adding to this picture is the fact that the archaeological data show no signs of extreme wealth among the urban residents of Sepphoris. An overview of the material remains of the inhabitants of Sepphoris presented by Reed illustrates the rather stark contrast between the wealth and pres-tige of this city in comparison to other major Greco-Roman cities in the region, such as Tyre, Caesarea, or Scythopolis.[27] The citizens of Sepphoris appear to have been unable to afford most luxury items. There is evidence for some trade with outside regions in the form of imported fine wares, and there are various domestic decorations that imply attempts by some of the residents to try to reproduce signs of wealth with cheaper replicas (one example being the fresco remnants and painted plaster molding found in the ruins of a first-century house). However, there are no large quantities of imported marble and no major public building projects such as a hippo-drome, temple, or gymnasium that date to the early first century.

---

[23] Edwards, "Socio-economic and Cultural Ethos of Lower Galilee," 72.

[24] Richardson, *Herod,* 175–76.

[25] Regarding the general lack of evidence for non-Jewish people, including members of the Roman military, see Mark A. Chancey, *The Myth of a Gentile Galilee* (SNTSMS 118; Cambridge: Cambridge University Press, 2002).

[26] Eric Meyers, "Sepphoris on the Eve of the Great Revolt (67–68 C.E.): Archaeology and Josephus," in *Galilee through the Centuries* (ed. E. Meyers; Winona Lake, Ind.: Eisenbrauns, 1999), 114, 120–22.

[27] Reed, *Archaeology and the Galilean Jesus,* 117–31.

The trade connection with regional village sites evidenced by the pottery distribution in Galilee, along with the lack of Roman military personnel and relative lack of wealth in the urban centers, combine to suggest the need for restraint when considering the impact of the urbanization of Galilee. The typical theory of the impact of the ancient city on the surrounding countryside that was stated by Moses I. Finley (based on the work of Max Weber), that the major characteristic of an ancient city was its consumer or parasitic nature, has not been undermined,[28] but Edwards has provided a reasonable modification in light of the Galilean evidence.

I have regularly asked students to read Edwards's essays in conjunction with several selections from the recent publications of Richard Horsley. Although both scholars are interested in how archaeology can help us understand the Galilean economy and its impact on the earliest Christians in the region, their conclusions are distinct. For instance, in contrast to Edwards, Horsley has stressed the role of urban centers as administrative centers with close ties to the elite administrative center of Jerusalem. In his book *Archaeology, History and Society in Galilee,* he has argued that the cities of Sepphoris and Tiberias were primarily centers of taxation and reminders of the power of the Jerusalem based elite of the "tributary political-economic" center, providing little (if any) economic benefit for the rural peasant population.[29] His argument is based on the construction of society in the Galilee that was primarily agrarian and agricultural in nature. In his view, the rise of the *polis* would have had little impact on the actual market practices, since the agrarian lifestyle is understood as mainly self-sufficient, with little need to buy or sell goods in the large market centers.[30] Thus, the fact that Herod Antipas built a city such as Sepphoris was not representative of a major shift in the socioeconomic setting, particularly with regard to the markets, but is understood to be a center of elite, urban life that would have caused a negative response from the stable agrarian residents of Galilee. Horsley suggests that there was an active opposition to the city by the villagers, a theory that is based on his contention that the villagers in Galilee were primarily descendants of an Israelite heritage,

---

[28] Moses I. Finley, "The Ancient City: From Fustel de Coulanges to Max Weber and Beyond," *Comparative Studies in Society and History* 19 (1977): 305–32.

[29] Richard Horsley, *Archaeology, History and Society in Galilee: The Social Context of Jesus and the Rabbis* (Valley Forge, Pa.: Trinity Press International, 1996). See particularly Horsley's description of Galilean economics in ch. 3, "Trade of Tribute: The Political Economy of Roman Galilee," 66–87.

[30] Horsley, *Archaeology, History and Society in Galilee,* 76–85, 118–130; and see Richard Horsley, "Social Conflict in the Synoptic Sayings Source Q," in *Conflict and Invention: Literary, Rhetorical, and Social Studies on the Sayings Gospel Q* (ed. J. S. Kloppenborg; Valley Forge, Pa.: Trinity Press International, 1996), 37–52.

while the new urban centers were inhabited by people from Judea, with ties to Jerusalem and the Herodian authorities. While this thesis is intriguing because it provides a clear identity for the inhabitants of Galilee separate from the region of Jerusalem, this dichotomy is not supported by the archaeological material. Jonathan Reed has well illustrated the lack of evidence for a continuous occupation of Galilee by descendants of the Israelites and has proposed instead that the archaeological material suggests that the residents of the region had moved there from Judea.[31] Regardless of the exact ethnicity of the Galileans (a topic discussed further below), what Horsley provides is useful in a classroom setting as a rejoinder to Edwards's more optimistic view of urban-rural relations.

Arnal's contribution to the area of archaeology and New Testament studies is in many respects more specialized than those previously mentioned, but his presentation of the material is thorough, accessible to students, and easy to integrate into classroom discussions of how archaeological research is being used to redescribe Christian origins. In his recent publication, *Jesus and the Village Scribes,* Arnal provides an admirable overview of the socioeconomic setting of Early Roman Galilee. His study of coinage, monetization, debt, and taxes is particularly useful for discussions of Jesus' sayings that mention tenant farmers, landlords, and debtors (Matt 6:12; 18:23–34; 20:1–15; Mark 12:1–11; Luke 12:16–20; 16:1–17).[32] Due to the proximity of the new administrative centers of Sepphoris and Tiberias, Arnal illustrates the possible ways that the village citizens of Galilee were pressed into debt. He points out that, with the rise in taxes that typically accompanied tighter administrative oversight,

> the peasants' tenuous hold on the land is threatened, and they begin a cycle of debt, monetization, loss of land, tenancy, and further monetization, all of which serve to benefit the local elites and the imperial administration. By the political imposition of taxes, the region in question is drawn into an empirewide orbit of money and trade, and must redirect its own local resources accordingly.[33]

Many other sayings of Jesus are intriguing to read within the context of the growth of the Herodian cities. For example, I have found it useful in my New Testament introduction courses to coordinate a discussion of the Beatitudes (Q/Luke 6:20–23; Matt 5:1–4, 6, 11–12) and several of the Woes (Q/Luke 11:42–43, 46; Matt 23:4–7, 23) with a presentation of the economic

---

[31] Reed, *Archaeology and the Galilean Jesus,* 23–61.

[32] William E. Arnal, *Jesus and the Village Scribes: Galilean Conflicts and the Setting of Q* (Minneapolis: Fortress, 2001), 97–155.

[33] Ibid., 146.

shifts that likely accompanied the growth of the new urban centers. I have consistently found that when students are introduced to the archaeological material they become interested in reading these sayings through the lens of the economic setting of Roman Galilee. Having integrated material from Reed, Edwards, Horsley, and Arnal into the course reading list, information about the shift in the socioeconomic setting of Galilee can enliven and improve teaching about the Gospels and the historical Jesus.

CULTURAL AND RELIGIOUS INFLUENCES IN GALILEE

Several recent studies provide students and teachers with a wealth of information about the possible ethnic and religious makeup of the region of Galilee during the time of Jesus. A useful summary is found in a recent article by Freyne.[34] Drawing primarily on the archaeological evidence, he argues that an identifiable localized area of Galilee was predominantly occupied by Jewish settlements. This included the region around Sepphoris, including the urban site itself, the area north of Sepphoris (often referred to as Upper Galilee), and most of the western shore of Lake Kinneret. These areas are the main places where Jesus is said to have lived and traveled.[35] Other localized regions surrounding these sections of Galilee have produced materials that indicate either much more of a mixture of religious traditions or primarily a non-Jewish or "pagan" population.[36] However, one should not overstate the isolation of the various localized regions; "the Jewish and non-Jewish areas were not hermetically sealed from one another."[37] The predominantly Jewish areas were well connected to their larger regions, especially as the road systems were continuously being expanded and enhanced during the Early Roman Period. After Herod had the major port city of Caesarea Maritima established in the first century B.C.E., not only was a better system of roads constructed in Galilee, but even more traffic crossed the region due to the large amount of commerce going to and from the new port.[38] In Galilee, access to the larger Roman world was not only accessible, but it was often unavoidable.

---

[34] Freyne, "Archaeology and the Historical Jesus," 132–38.

[35] For a complete survey of the evidence, see Chancey, *Myth of a Gentile Galilee.* Although this book probably contains too much detail for use as a classroom textbook, it is an excellent resource for teachers interested in the archaeological remains that have any bearing on the ethnic and religious identities of the inhabitants of Galilee.

[36] See Jürgen Zangenberg's essay in this volume for a discussion of the term "pagan" and an overview of the extant "pagan" materials in the region of Galilee.

[37] Freyne, "Archaeology and the Historical Jesus," 137.

[38] See Reed, *Archaeology and the Galilean Jesus,* 147–48.

Taking the city of Sepphoris as a test case, Reed's work on the ethnic markers that have been identified in the archaeological material is our primary source of information.[39] He argues that the material remains show that these residents of Galilee were quite similar to the residents of Judea, particularly Jerusalem, with regard to their "religious indicators." "Key aspects of the Galilean material culture of this period match that of Judea: stone vessels, *miqwaoth* in houses but no pork wherever bone profiles are published, and secondary burial with ossuaries in *kokhim*."[40] These are all signs of early Jewish practice in Judea; thus a clear argument can be made in favor of the Jewish inhabitants of Galilee being connected to—even descended from—the residents of Judea/Jerusalem. The aforementioned article of Chancey and Meyers ("How Jewish Was Sepphoris in Jesus' Time?") is another useful resource for presentations of this material in classroom settings.

Of related interest to the question of ethnic and/or religious identities in the region of Galilee is the somewhat surprising (and often referenced) lack of synagogues in much of the area that has been designated as Jewish. While the literary picture from the Gospel narratives suggests the presence of many synagogues in the region[41]—even in the small villages such as Nazareth—the archaeological material presents a stark contrast. No unquestionable synagogue remains are extant from the Early Roman period in Galilee. This fact from the archaeological record has led to a rethinking of the meaning of term *synagogue.* The majority scholarly opinion appears to be in favor of understanding the term to refer to a gathering of people in public spaces, courtyards, or private homes rather than as a reference to an actual building.[42] While the significance of this shift in definition may not be immense, this is arguably one of the clearest indications that archaeology is having a direct impact on the study of the historical Jesus and the Gospels. Our picture of Early Roman Galilee has literally been forced to change; there is no evidence for any synagogue building in the Galilean sites mentioned in the New Testament.

The archaeological picture, though still incomplete, suggests that the inhabitants of the immediate areas where Jesus is said to have lived were Jewish. These people were not isolated. Greco-Roman culture or Hellenism was not only plentiful in the many surrounding regions and cities in close proximity to the localized Jewish regions of Galilee, but quite

---

[39] Ibid., 23–61.

[40] Ibid., 52–53.

[41] Cf. Mark 1:39 par. Matt 4:23 and Luke 4:15.

[42] See the discussion, with references to the relevant secondary literature, in Freyne, "Archaeology and the Historical Jesus," 130–31; Chancey, *Myth of a Gentile Galilee,* 66–67.

clearly Hellenism was integrated into the daily world of most Galileans. Sepphoris and Tiberias were most likely primarily inhabited by people whom we would classify as Jewish, but this did not make them any less Hellenistic than their regional neighbors. The old dichotomy of Judaism in distinction from Hellenism is a thing of the past. Travel, trade, Herodian influences, the establishment of new urban centers, and the close proximity of major centers of non-Jewish inhabitants all suggest a world that cannot be neatly categorized by the modern notions of distinct ethnic and/or religious identities. What is the picture that archaeology is painting? Was Galilee Jewish? Yes! Was Galilee Hellenistic? Yes!

THE RELATIONSHIP BETWEEN GALILEE AND JERUSALEM

As noted above, students are often compelled to construct an image of Early Roman Galilee that is dominated by the Pharisees. There are several indications from the archaeological data, and even the literary material outside of the New Testament, that suggest that the Gospels have overstated the role of the Pharisees (and also the Sadducees). No doubt the inhabitants of some parts of Galilee (including Sepphoris) show signs of descent from a Judean tradition, but what can we know about the actual contacts between the regions during the Early Roman period? To a large extent, the material evidence that could be used to suggest direct contact between the regions is missing. For example, I can point students to various studies that observe that there is scarce evidence outside of the New Testament Gospels that suggests a widespread pattern of travel between the two areas, even for the holy days. For instance, Ze'ev Safrai has concluded, "Basically, each of the major regions of Eretz-Israel—Judaea, Peraea, Galilee and Samaria— were separate units. The impression that one gets from Talmudic tradition is that there was hardly any travel between the various regions."[43] No doubt some people traveled between the various regions for trade, entertainment, and holy days, but there is no evidence that supports the idea that Galileans were physically tied to Jerusalem in any significant way. The idea that large groups would travel together to Passover is not supported in the literature outside of Luke.[44]

Unfortunately, introductory textbooks in New Testament studies do not point out that there is little material evidence that would suggest significant commerce or travel between the two regions. Part of the argument depends on what has not been found in the excavations of Galilean sites.

---

[43] Ze'ev Safrai, *The Economy of Roman Palestine* (London: Routledge, 1994), 269.

[44] Sean Freyne, "Galilee-Jerusalem Relations according to Josephus' *Life*," *NTS* 33 (1987): 600–609.

For example, one might suspect that if individuals or groups were often going to Jerusalem there would be a quantity of Judean numismatic evidence (coins) or pottery remains found in Galilee. However, the trade from Galilee to the northwest, rather than toward Judea, is better attested. There is no reason to doubt that the ideas of the temple and the city of Jerusalem were influential in Galilee, but the contention that people often moved back and forth between the regions appears to be difficult to support in the archaeological record.

The lack of evidence for direct contact between the regions of Judea and Galilee suggests that Jerusalem-based groups such as the Pharisees and Sadducees were not as influential in Galilee as the Gospel narratives envision. While the debate over this issue will continue, it is safe to say that our archaeological evidence is mixed. There is no clear evidence of Jerusalem's direct impact on the region, outside of the above-mentioned signs of a Judean heritage for some of the residents. Since the Galileans had their own administrative centers, their own natural resources and manufacturing centers, and were connected to the Greco-Roman world through a road system that passed through the region, what can be said of the actual role of the Jerusalem authorities in the region? To date, the silence of the archaeological remains appears to be in agreement with the literary sources outside the New Testament: there were few close contacts between Galilee and Jerusalem in the Early Roman period.

CONCLUSION

The dialogue between the interpretations of the archaeological data and the literary remains from the Early Roman period has the potential to be a great stimulant for everyone who teaches courses on the New Testament. I have briefly outlined some of the topics that are promising areas of research, particularly where the archaeological material informs the reconstruction of life in ancient Galilee. While archaeological research is restricted by several factors (e.g., the lack of useable published resources and the relatively few sites that have been excavated), the growing body of literature that lets archaeology have a right to be heard, encouraging a separate reconstruction from that which is derived from the literary sources, is a hopeful sign of life in New Testament studies. In the classroom, I have found that the more I am able to integrate this material into my teaching, the more students are able fully to grasp the settings and meanings of the New Testament texts, and, no doubt the interdisciplinary approach that is necessitated by the integration of the archaeological data provides students with more of an ability to form reasonable historical reconstructions of the rise of earliest Christianity.

Teaching Second Temple Judaism
in Light of Archaeology

Eric M. Meyers
Duke University

Although there has been enormous interest in recent years in the topic of Second Temple Judaism, reflected in the wide range and number of publications on this subject, it is remarkable that there has been an inconsistent use of archaeology for the reconstruction of this important era in the history of religion. The first thing to do, however, is to state the precise chronological time frame about which we are concerned: 515 B.C.E. to 70 C.E. The beginning date is determined by the rededication of the temple in Jerusalem in the days of Joshua the high priest and Zerubbabel the governor.[1] Its ending date in 70 C.E. is related to the destruction of the temple at the hands of the Romans at the end of the First Revolt on the ninth of Ab according to Jewish tradition (Josephus, *War* 6.164–253; *m. Ta'anit* 4:6). During the course of those 585 years, the tiny nation of Judea, first known as Yehud, survived under three different world empires: the Persian (515–332 B.C.E.), the Greek (332–63 B.C.E.), and the Roman (63 B.C.E.–70 C.E.), which continued to administer Palestine, including Judea and other territories, until the reign of Constantine the Great (306–337 C.E.). The fact that these six centuries witnessed such epochal changes makes it especially important to keep track of the material culture of the region and to observe the degree to which it reflects those changes.

The predominant approach to presenting the history of this period aside from special studies has been to focus on the main literary compositions associated with each era or the major trends and movements attributed to Second Temple Judaism. This is true even with the well-received small volume by James VanderKam on early Judaism, which is virtually entirely focused on literature.[2] Few have ventured the task of

---

[1] Carol. L. Meyers and Eric M Meyers, *Haggai, Zechariah 1–8* (AB 25B; Garden City, N.Y.: Doubleday, 1987), xxi, 9–17, 193–95.

[2] James. C. VanderKam, *An Introduction to Early Judaism* (Grand Rapids: Eerdmans, 1999).

151

integrating or "mainstreaming" archaeology, although all scholars are to a high degree dependent on inferences and conclusions that rely on archae-ological information. It may come as a surprise to readers that we are particularly well informed about the Persian and Roman portions of Second Temple archaeology and that the Hellenistic or Greek period is the least well-known component of Second Temple history. So it is all the more surprising to find so many of the biblical "minimalists" place so much of biblical writing in an era about which we know so little except from the point of view of Josephus, the first-century Jewish historian. On the other hand, some of the most distinguished scholars in the field of Syro-Palestin-ian archaeology have provided very detailed accounts of the material culture of their fields, especially the recent study of Ephraim Stern on the Persian period[3] or the excellent summary of Andrea Berlin on the Hel-lenistic period,[4] and there are numerous specialized studies including the archaeology of the period from Pompey's invasion of Palestine (63 B.C.E.) to the fall of the Second Temple in 70 C.E.

One scholar who has made great advances in putting archaeology together with the literary evidence and allowing both databases to influ-ence his conclusions is Lee Levine, especially his Stroum Lectures at the University of Washington.[5] In that work Levine undertakes to evaluate the degree to which Second Temple Judaism and post-70 early Judaism has accommodated many aspects of Hellenistic civilization in both its religious makeup and material world. Reed has recently done this for New Testament studies in a very accessible fashion.[6] I have attempted to do this in a long essay in the new Schocken cultural history of the Jewish people.[7]

The purpose of the present essay, then, will be to demonstrate the importance of integrating archaeological materials into the teaching of the Second Temple period. I will present my arguments by period and will offer some concluding remarks at the end of the presentation. While the bibliography is selective, it is intended to introduce and guide the reader

---

[3] Ephraim Stern, *Archaeology of the Land of the Bible, Volume II: The Assyrian, Babylonian, and Persian Periods (732–332 B.C.E.)* (New York: Doubleday, 1999).

[4] Andrea M. Berlin, "Archaeological Sources for the History of Palestine: Between Large Forces: Palestine in the Hellenistic Period," *BA* 60 (1997): 2–51.

[5] Lee I. Levine, *Judaism and Hellenism in Antiquity: Conflict or Confluence?* (Samuel and Althea Stroum Lectures in Jewish Studies; Seattle: University of Washington Press, 1998).

[6] Jonathan L. Reed, *Archaeology and the Galilean Jesus* (Harrisburg, Pa.: Trinity Press International, 2000); and John Dominic Crossan and Jonathan L. Reed, *Excavating Jesus: Beneath the Stones, Behind the Texts* (San Francisco: HarperSanFrancisco, 2001).

[7] Eric M. Meyers, "Jewish Culture in Greco-Roman Palestine," in *Cultures of the Jews: A New History* (ed. D. Biale; New York: Random House/Schocken, 2002), 1:135–79.

through these centuries so that he or she is able to place movements associated with those texts within the appropriate material and social context in which they emerged.

The Persian Period (515–332 b.c.e.)

The first item to be pointed out has to do with nomenclature. Any keen observer of the archaeology of ancient Israel will notice that the earlier periods of Israel's history are identified in the literature by the material in predominant use or that had a major influence on the people of those periods. For the ancient Near East and Israel in the historical periods that material was bronze and iron and the periods known as the Bronze and Iron Ages. With the emergence of the Persian Empire, however, in the mid-sixth century b.c.e., succeeding eras have been identified in nomenclature by the imperial government that dominated the region. However, the reader is cautioned not to necessarily associate Persian domination of the Near East either with Persian ethnicity or Persian-type material culture. The imposition of an imperial rule in any of the succeeding periods did not necessarily cause a widespread transformation of local culture, and some artifacts should merely be understood in terms of their inherent value and function as objects related to a specific time and not necessarily to a particular people. Indeed, the Persian period is when we begin to find black Attic-ware pottery sherds and Greek-looking statues even though the Persians and Greeks were at war.

Rather than give a systematic review of all the relevant data for each period, I will highlight some of the most important items, which, when properly taken into account, will greatly influence one's understanding of the entire social setting of the era. It can hardly be doubted that the Elephantine papyri have contributed greatly to our understanding of the Jewish community in Egypt and their assimilation to Canaanite and Egyptian culture.[8] However, even more than that, their texts demonstrate and illustrate their loyalty to their Jewish colleagues in Palestine and their deference to them on matters of observance.[9] Needless to say, their

---

[8] Bezalel Porten, "Egyptian Aramaic Texts," *OEANE* 1:213–29.

[9] James B. Pritchard, *The Ancient Near East: An Anthology of Texts and Pictures* (Princeton: Princeton University Press, 1973), 278–81 (also available in *ANET,* 491–92). The so-called "Passover Papyrus" indicates the degree to which the Jews in Elephantine were concerned about proper observance of the pilgrim festivals, which apparently had to be approved by the Persian authorities. The letter is written by Hananiah, secretary for Jewish affairs to Arsames, satrap in Egypt 455/454–407 b.c.e. A copy of the authorization to rebuild the temple of Yaho there illustrates the continuing importance of their cult, which the governors or Judah and Samaria approved for "meal-offering and incense."

discovery has also led to the illumination of key biblical texts of the post-exilic era.[10]

The purchase of a postexilic cache of bullae and their publication by Nahman Avigad is the kind of archaeological corpus of artifacts that has enabled us to fill in the so-called governor gap from Zerubbabel to Nehemiah and allowed us to reconstruct the series of civil authorities or governors (*peḥâ*) in Yehud[11] and to clarify the role of Shelomith, *'āmâ* of Elnatan (ca. 510–490 B.C.E.).[12] Supplemented by the jar-handle sealings found at Ramat Rahel and Tell en-Nasbeh, we are now able to link up directly with the governorship of Nehemiah by adding two Judean governors, Yehoezer and Ahzai.[13] All of these governors served against the backdrop of the Greco-Persian wars, Elnatan's final year of his term coinciding with Darius I's greatest defeat at Marathon.

Kenneth Hoglund has examined Persian imperial policies and the forts that were built as part of the infrastructure connected with the extensive roads that the Persians constructed in the fifth century B.C.E., a study that has enabled students better to comprehend the full import of the changes that Persians brought to their rule in the ancient Near East.[14] To this we should also add that a network of royal granaries in Palestine, together with the forts that were constructed, was introduced along the coast to control the port cities.[15] It is too simplistic to conclude that Persian indirect rule was totally benign, but the fact that they allowed conquered peoples and former nations to exert a kind of quasi-autonomy, albeit without the normal trappings such as with a king, enabled local cultures to grow and flourish in new and unexpected ways. Perhaps this is why the Hebrew Bible greets Cyrus's kingship with messianic expectation (Isa 44:28; 45:1). It is difficult to imagine understanding the late sixth or fifth centuries

---

[10] The Elephantine corpus is especially relevant to understanding the organization of Samaria and Judah during Nehemiah's governorship (Lester L.Grabbe, *The Persian and Greek Periods* [vol. 1 of *Judaism from Cyrus to Hadrian;* Minneapolis: Fortress, 1992], 54–55, 131–36).

[11] Nahman Avigad, *Bullae and Seals from a Post-exilic Judean Archive* (Qedem 4; Jerusalem: Hebrew University, Institute of Archaeology, 1976).

[12] Eric M. Meyers, "The Shelomith Seal and the Judean Restoration: Some Additional Considerations," *ErIsr* 18 (1985): 33–38. Assuming Shelomith of the Elnatan bulla can be identified with the daughter of Zerubbabel in 1 Chr 3:19, the governor Elnatan, by marrying a descendant of the David house, would have strengthened his position in a time when civil authority was giving way to increasing priestly power.

[13] Mary Joan Winn Leith, "Israel among the Nations: The Persian Period," in *The Oxford History of the Biblical World* (ed. M. D. Coogan; New York: Oxford University Press, 1997), 394, 402–3.

[14] Kenneth Hoglund, *Achaemenid Imperial Administration in Syria-Palestine and the Missions of Ezra and Nehemiah* (SBLDS 25; Atlanta: Scholars Press, 1992).

[15] David F. Graf, "Palestine in the Persian through the Roman Period." *OEANE* 4:224.

without having a real sense of what the Persians were doing at home and in their holdings, organized as satrapies. The opportunity to bring to bear Greek and Persian historical writings and archaeology on the early post-exilic age enables one to appreciate more fully the growing influence of the temple and priestly establishment on the Jewish community of Yehud and how it is reflected in the realia of the period.[16]

Charles Carter published the results of his innovative, social-scientific work on the recent archaeological surveys of Israel and their importance in understanding the two main phases of the Persian period, early postexilic and mid-fifth century and later, and for estimating the size of the Jewish population of Yehud.[17] Among the most surprising conclusions are the sparse numbers of returnees in the era of Zerubbabel and after, and even in the time of Second Zachariah (Zech 9–14).[18] It is striking how an awareness of these new data enables one to view the biblical sources, and even the extrabiblical written evidence mentioned, in an entirely new light when placed against the demographic picture reconstructed from archaeology. The struggle to maintain one's ethnic identity, let alone religion, in the face of an under-population of Jews in this period allows us better to understand the reforms of Ezra and Nehemiah.

How one introduces this material to students is a matter for the individual teacher to decide. How much visual material is needed to make these points? How many articles should supplement a text or reader? At the moment one has to pick and choose, and I have given a few new approaches to familiar material.[19] These new materials are intended to offer

---

[16] Graf's summary of the period ("Palestine," 4:222–24), and Grabbe's detailed treatment (*Persian and Greek Periods*, 27–146) are convenient entry points for study. Similarly, Leith's ("Israel among the Nations," 367–419) treatment is more synthetic and mindful of the biblical materials.

[17] Charles E. Carter, *The Emergence of Yehud in the Persian Period: A Social and Demographic Study* (JSOTSup 294; Sheffield: Sheffield Academic Press, 1999).

[18] Carter's population figures for the Persian I period (ca. 515–450 B.C.E.) are thirteen thousand and for the remainder of the Persian period (Persian II ca. 450–332 B.C.E.) twenty thousand (*Emergence of Yehud*, 201). More recent studies on the population of Yehud, however, suggest that Carter's figures are too low. See now the essays in Oded Lipschits and Joseph Blenkinsopp, eds., *Judah and the Judeans in the Neo-Babylonian Period* (Winona Lake, Ind.: Eisenbrauns, 2003), especially 323–76. The implications of Carter's work for the study of the Persian-period biblical materials is enormous. The Anchor Bible commentary on Haggai and Zech 1–8 with C. L. Meyers and the successive volume of Zech 9–14 (*Zechariah* 9–14 [AB 25C; Garden City, N.Y.: Doubleday, 1993]) reflect the influence of Carter on our thinking, especially the latter volume. See my most recent essay (Meyers, " Jewish Culture in Greco-Roman Palestine," 139–42) in addition to Carter (*Emergence of Yehud*, 294–324).

[19] Depending on the course one is teaching, one may turn to biblical handbooks such as Coogan, *Oxford History of the Biblical World*, encyclopedias (*OEANE* or *NEAHL*), or the scholarly literature for materials. Note the special resources listed in this volume by Aubin.

a new avenue of entry for a teacher who has had difficulty making this important period come alive. To illustrate the variety of material culture in Persian-period Palestine (Judah and Samaria still remaining under the influence of Egypt and Mesopotamia, the coastal plain and Galilee reflecting the ongoing influence of Greek and Phoenician culture),[20] I would recommend turning to Stern's definitive new study already mentioned.[21]

THE HELLENISTIC PERIOD (332–63 B.C.E.)

We have already indicated that it would be incorrect to conclude that the Persian period may be characterized only by "Persian" material culture. If anything, especially on the coast, Palestine was beginning to reflect the growing cultural influence of Hellenistic culture and civilization, which was edging its way closer to Near Eastern lands. The appearance of the Philisto-Arabian Attic-type coin, with its Attic standard, in the Persian period in Gaza and inland at sites in Yehud and elsewhere, along with black Attic sherds, proclaimed the coming of Hellenism long before Alexander led his armies south from Cilicia toward Egypt. Though he had his eyes on Persepolis, capital of the Persian Empire, Alexander was wise to soften up his southwestern flank by heading down the Phoenician coast and the coastal plain in Palestine toward the strongest of the satrapies, Egypt. Since most books and essays on this era speak of "Alexander the Great's conquest of the ancient Near East," it should be noted right away that his coming to Palestine was largely peaceful. The earlier Assyrian and Babylonian wars (eighth and sixth centuries) had left large swaths of Palestinian territory reduced in population (Judea, Samaria, and Galilee), with the jurisdiction of the Phoenician city of Tyre extending down to Akko and its adjoining lands, the Phoenician city of Sidon extending its administrative control to the plain between Dor and Joppa, and Ashkelon remaining under Tyrian authority.[22] These areas were the first to recover from the earlier wars and to be repopulated in the course of the Persian period. It should be stressed that since so much of biblical literary history is assigned to either the Persian or Hellenistic period it is especially important for teachers to be mindful of the larger demographic picture of Palestine that can only be inferred from archaeological data. By the time Ezra had reestablished the Torah in Israel, in the second half of the fifth century, there were twenty to thirty thousand Jews in all Yehud—the vast majority of Jews were living in the Diaspora.[23]

---

[20] Graf, "Palestine," 4:224.

[21] Stern, *Archaeology of the Land of the Bible.*

[22] Berlin, "Archaeological Sources for the History of Palestine," 3.

[23] Unfortunately, there is no single work that deals with the "early" Jewish Diaspora. Judging from Carter's low population estimates for Palestine and combining the populations

Within such a context, the impact of Alexander's taking control of Syria-Palestine and neighboring lands was even more significant. I have noted how the indirect rule of the Persians facilitated indigenous, conquered peoples and cultures to continue and even flourish, albeit under foreign hegemony. Alexander, however, had a vision of bringing Hellenistic culture and Greek language to his newly adopted and conquered territories in hopes of bringing the world closer together. The process by which those new peoples and places were to become acculturated to this new idea we call "Hellenization," the movement "Hellenism." Accommodation to such a worldview was made possible as Greek settlers and mercenaries were moved into old established cities and new colonies were founded.[24] Seeing the transformation of one of these cities, such as Dor and its fortification wall that previously had been Phoenician in design and construction technique, would be a good way to demonstrate the kind of cultural shift that took place early in the Hellenistic era, at least by the mid-third century B.C.E. The new "header" stone construction, with its narrow ends facing out and a series of large square towers projecting out from the wall at forty-meter intervals, demonstrates such a transition.[25]

It is well known that two of Alexander's generals established two Hellenistic empires in the Near East after his death: Ptolemy in Egypt and Seleucus in Syria. These smaller empires became the vehicles through which Greek culture continued to filter into Palestine and Egypt as well. The Ptolemies influenced Palestine through a variety of means, but its mercantile center became Gaza, through which all manner of goods and services flowed. The stepped-up economic activity is reflected in the Zenon papyri, which notes Gaza's central role in the caravan trade. The new activity also brings to notice the Nabateans, who became active in the trans-Negev (E–W) trade from Petra to Gaza.[26] The impact of these activities is reflected in the earliest bilingual (Aramaic and Greek) inscriptions from Khirbet el-Qom in Idumaea, in the northern Negev, six in all, and dated to the fourth and early third century.[27] Secular Jewish coins of the

---

of the Egyptian Jewish community, the exiles in Babylonia, and others outside the land of Israel, it is not difficult to see how the majority of Jews lived outside the land.

[24] The best article by far on integrating archaeology with history is Berlin ("Archaeological Sources for the History of Palestine") and the bibliography there, but see also Greenspoon, who fills in on the intertestamental side (Leonard J. Greenspoon, "Between Alexandria and Antioch: Jews and Judaism in the Hellenistic Period," in Coogan, *The Oxford History of the Biblical World,* 421–66).

[25] Berlin, "Archaeological Sources for the History of Palestine," 5.

[26] See David Graf, "Nabateans," *OEANE* 4:82–85; Berlin, " Archaeological Sources for the History of Palestine."

[27] For the best known of the El-Qom bilinguals, see Lawrence T. Geraty, "The Khirbet el Kôm Bilingual Ostracon," *BASOR* 220 (1975): 55–61.

Ptolemaic era lack the secular designation of *peḥâ* or governor, familiar to us from the Persian era, and signal a shift toward the temple and the high priesthood. While the Ptolemies allowed the Jews to mint coins, it is also quite clear that they had no intention of granting the Jews autonomy.

All in all the transition to the Hellenistic age, though peaceful, surely brought with it the trappings of a paradigm shift. While we cannot speak of a uniform spread of Hellenism, we note Hellenism's clear imprint on the coast and in places such as Marissa, some forty kilometers southwest of Jerusalem, where the Ptolemies installed a Sidonian colony and laid out the city on a Greek grid. Jerusalem and other sites in the Judean heartland do not at this time reveal such signs of Hellenization, however, which means at least that Hellenism's advance was uneven and affected by regional trade systems and economies. Moreover, it indicates possibly that there were pockets of resistance to Hellenization, and many of those resurfaced in the time of the Maccabean revolt. The stamped jar handles with YHD ("Yehud") in Paleo-Hebrew and the other group with YRSLM on them ("Jerusalem") that date to mid-third century may point to a more conservative group in charge of the complex system of taxation that was introduced by the priests.[28]

The flourishing of trade and rise in the economy during Ptolemaic rule over Palestine resulted in the rise of a new Jewish middle class and began the transformation of society as a whole that continued for centuries.[29] The emergence of the Tobiad clan as a wealthy Jewish family that served the interests of the Ptolemies, mentioned in the Zenon papyri and embellished in Josephus's treatment of them,[30] erected a monumental trading facility and castle in Ammon in Transjordan at a site called Arak el-'Amir, decorated with gorgeous felines in its four corners and dated to the end of the third century or beginning of the second century B.C.E.[31]

Only in the context of what I have described is it possible, for example, for a teacher of Hebrew Bible/Old Testament to appreciate the appearance in Egypt in the time of Ptolemy Philadelphus (288–247 B.C.E.) of the publication of the Greek Bible, the Septuagint. Certainly the old Greek translation is one of the most important literary creations of all antiquity and is a major by-product of the process of Hellenization of the

---

[28] See Meyers, "Jewish Culture in Greco-Roman Palestine," 143.

[29] Robert K. Harrison, "Hellenization in Syria-Palestine: The Case of Judaea in the Third Century B.C.E.," *BA* 57 (1992): 98–108.

[30] The Josephan narrative of the Tobiad family, but primarily concerning Joseph and his son Hyrcanus, occurs in Josephus, *Ant.* 12.157–236. Though full of many novelistic elements, the narrative remains useful for understanding the Ptolemaic era.

[31] Fawzi Zayadine, "'Iraq el-Amir." *OEANE* 3:177–81.

ancient Near Eastern world. Though it was composed in Egypt, it is a sign of how central Greek language had become and was to become in Palestine in succeeding centuries.

No matter what one's opinion is about how much of the Hebrew Bible was composed or edited in the Hellenistic period, the transfer of Palestine to Seleucid control at the beginning of the second century had momentous import for the second half of the Hellenistic period. If anything, the pace of Hellenization accelerated, and archaeological evidence exhibiting accommodation to Hellenism may be noted in the presence of more than a thousand Greek (Rhodian) stamped jar handles from Jerusalem and the coins of this era, as well as two long Greek inscriptions from Jerusalem dating to the time of Antioclus Epiphanes, and possibly a third tariff inscription.[32] Despite the obvious trappings of Greek culture that began to envelop the Jewish heartland, not all Jews agreed that accommodation to Hellenism was the appropriate way to truly prosper. Thus a rift developed between those who were in favor of cultural compromise, the pro-Hellenizers, and the more conservative group who saw the old ways threatened. Among the latter were the Hasidim, the pietists and the clan of Hashman, the later Hasmoneans.

In resisting foreign involvement in their internal affairs Judeans expressed their suspicions regarding outsiders. Antiochus's struggle with the Ptolemies did not end in 200 B.C.E., and in retreat from Egypt he looted the temple treasury (1 Macc 1:21–24), then two years later fortified the City of David with a citadel, called the Akra, and placed a Macedonian garrison there (Josephus, *Ant.* 12.252). Some Jews decided to live in this fortified section of Jerusalem, while others continued to live in their traditional neighborhoods. The obvious tension between the two groups of Jews now embroiled in major civil unrest forced Antiochus to desecrate the temple (1 Macc 1:44–50), and when the pro-Seleucid group failed to react and condemn him, unrest gave way to civil war. The struggle is known as the Maccabean rebellion (ca. 167–164 B.C.E.).

The book of Daniel can hardly be understood without appreciating the complexity of the events surrounding the revolt and the success of the Maccabees. It would be incorrect, however, to view the struggle simply as one between Hellenism and Judaism, and if anything the archaeology of this period shows that the adoption of Hellenistic culture already in process for centuries proceeded and increased regardless of the position adopted by the Hasmoneans. If anything, the Hasmoneans within a very short time became the main purveyors of Hellenistic culture as they reinstalled the office of king, merging it with the high-priest position already

---

[32] Berlin, "Archaeological Sources for the History of Palestine," 17.

assumed by Jonathan in 152 B.C.E. Surprisingly, however, the Hasmoneans in their coinage and in their public architecture eschewed figural art consistently.[33] Since they were neither descended from King David or the high priest Zadok, their adoption of Paleo-Hebrew script on their coins or seals did little to assuage the traditionalists in the Jewish community that they were interlopers. Here the archaeology of the era must be balanced with a judicious look at the literary sources, especially Josephus. Opposition to Hasmonean leadership arose not so much in reaction to the Hellenistic ways they came to adopt but rather because of their violation of biblical precedent, cruelty in office, and nepotistic ways. The end of the Hellenistic era in Palestine converges with Pompey's annexation in 63 B.C.E. while two Hasmonean descendants waged civil war over the issue of dynastic succession. It is no wonder that so many Jews welcomed Rome's involvement at this time. The Hellenistic era, like the preceding Persian period, proved to be of major significance for the Jewish people and for the shaping of ancient Palestine.

THE ROMAN PERIOD (63 B.C.E. TO 70 C.E.)

It is impossible to summarize all the materials relevant to consider the import of archaeology on the last 133 years of the Second Temple period. For a treatment of Khirbet Qumran and the Dead Sea Scrolls, for example, I refer the reader to the article in this volume by Daniel Falk. What is important for all teachers to remember is that by the turn of the common era and in its first decades Palestine gives witness to the birth of Jesus of Nazareth and his followers, significant developments in nascent Judaism under Hillel the Elder, and the continuing literary output of individuals in all sectors of society, including the sectarians at Qumran. Moreover, during this unprecedented burst of spiritual, literary, and religious ferment Jerusalem and the temple underwent a major, if not historic, renovation and rebuilding campaign, launched first by Herod (37–4 B.C.E.), which continued through the first century before the fall of the city and temple in 70 C.E. It is unusual in biblical and Palestinian history to observe a time in which both material culture and spiritual or literary creativity occur simultaneously, and it would be foolish to draw too many conclusions, especially when the major activity occurred under Herod the Great. Still, as

---

[33] So Meyers, "Jewish Culture in Greco-Roman Palestine," 147; and Levine, *Judaism and Hellenism in Antiquity*, 44. However, whether such aniconic behavior was deliberate and widespread is certainly debatable. The use of the Tyrian shekel with the bust of the king on one side and an eagle on the other throughout this period suggests that the issue is more complex.

a backdrop for studying Jewish and Christian origins, the setting is helpful in re-creating the atmosphere of the times. In those times, it is quite clear to say the effects of centuries of accommodation to Hellenistic civilization were everywhere in evidence in Jerusalem, and from the time of Zerubbabel to Herod the size and population of Jerusalem had grown more than ten times.[34]

One of the major reasons for Jerusalem's more international flavor and Hellenistic character was the nature of the Roman Empire itself. Jerusalem was linked to other urban centers in the East by trade, commerce, and as a Jewish religious site, and Herod as a client king labored greatly during his life to integrate the capital city into the larger Roman world. His family and court, like the Hasmoneans before him, bore Greek or Latin names. In his attraction to Roman society Herod was joined by the upper classes and priests, whose lavish homes have now been excavated and restored.[35] Moreover, Herod and his sons often avoided figural art in the main, used Greek on their coins, and employed the best artisans and architects in their construction and renovation projects, many of them from abroad. Gifts from Diaspora Jews greatly assisted the task of beautifying Jerusalem, and many of them established small enclaves of permanent residency in the city itself.[36] Herod's pagan building projects in sports, theater, and spectacle he kept at a distance from the Jewish population while assuaging the foreign elements in their cities. In this strategy Herod was prescient, and his sensitivity or political savvy presents an ironic twist to these fateful times.

The language situation in Jerusalem in this period reflects the increased diversity of greater Palestine. The four major languages attested are Hebrew and Aramaic, Greek and Latin. No doubt Aramaic and Greek were the most used languages, and certainly large segments of the Jewish community knew a good deal of Hebrew. Latin, on the other hand, was known only in the Roman military ranks and among imperial officials.[37] The prevalence of Aramaic and Greek in contemporary epigraphy leaves little doubt about whether or not Jesus was bilingual: the more relevant question is, To what degree was he trilingual? For the major archaeological discoveries of the first century and how they relate to the reconstruction of the life of Jesus and the setting of early Palestinian Christianity, I refer the reader to Crossan and Reed, *Excavating Jesus.*

---

[34] Levine, *Judaism and Hellenism in Antiquity*, 35, n. 4.

[35] For a review of the work up to 1994, see the collections of essays in Hillel Geva, ed., *Ancient Jerusalem Revealed* (Jerusalem: Israel Exploration Society, 1992); and its predecessor volume that appeared in 1975: Yigael Yadin, ed., *Jerusalem Revealed: Archaeology in the Holy City, 1968–1974* (Jerusalem: Israel Exploration Society 1975).

[36] Levine, *Judaism and Hellenism in Antiquity*, 54.

[37] Ibid., 72–73.

In suggesting how deeply Hellenized Jerusalem was in the Early Roman period, I do not mean to suggest that the prevailing ethos was not Jewish. The recent excavation of large houses and villas there leaves no doubt as to the degree to which Jews observed the laws of purity, not only reflected in the ritual baths that have been revealed but also through the stone vessels associated with them. In teaching students about this era it is important to stress that just as most of the literary texts that survive are products of elite groups, so too the archaeology of Jerusalem presents a picture of elite groups. In order to get a more reliable database one has to examine tomb remains, including inscriptions, ossuaries, and sarcophagi and the finds associated with them.[38] When one turns to other cities and regions from the same era, one should expect to find important differences. The Galilee, for example, is not as Hellenized as Jerusalem and parts of Judea and the coastal plain until much later, that is, in the second century C.E., after the demographic shift from south to north that began with the fall of Jerusalem in 70 C.E.[39]

In discussing the rise of Palestinian Christianity pre-70 C.E., it is quite important to emphasize the absence of identifiable "Christian" remains. In part because there did not exist a symbolic vocabulary for the first Christians but mainly because the overwhelming material is either Jewish or pagan, the material evidence contextually considered points to the bold fact that the earliest Christians in Palestine were obviously at home in the Jewish matrix in which they emerged. Keeping in mind that there was not yet a fixed "canon" of scripture and that the Ketubim or Hagiographa was still very much in flux, the kind of picture that derives from material culture is greatly similar, namely, that Palestine was a multicultural land in which Jewish culture thrived amidst great diversity. I believe this powerful message can only be properly conveyed when taking archaeology fully into account.

CONCLUSION

The main point of this essay has been to demonstrate that archaeology is an essential tool for studying biblical history and, in particular, the Second Temple period. In dividing up this period (515 B.C.E.–70 C.E.) into its three main units, Persian (515–332 B.C.E.), Hellenistic (332–63 B.C.E.), and Early Roman (63 B.C.E.–70 C.E.), I have hopefully been able to illustrate in

---

[38] The material on this subject is vast. One has to be somewhat selective in dealing with the materials and consult the various handbooks. On Jerusalem, see Levin, *Judaism and Hellenism in Antiquity,* 61–67.

[39] Meyers, "Jewish Culture in Greco-Roman Palestine," 155–62.

specific ways how such information derived from material culture can alter or transform traditional views. In recent years, when many scholars have become more vocal in calling for an early or late Second Temple dating for large portions of the Hebrew Bible, it is especially important to understand the social setting of those periods. Without archaeology, it is virtually impossible to come to any refined notion about Palestinian society or Second Temple Judaism.

How one introduces such material into one's teaching without having to do so in a separate course is certainly the main challenge for most academics. I have suggested that "mainstreaming" is the best way to do this. In other words, if someone is teaching "Introduction to Hebrew Bible," for example, I would urge that person to introduce significant archaeological materials where it alters or supplements in a significant way the literary materials being used to present a historical overview. Archaeological materials, when properly used, enable the instructor to avoid the pitfalls of just doing straight history or political history and gets one pointed more in the direction of social-historical reconstruction.[40] In any case, as a major building block for contextual study, archaeology is the sine qua non of both good historical and good exegetical work. Passing on this idea to students, while not easy, is surely worth the effort. The best way to do this is through on-site study tours and fieldwork. In the absence of such a possibility, the instructor must rely on his or her own ingenuity in providing new readings, visual images that tell the story, and inferences that are not derived from text alone. If one can make such points, students are bound to listen better and remember longer.

---

[40] Carol L. Meyers and Eric M. Meyers, "Expanding the Frontiers of Biblical Archaeology," *ErIsr* 20 (1989): 140–47.

Text and Artifact:
The Dead Sea Scrolls and Qumran

Daniel Falk
University of Oregon

Qumran and the Dead Sea Scrolls present a classic case in the problem of relating text and artifact, both in research and teaching. Here we have a significant body of texts (the scrolls from Caves 1–11) and significant artifacts (the site of Qumran, material finds, skeletons) in close temporal and geographic proximity that arguably should help interpret each other. Furthermore, there are external texts about a particular Jewish group—the Essenes—that arguably relate to both the Dead Sea Scrolls (by describing the same distinctive practices and beliefs) and the site of Qumran (Pliny, by describing Essenes living in the same vicinity). From early on, these links were foundational to the understanding of Qumran and the Dead Sea Scrolls, leading to a compelling and dominant view that Qumran was a sectarian Essene settlement whose communal life is also reflected in some of their writings among the scrolls found in the nearby caves. In recent years, a growing number of scholars have questioned each link of this triangular model, and there have been strident criticisms of the process of scholarship by which this model came to dominate. These criticisms have often been unfair and have so far failed to offer a more convincing alternative. Still, there are lessons to learn from the fascinating and at times rancorous conversation among scholars over the interpretation of Qumran. This essay surveys the implications— both negative and positive—of the triangular model, particularly for the problem of how one relates text and artifact in the process of research and instruction.

The Vicious Triangle

To put things in perspective, it is helpful to recall the situation about half a century before the discovery of the Dead Sea Scrolls. The mysterious Essenes mentioned by various ancient authors were a subject of scholarly and popular fascination, and there were attempts to relate various newly recovered Jewish documents with them.[1] Scholars were aware of the ruins near Wadi Qumran since the description of Ferdinand de Saulcy in 1861, but apart from a brief survey and excavation of two tombs by C. Clermont-Ganneau in 1873 and various speculations to identify it with one of the cities mentioned in the Hebrew Bible (Gomorrah, City of Salt, etc.), the site did not attract a detailed investigation.[2] Also before the close of the nineteenth century, Solomon Schechter had discovered two medieval copies of what is now known as the *Damascus Document* among the mass of manuscripts long forgotten in the genizah of a Karaite synagogue in Cairo.[3] When Schechter published the document in 1910, it sparked immediate excitement among scholars, although no one could have predicted that ten copies from around the turn of the era would later appear in caves near Qumran. Schechter attributed the work to a Zadokite sect. Others related this previously unknown Jewish group with Pharisees or Sadducees.[4] In hindsight it is surprising, but nothing about the site of Qumran or even a key "sectarian" document particularly suggested Essenes. All of that changed dramatically after the discovery of scrolls near Khirbet Qumran in 1947.

Among the first scrolls published, numerous elements in the *Community Rule*—especially the initiation procedures—recalled to scholars the descriptions of the Essenes by ancient authors. Even before copies of the *Damascus Document* came to light in Qumran Cave 4 in 1952, scholars recognized that this document belonged with the new texts and, by implication, somehow with the Essenes: it contains similar laws to the *Community Rule,* and its mysterious "Teacher of Righteousness" (CD 1:11; 20:28) features prominently in the *Habakkuk Pesher.* Second, the scrolls awakened interest in the nearby ruins of a settlement at Qumran that Father Roland de Vaux excavated in 1951 and 1953–56. Seen now as possibly related to Essene scrolls, this site seemed to match Pliny's description

---

[1] E.g., Christian D. Ginsburg, *The Essenes: Their History and Doctrines* (London: Longman, Green, Longman, Roberts, and Green, 1864); see the bibliography in Emil Schürer, *The History of the Jewish People in the Age of Jesus Christ (175 B.C.–A.D. 135)* (rev. and ed. G. Vermes, F. Millar, and M. Black; Edinburgh: T&T Clark, 1973–87), 2:555–56.

[2] Phillip R. Davies, *Qumran* (Cities of the Biblical World; Guildford, Surrey: Lutterworth, 1982), 30–32.

[3] Stefan C. Reif, "The Damascus Document from the Cairo Genizah: Its Discovery, Early Study and Historical Significance," in *The Damascus Document: A Centennial of Discovery: Proceedings of the Third International Symposium of the Orion Center for the Study of the Dead Sea Scrolls and Associated Literature, 4–8 February, 1998* (ed. J. M. Baumgarten, E. G. Chazon, and A. Pinnick; STDJ 34; Leiden: Brill, 2000), 113–15.

[4] Philip R. Davies, *The Damascus Covenant* (JSOTSup 25; Sheffield: JSOT Press, 1983), 5–14.

of a community of Essenes living near the Dead Sea south of Jericho.[5] Thus, these three subjects—ancient descriptions of Essenes, the ruins at Qumran, and a body of sectarian writings—quickly became tied together in a triangular relationship of mutual illumination.

De Vaux's interpretation of the archaeological evidence at Khirbet Qumran, presented in a series of field reports and a set of lectures to the British Academy in 1959, published in French in 1961 and in a revised English edition in 1972, has had pervasive influence and is still fundamental for understanding the site.[6] He distinguished two main periods of occupation of the site in the Hasmonean and Early Roman periods, each brought to an end by a fiery destruction. At the beginning of the first period, a very small community resettled the site of a modest Iron Age fort, but after a brief time they greatly expanded with many new buildings. De Vaux differentiated these two phases as Periods Ia and Ib, although there were no coins to associate with Period Ia and no grounds for distinguishing any of the pottery from Period Ib. On the basis of the coin evidence, de Vaux concluded that "it is certain that the buildings of Period I*b* were occupied under Alexander Jannaeus" (103–76 B.C.E.) and that it could be "possible" to push back the date of the expansion to the reign of John Hyrcanus (135–104 B.C.E.).[7] His differentiation of a preexpansion settlement of "short duration"—Period Ia—allowed him to extend the origins of the first period of occupation slightly earlier yet, at the outer limits and with acknowledged difficulty to the middle of the second century B.C.E.[8] The coin evidence for the end of the first period of occupation was ambiguous, most notably four coins of Antigonus Mattathias (40–37 B.C.E.), ten coins of Herod the Great from "mixed levels," and a hoard of coins in three pots found beneath the ash marking the end of Ib containing silver tetradrachmas with dates ranging from 126 to 9/8 B.C.E.[9] He argued that the Herodian coins and the hoard properly belonged to Period II and instead dated the destruction of Ib to 31 B.C.E. by connecting the fire with evidence of an earthquake, which he identified with the one mentioned by Josephus (*Ant.* 15.121–147; *War* 1.370–380). Accumulated sediment in the water system betrays a period of abandonment, which de Vaux suggested lasted until near the turn of the era because of the scarcity of Herodian coins in the

---

[5] Pliny, *Natural History* 5.73. See Geza Vermes and Martin D. Goodman, eds, *The Essenes according to the Classical Sources* (Oxford Centre Textbooks 1; Sheffield: JSOT Press, 1989), 32–33.

[6] Roland de Vaux, *Archaeology and the Dead Sea Scrolls* (rev. ed.; Schweich Lectures of the British Academy 1959; London: Oxford University Press, 1973).

[7] Ibid., 19, cf. 5.

[8] Ibid., 5, 116–17.

[9] Ibid., 22–23, 34–35.

ruins. That is, the settlement was abandoned roughly the duration of the reign of Herod the Great, about thirty years. Between 4 and 1 B.C.E., the same group resettled the site in Period II, as suggested by the similarity in pottery types and distinctive burials of animal bones under pottery sherds in both Periods Ib and II. The end of Period II is again marked by a destruction layer of ash. Roman arrowheads and Jewish coins from the second and third years of the Jewish Revolt—but none from the fourth—suggest that this period of occupation of Khirbet Qumran came to a violent end in 68/69 C.E. A limited occupation following this destruction, probably Roman soldiers, lasted at least until the fall of Masada in 73 C.E.

De Vaux emphasized several notable features about the settlement: it consisted almost exclusively of communal facilities, including a large hall with an adjoining pantry containing over one thousand vessels; there were impressive water installations, including several baths; two inkwells and the remains of tables and benches had come from an upper room; nearby was a cemetery with about twelve hundred individual shaft graves carefully arranged in rows and oriented (predominantly) south-north; a small sample of excavated graves contained a disproportionately small number of women and children; an agricultural and industrial center three kilometers to the south at Ein Feshkha were related to the settlement at Qumran during Periods I–II; and the nearby caves in which scrolls were found are connected with Qumran by similar pottery.

On the basis of the material evidence, de Vaux depicted a Jewish community of up to two hundred (mostly or exclusively) men who lived in nearby caves and tents but shared a communal life. They farmed nearby and labored at communal workshops at Qumran and Ein Feshkha. They ate meals together in a "refectory," prepared and/or copied scrolls in a "scriptorium," and observed purification rites.

Although de Vaux was convinced that there were sound archaeological reasons for confidence that the scrolls from nearby caves were related to the settlement at Qumran, he was careful to note that "archaeology cannot prove that the people of Qumran were Essenes or were related to them. That is a question of doctrine, and the answer to it is to be sought from the texts rather than from the ruins."[10] Moreover, he stated that the question of whether the material evidence from Qumran contradicts or corroborates the theory that the scrolls are related to the Essenes is "inconclusive." Still, he did seek to relate his archaeological findings to theories about the scrolls and the Essenes. His time frame just allowed, at its outer limits, for a founding of the settlement at the time of Jonathan (152–143 B.C.E.) or Simon (143–34 B.C.E.), to accommodate theories that one of these was the

---

[10] Ibid., 128.

"Wicked Priest" mentioned in the scroll.[11] The "scriptorium" accounted for the large number of scrolls. The ancient descriptions of the Essenes as celibate seemed to be consonant with the cemetery, in which only a small number of women and children were buried, and then on the peripheries. Pliny's description of the Essenes near the Dead Sea south of Jericho, with Ein Gedi "below"—if this is understood to mean further in the direction of downstream—aptly fit the location of Qumran.

In its main outlines, de Vaux's interpretation of Khirbet Qumran has enjoyed the acceptance of most scholars and become part of a broad consensus that Qumran, the scrolls, and the Essenes are interrelated. Over the last decade, there has been renewed interest in the archaeology of Qumran, and much effort at reevaluating the evidence.[12] Several competing theories have rejected links between the three points of our triangle, most notably Khirbet Qumran as a Hasmonean fortress and the scrolls as collections smuggled out of Jerusalem;[13] Khirbet Qumran as a Hasmonean villa;[14] and Khirbet Qumran as a trading entrepôt.[15] None of these have proved persuasive overall.

Nevertheless, even apart from more radical revisionist theories of Qumran, serious challenges remain over several details of de Vaux's

---

[11] Ibid., 116–17.

[12] Interpretation of Qumran archaeology was the subject of lively and at times heated debate at a conference in New York in 1992; see Michael O. Wise et al., eds., *Methods of Investigation of the Dead Sea Scrolls and the Khirbet Qumran Site: Present Realities and Future Prospects* (Annals of the New York Academy of Sciences 722; New York: New York Academy of Sciences, 1994), 1–111. In 1994, the first volume of a project to complete a final report on the Qumran excavations by de Vaux was published: Jean-Baptiste Humbert and Alain Chambon, *Fouilles de Khirbet Qumrân et de Aïn Feschkha*, vol. 1 (NTOA Series Archaeologica 1; Fribourg: Éditions Universitaires; Göttingen: Vandenhoeck & Ruprecht, 1994). The site has undergone several new surveys, the skeletons have been reexamined, several international conferences have been devoted to the archaeology of Qumran, and numerous new theories have been proposed. Jodi Magness has emerged as one of the most prominent interpreters of the site, and her recent book provides references to much of the literature; see Jodi Magness, *The Archaeology of Qumran and the Dead Sea Scrolls* (Studies in the Dead Sea Scrolls and Related Literature; Grand Rapids: Eerdmans, 2002).

[13] Norman Golb, "Khirbet Qumran and the Manuscripts of the Judean Wilderness: Observations on the Logic of Their Investigation," *JNES* 49 (1990): 103–14; Norman Golb, "Khirbet Qumran and the Manuscript Finds of the Judaean Wilderness," in *Methods of Investigation of the Dead Sea Scrolls and the Khirbet Qumran Site: Present Realities and Future Prospects* (ed. M. O. Wise, et al.; Annals of the New York Academy of Sciences; New York: The New York Academy of Sciences, 1994), 51–72.

[14] R. Donceel and P. Donceel-Voûte, "The Archaeology of Khirbet Qumran," in Wise, *Methods of Investigation of the Dead Sea Scrolls*, 22–32; see the critique by Jodi Magness, "A Villa at Khirbet Qumran?" *RevQ* 16 (1994): 397–419.

[15] Alan D. Crown and Lena Cansdale, "Qumran: Was It an Essene Settlement?" *BAR* 20/2 (1994): 24–35, 73–78.

interpretation of Khirbet Qumran. The most important concern the validity of Period Ia, the date of the end of Period Ib, the length of the period of abandonment, the interpretation of the cemetery, and the language that de Vaux used to describe the site. Concerning Period Ia, both Davies and Magness have noted that de Vaux's own report of the data (primarily coins) shows no concrete evidence for a resettlement earlier than the early first century B.C.E. (that is, Alexander Jannaeus's reign), and they consequently reject the idea of a Period Ia altogether.[16] Davies suggests that the positing of Period Ia was a case of pushing the limits of the material evidence (as far as the middle of the second century B.C.E.) to accommodate theories of the history of the sect based on texts of the Dead Sea Scrolls, namely, that this settlement was founded out of a persecution by either of the Hasmoneans Jonathan or Simon. This assumes that the literary descriptions of the history of the sect can be read as historical data and related to the settlement at Qumran. If, instead, the scrolls are treated as artifacts rather than merely as texts, their dating (based on paleography and supported by recent radiocarbon tests) points to roughly the same period of activity as the coins.[17] The greatest body of manuscripts date from the first century B.C.E., and the sectarian documents range in date from the rule of Jannaeus to the time of Herod's reign.[18] That is, "this work suggests that the group that copied these documents was active throughout the first century B.C.E. and perhaps into the first century C.E., and could be associated with Kh. Qumran's Period Ib–II."[19]

Numerous scholars have also questioned the connection de Vaux accepted between the earthquake and the fire that destroyed the community at the end of Period I: Why would an earthquake cause a group to abandon their settlement completely, and then why would they come back to the same place after thirty years? Magness has presented the most plausible chronology, which pays careful attention to the coin and pottery evidence.[20] On the grounds that hoards are usually lost because they are

---

[16] Jodi Magness, "Qumran Archaeology: Past Perspectives and Future Prospects," in *The Dead Sea Scrolls after Fifty Years: A Comprehensive Assessment* (ed. P. W. Flint and J. C. VanderKam; Leiden: Brill, 1998), 1:64–65; Philip R. Davies, "How Not to Do Archaeology: The Story of Qumran," *BA* 51 (1988): 204–5.

[17] Georges Bonani et al., "Radiocarbon Dating of the Dead Sea Scrolls," *Atiqôt* 20 (1991): 27–32; Greg Doudna, "Dating the Scrolls on the Basis of Radiocarbon Analysis," in Flint and VanderKam, *Dead Sea Scrolls after Fifty Years*, 1:430–71.

[18] P. R. Callaway, *The History of the Qumran Community: An Investigation* (JSPSup 3; Sheffield: JSOT Press, 1988), 199–200.

[19] John R. Bartlett, "The Archaeology of Qumran," in *Archaeology and Biblical Interpretation* (ed. J. R. Bartlett; London: Routledge, 1997), 82–83.

[20] Magness, "Qumran Archaeology," 1:57–61; idem, *Archaeology of Qumran*, 63–69.

hidden at a time of danger, she argues that the hoard of coins with dates ranging to 9/8 B.C.E. belongs to the stratum of Period I, where they were actually found. Thus, the community repaired and continued on at Qumran after the earthquake of 31 B.C.E., until they were attacked around 9/8 B.C.E. and their settlement destroyed. The abandonment was thus short, with the community returning following 4 B.C.E. early in the reign of Herod Archelaus.

Most contentious of all is the cemetery at Qumran. Critics of de Vaux have charged that his description of the cemetery inappropriately marginalized the presence of women and children under the influence of the view of Essenes as celibate found in Pliny, Philo, and Josephus.[21] However, equally vocal are supporters of the view that this was a cemetery for celibate Essenes, with a few anomalous burials of women and children.[22] This debate, heated at times, is part of a larger issue of the use of language. Some have criticized de Vaux's use of monastic language such as "refectory" and "scriptorium" as inappropriately depicting the community on the model of celibate monks living a vow of poverty.

Common to such criticisms are concerns that interpretation of material remains was influenced by the interpretation of texts and by preconceptions.[23] It is indeed worth pondering how Qumran might have been described if excavated before the discovery of the Dead Sea Scrolls and without reference to Pliny's description of the Essenes—but we shall never know. It was excavated because scrolls were found nearby and with a concern to identify the authors of the scrolls, who were already suspected to be Essenes. Nor is this to imply that archeologists should ignore texts, but it is essential clearly to differentiate between secure data from material finds and hypotheses about how these might relate to other (e.g., textual) evidence. For the most part, de Vaux was careful to make this distinction explicit, although inevitably there were instances where synthesis influenced his

---

[21] Joan E. Taylor, "The Cemeteries of Khirbet Qumran and Women's Presence at the Site," *DSD* 6 (1999): 285–323; Eileen Schuller, "Women in the Dead Sea Scrolls," in Flint and VanderKam, *Dead Sea Scrolls after Fifty Years*, 2:139–41; Linda Bennet Elder, "The Woman Question and Female Ascetics among Essenes," *BA* 57 (1994): 220–34.

[22] Magen Broshi, "Was Qumran, Indeed, a Monastery? The Consensus and Its Challengers: An Archaeologist's View," in *Caves of Enlightenment: Proceedings of the American Schools of Oriental Research Dead Sea Scrolls Jubilee Symposium (1947–1997)* (ed. J. H. Charlesworth; North Richland Hills, Tex.: Bibal, 1998), 19–37; Joseph E. Zias, "The Cemeteries of Qumran and Celibacy: Confusion Laid to Rest?" *DSD* 7 (2000): 220–53.

[23] Davies, "How Not to Do Archaeology"; Allan Rosengren Petersen, "The Archaeology of Khirbet Qumran," in *Qumran between the Old and New Testaments* (ed. F. H. Cryer and T. L. Thompson; JSOTSup 290; Copenhagen International Seminar 6; Sheffield: Sheffield Academic Press, 1998), 249–60.

description of data. Throughout the history of Qumran scholarship, however, the distinction has often been blurred, so that hypotheses reached by interpreting archaeology and texts in the light of each other are then treated as hard archaeological data to use in further interpretation.

In this way, the triangular relation model has often become a vicious circle of self-confirming data. To highlight but one example, in his attempt to read religious significance from the Qumran burials, Puech notes that "archaeology gives a basis for the scrolls and the scrolls help to interpret archaeological data. Archaeology *and texts* show that Essene burials existed *undoubtedly,* at least at Qumrân, 'Ain el-Ghuweir, Jericho, and Jerusalem."[24] As discussed further below, it is highly debatable whether we are dealing with a consistent form of burial unique to one particular social grouping. Furthermore, no texts discuss or provide explanations for the distinctive burials seen at Qumran and some other sites, but Puech accepts the burials as firm archaeological evidence of religious ideas found in the Dead Sea Scrolls:

> It *clearly* indicates an intentional use of the graves by a group who wanted to separate tombs of men from those of women and children. These scrupulous observations *turn into fact* the religious belief of the Essene community in an afterlife.... the necropolis of *Khirbet* Qumrân had special significance for the Essenes in terms of the benefit of future salvation and probably also for resurrection.[25]

The predominant south-north orientation "indicates a rejection of an east-west orientation ... that is, towards Jerusalem, because the holy city was defiled for an Essene."[26] Following Milik, Puech explains the south-north orientation theologically as reflecting a view that "Paradise was in the north," on the basis of the Enochic Book of Watchers, which was revered at Qumran. This explanation is certainly attractive and could be possible, but it risks the "dangers of over-interpretation" that Davies warns about, when "preconceptions shape analysis."[27] A clear differentiation between data and hypothetical synthesis is necessary.

LANGUAGE AND IMAGE

The special appeal of archaeology has to do with the very concreteness of its evidence: it has the potential to bring a site to life with powerful images and lends the impression that one is dealing with "hard" facts, since

---

[24] Emile Puech, "The Necropolises of *Khirbet* Qumrân and Ain el-Ghuweir and the Essene Belief in Afterlife," *BASOR* 312 (1998): 29, emphasis added.

[25] Ibid., emphasis added.

[26] Ibid.

[27] Davies, "How Not to Do Archaeology," 205–6.

stones do not lie. However, stones by themselves are also silent, and any description is inherently interpretive. The language adopted in archaeological reports has a great deal to do with the image formed in the mind. Nowhere has this come more into play in Qumran research than with regard to the cemetery. De Vaux distinguished between "the main cemetery," which was carefully ordered in rows with a consistent form and contained only males, and "extensions" to the east and "secondary cemeteries" to the north and south that were less regular and contained some skeletons of women and children.[28] De Vaux acknowledged one skeleton in the "main" cemetery that was certainly female, but he described this burial as "abnormal in type and situated apart from the rows."[29] As Joan Taylor and others have pointed out, de Vaux's language in describing the cemetery effectively marginalized the graves containing women and children.[30] This valuing language with regard to the graves—distinguishing membership or status—has so influenced the resulting image of the cemetery that it is not uncommon to find summaries by other scholars giving the impression that the absence of women and children at Qumran is hard evidence from the material remains.

Even on the basis of evidence from the first excavations this language was arguably misleading. Aerial photographs show that the cemetery merely follows the irregular contours of the ground to the east of the settlement: there is one large cemetery that extends onto three projecting plateaus and one hillock to the east, and close by is a small cemetery to the south and a further one to the north.[31] Nothing in the large-scale layout clearly indicates an intent to demarcate separate burial areas, and in each area there is both consistency and variation in burial form, including orientation. Thus, apart from the discovery of female skeletons and the theory of celibate Essenes, is there any material basis for distinguishing a "main" cemetery from "extensions" and "secondary" cemeteries? We may note that the language of differentiation does not seem to have arisen until after the discovery of female skeletons.

In the last few years, the cemetery has become the focus of considerable reevaluation: the site has been newly surveyed, and many of the skeletons excavated by de Vaux have come to light and been submitted to new analysis.[32] Thus far there is still considerable debate over what may or

---

[28] Vaux, *Archaeology and the Dead Sea Scrolls,* 45–48, 57–58, 128–29.

[29] Ibid., 47.

[30] Taylor, "Cemeteries of Khirbet Qumran," 288–99.

[31] Rachel Hachlili, "Burial Practices at Qumran," *RevQ* 16 (1993): 247–64; Humbert and Chambon, *Fouilles de Khirbet Qumrân,* plates 8, 442–44, 448.

[32] Olav Röhrer-Ertl, Ferdinand Rohrhirsch, and Dietbert Hahn, "Über die Gräberfelder von Khirbet Qumran, insbesondere die Funde der Campagne 1956.I: Anthropologisch

may not be established on the basis of the cemetery, but several observations are noteworthy. (1) There is a greater tendency to treat the cemetery
as a whole and to avoid prejudicial language such as "extensions" and "secondary." (2) On the basis of new excavations, Eshel and Broshi now argue
that a building at the eastern edge of the Middle Finger was a mourning
enclosure.[33] Contrary to previous assumptions that the western sector was
the most important part of the cemetery for the Qumran community and
that the "extensions" to the east were merely "secondary" and for outsiders
or those of lesser status, this conclusion would suggest that the eastern part
of the cemetery could be the most important, and at least the Middle Finger
for persons of highest status. (3) Some of the skeletons have been resexed:
there are now two skeletons from the "main" cemetery classified as female
(T22, T24b), both oriented south-north, as well as ten further female skeletons from other sectors of the cemetery. This represents about 40 percent of
the total of skeletons whose sex has been determined (twenty-nine
males).[34] (4) J. Zias has argued that the east-west graves are recent bedouin
burials. If true, this would apply to six female and three male skeletons and
would reduce the female-male ratio in the community cemetery to about 23
percent. (Zias also resexes some female skeletons as male and so virtually
eliminates Jewish women from the cemetery altogether, but this is questionable.) (5) The new and more detailed surveys of the cemetery reveal greater
variation among the burial forms than previously appreciated. The basic
"Qumran-type" burials are vertical shaft tombs generally aligned south-
north, with mounds of stone markers on the surface. Usually a single
person is interred in each tomb, often in a side niche at the bottom covered
with stones or mud bricks. The skeletons are mostly oriented with the head
to the south, and there are usually no grave goods. De Vaux isolated the
female skeletons on the basis of what he regarded as irregularities, but there
are considerable variations among all of these features, so that it becomes
questionable whether one can speak of a strictly uniform practice from
which a few can be regarded as deviations setting them apart.[35] (6) There is

---

Datenvorlage und Erstauswertung aufgrund der Collectio Kurth," *RevQ* 19 (1999): 3–47;
Zias, "Cemeteries of Qumran and Celibacy"; Susan Guise Sheridan, "Scholars, Soldiers,
Craftsmen, Elites? Analysis of French Collection of Human Remains from Qumran," *DSD* 9
(2002): 199–248; Hanan Eshel et al., "New Data on the Cemetery East of Khirbet Qumran,"
DSD 9 (2002): 135–165.

[33] Eshel et al., "New Data on the Cemetery," 147–54.

[34] These figures follow the statistics of Eshel et al., "New Data on the Cemetery," 147–54,
not including the controversial identifications of Steckoll.

[35] Jürgen Zangenberg, "Bones of Contention: 'New' Bones from Qumran Help Settle Old
Questions (and Raise New Ones)—Remarks on Two Recent Conferences," *QC* 9 (2000): 67–70;
Eshel et al., "New Data on the Cemetery," 156–60.

also a growing appreciation of how the cemetery, as well as Qumran generally, fits into its regional context more broadly. Similar shaft burials of the "Qumran type" have come to light at Ein el-Ghuweir and Ḥiam el-Sagha to the south, but also at Beit Safafa in Jerusalem and at Khirbet Qazone in Jordan.[36] The cemetery at Khirbet Qazone is the most significant, because it is Nabatean and shows that we are not dealing with a type of burial unique to a particular group of Jews. This also makes it very problematic to read religious significance from the form of burial.

Debates over the cemetery will continue, and perhaps without further exhumations some questions will remain unresolved. Nevertheless, however one interprets Qumran one must deal with the fact that there were women buried in the Qumran cemetery and that there are as yet no solid archaeological grounds for isolating these as marginal. On the other hand, there is a lower ratio of women and children to adult males than expected in a typical population, although not nearly as low or as anomalous as often represented. There seems to be something unusual about the makeup of this community, but it is not clearly a celibate community. It is possible, as Zias has argued primarily on the basis of orientation, grave depth, and grave goods, that the east-west burials are of bedouin from more recent times, but this is not proven and still does not change the fact that there are some women buried there. The form of burial is neither as consistent nor unique as previously regarded. Some scholars have found in the cemetery testimony to an isolated community, the lack of family units, rejection of wealth, and particular religious beliefs about resurrection.[37] It is important to be clear that such explanations of motivation remain open questions. The archaeological evidence by itself is ambivalent, and any proposed links between these material features and texts remain hypotheses, not archaeological data. There is an important lesson here: in describing archaeological data one should avoid language that implies an interpretation.

CONTROLLING QUESTIONS AND FILTERED DATA

In any investigation, the questions that one asks to a certain extent control the data that are discovered and the way these data are presented.

---

[36] Magness, *Archaeology of Qumran,* 173–75, 187; Taylor, "Cemeteries of Khirbet Qumran," 310–13. See the reports by Boaz Zissu, "'Qumran Type' Graves in Jerusalem: Archaeological Evidence of an Essene Community," *DSD* 5 (1998): 158–71; Boaz Zissu, "Odd Tomb Out: Has Jerusalem's Essene Cemetery Been Found?" *BAR* 25/2 (1999): 50–55, 62; Hanan Eshel and Zvi Greenhut, "Ḥiam el-Sagha, a Cemetery of the Qumran Type, Judaean Desert," *RB* 100 (1993): 252–59; Hershel Shanks, "Who Lies Here? Jordan Tombs Match Those at Qumran," *BAR* 25/5 (1999): 48–53, 76.

[37] E.g., Hachlili, "Burial Practices at Qumran," 263; Puech, "Necropolises."

With regard to the Dead Sea Scrolls, the controlling questions for the first decades were predominantly related to the interpretation of the New Testament and early Christianity, such as the nature of messianic belief. It took three decades (until the publication of the *Temple Scroll*) before scholars started to pay significant attention to legal interpretation, which is a much more central concern in the sectarian texts. In the case of the archaeology of Qumran, controlling questions from the beginning had to do with the relationship to the scrolls and identifying the community in the light of the descriptions of the Essenes in antiquity.

On the one hand, these controlling questions influenced how the site of Qumran was described: an emphasis on isolation and austerity, marginalizing of evidence for women, and use of language associated with monasticism. On the other hand, they also influenced what data were included in the picture. That is, data that reinforced or affirmed features in the scrolls or in ancient descriptions of the Essenes were highlighted, and other data received comparably less attention. For example, only in the course of sifting through de Vaux's excavation notes and collections of artifacts from Qumran in preparation for a final publication of the archaeology of Qumran (a team appointed in 1986) did the full extent of fine pottery and glass and stone ware from Qumran come to light, of a quantity and quality completely unexpected from the descriptions of the austerity of the site.[38] Much of this material escaped comment in the published reports of de Vaux.

A certain amount of filtering of data is inevitable, especially with regard to the weighing of relevant data. In his book de Vaux referred to only one female skeleton identified in what he called the "main cemetery," without repeating that his anthropological expert, H. Vallois, reported skeletons of "several women" there.[39] The filtering of relevant data on the basis of a hypothesis can have dramatic implications, as in another example concerning the sex of skeletons. In a fresh examination of some of the skeletons, O. Rohrer-Ertl had reclassified three skeletons as female: two from the "main cemetery" (T22 and T24b) and one from one of the extensions (T37).[40] J. Zias argues that all of these reclassifications should be overturned primarily because the estimated statures of the skeletons (163 cm, 159 cm, and 159 cm) are too large for females.[41] He provides statistics for the estimated stature of Jewish females at four other contemporary sites (Ein Gedi, Meiron, Mount Scopus, Gush Halav), with an average mean of

---

[38] Donceel and Donceel-Voûte, "The Archaeology of Khirbet Qumran," 7–13.

[39] de Vaux, *Archaeology and the Dead Sea Scrolls*, 47.

[40] Röhrer-Ertl, Rohrhirsch, and Hahn, "Über die Gräberfelder von Khirbet Qumran," 47.

[41] Zias, "Cemeteries of Qumran and Celibacy," 232–34.

148.7 cm and an average range of 143.9–153.8 cm, and compares this with the estimates for eleven male skeletons at Qumran, with an average of 164 cm and a range of 159–168 cm. On this comparison, Zias makes an apparently strong case for regarding the three disputed skeletons as probably male rather than female. However, it is problematic that he does not include data drawn from other female skeletons at Qumran: the statures of the four female skeletons of Q32–35 range from 152–162 cm. If this were the comparison, then the disputed skeletons would be seen as at the upper end of the range for female stature at Qumran.[42] Zias did not use these comparisons because he regards the burials at Q32–35 to be recent bedouin burials; he cites evidence for this view, but it is still an unproven and disputed hypothesis.[43] There is thus some circularity to the arguments by which Zias eliminates Jewish women from the cemetery.

The greatest problem with controlling questions coming from texts is the neglect of unique data presented by material evidence. Archeology provides data relevant to often completely different sets of questions than those addressed by texts. It allows opportunities to explore anthropological and sociological issues on which texts are often silent: diet, living conditions, tools, domestic arrangements, and the like. Controlled by the question whether or not this community was celibate, women were primarily categories to include or exclude, and once women were marginalized, evidence related to them was largely ignored (besides skeletons, there were found two spindle whorls, a wooden comb, and a small amount of jewelry). Only in the last decade have a few scholars even attempted to explore the conditions and role of women at Qumran.[44]

Another avenue that has hitherto received too little attention is the scrolls themselves as artifacts rather than as merely texts.[45] Especially Emanuel Tov has done a considerable amount of work on scribal features of the scrolls,[46] but much of this activity has been turned to understanding

---

[42] Sheridan gives as the range for female skeletons at Qumran 152–163 cm. Sheridan, "Scholars, Soldiers, Craftsmen, Elites," 236–37.

[43] See Zangenberg, "Bones of Contention," 60–76.

[44] Lawrence H. Schiffman, *Reclaiming the Dead Sea Scrolls: The History of Judaism, the Background of Christianity, the Lost Library of Qumran* (Philadelphia: Jewish Publication Society, 1994), 127–43; Elder, "Woman Question and Female Ascetics among Essenes"; Schuller, "Women in the Dead Sea Scrolls"; Taylor, "Cemeteries of Khirbet Qumran"; Mayer I. Gruber, "Women in the Religious System of Qumran," in *The Judaism of Qumran: A Systemic Reading of the Dead Sea Scrolls* (part 5 of *Judaism in Late Antiquity;* ed. A. J. Avery-Peck, J. Neusner, and B. D. Chilton; Handbook of Oriental Studies, The Near and Middle East 56; Leiden: Brill, 2001), 1:173–96; Magness, *Archaeology of Qumran,* 163–87.

[45] Petersen, "Archaeology of Khirbet Qumran," 256–59.

[46] E.g., Emanuel Tov, "Scribal Practices and Physical Aspects of the Dead Sea Scrolls," in *The Bible As Book. The Manuscript Tradition* (ed. J. L. Sharpe III and K. van Kampen;

the text (text types, corrections, sense divisions, etc.) and the question of provenance: Which are sectarian texts? Beyond this, the scrolls are prime data for fascinating sociological questions of literacy, scroll production and preservation, and the like that have barely begun to be pursued.[47]

TEACHING QUMRAN

It needs to be made clear that the examples discussed above do not represent attempts by scholars to deceive or skew the results of research. On the contrary, it is a testament to the remarkable quality of Roland de Vaux's excavation of Qumran that the majority of his observations still stand. The purpose of this essay is rather to draw lessons from what is to a certain extent inevitable: it is never possible to research any subject with a *tabula rasa*. Whether one is conscious of it or not, there will always be controlling questions that influence how one filters data and presents results. The best that one can do is to be aware of the pitfalls, to be as explicit as possible about distinguishing data from hypotheses, and continually to be prepared to ask new questions and to revise old hypotheses.

These problems related to research call for humility and caution on the part of the teacher, as Nickelsburg admonished: "Of course, like Socrates, we know that we don't know. But do we act and teach in this mode, or do we present our hypotheses with more than a tinge of positivism, and do we put forth our generalizations as representations of the real thing, rather than as models ?"[48]

For integrating archaeology into teaching, I would distill the following lessons from the example of Qumran. First, beware of the vicious circle of hypothesis becoming data. One must clearly distinguish between material data and synthetic hypotheses. Second, beware of the influence of language and the power of·image to mislead. Particularly to nonspecialist students, the presentation of archaeological data can give the impression of concrete and incontrovertible proof for a particular view. One must be clear about the limits of knowledge and the ambiguity of material evidence.

London: British Library; Newcastle, Del.: Oak Knoll, in association with the Scriptorium, Center for Christian Antiquities, 1998), 9–33; idem, "Scribal Practices Reflected in the Texts from the Judaean Desert," in Flint and VanderKam, *Dead Sea Scrolls after Fifty Years*, 1:403–29.

[47] Stegemann argues that one of the major functions of the Qumran community was scroll production: Hartmut Stegemann, *The Library of Qumran: On the Essenes, Qumran, John the Baptist and Jesus* (Grand Rapids: Eerdmans; Leiden: Brill, 1998), 51–55.

[48] George W. E. Nickelsburg, "Currents in Qumran Scholarship: The Interplay of Data, Agendas, and Methodology," in *The Dead Sea Scrolls at Fifty: Proceedings of the 1997 Society of Biblical Literature Qumran Section Meetings* (ed. R. A. Kugler and E. Schuller; SBLSymS 15; Atlanta: Scholars Press, 1999), 97.

Third, beware of the fallacy that naming equals understanding. With regard to Qumran, a great deal of emphasis has been focused on whether or not the community was Essene, as if that identification would convey real insight. More important is understanding the nature of this community, whether or not they could be called Essene in any particular way. Fourth, beware of using archaeology as a "proof text" for questions raised on the basis of texts. Rather, one should seek to let archaeological evidence set its own questions and to give its own insights to the lives and diversity of the people who left their marks on the material record.

Realizing Diversity: Reflections on Teaching Pagan Religion(s) in Late Hellenistic and Early Roman Palestine

Jürgen Zangenberg
University of Wuppertal

Acknowledging the Existence of the "Other": What We Mean by "Pagan"

To many people ancient Palestine is perceived and portrayed as a country populated by Jews, Samaritans and later a growing number of Christians. Palestine, after all, still is the "Holy Land" even to many people in the Western world. It is often overlooked that alongside and in many respects together with these three offshoots of "biblical religion," a large number of people lived in the region who did not at all adhere to this biblical tradition. Usually these groups are collectively labelled as "pagans" or "Gentiles."

The problem of teaching "pagan religions" in Hellenistic and Roman Palestine does not start with finding *their* habitats and mapping them; it starts with becoming aware of how *we* address them, what *we* call them: it starts with terminology and nomenclature. I will certainly not surprise anyone with my suspicion that reflecting upon the difficulties in trying to find or coin an appropriate expression for "paganism" should indeed teach us more about how we perceive foreign religions and how much *our* perceptions are bound up with our own tradition than they bring us any closer to what pagans thought of themselves. Moreover, since every terminology indicates how its inventors and users structure the world and their place in it, talking about pagans opens insights into our worldview as well.

So what do we mean with the term "pagans"? It is notoriously difficult to subsume all these different religious groups under a single term, even more so because the two terms we frequently use in colloquial or academic language betray our Christian background. The English word *pagan* comes from the Latin *paganus,* which originally meant "living on the countryside" and therefore "uneducated, uncivilized." It is clear that *paganus* cannot be a self-expression but must come from nonpagans, respectively, Christians. The word reflects the fact that in late antiquity most Christians lived in cities, while often the countryside was still populated by adherents of the old religious world. Consequently, *paganus,* just like the Germanic equivalent *heathen,* soon became a mostly derogatory expression for non-Christians. The word Gentile is directly influenced by biblical language where (in the Old Testament) non-Jews and (in the New Testament) also non-Christians are often collectively addressed as "the nations" (Hebrew *gôyīm*). The English word *Gentile* is a direct derivation from Latin *gentilis* ("belonging to the nations"). Using the term *non-Christian* is also not helpful because it still takes Christianity as the focal point and levels out all differences of the "others." No "pagan" would have wanted to be addressed with a term that was foreign to his or her own religious self-understanding.

Moreover, there certainly is no general, all-encompassing term for "paganism" in the ancient languages themselves, apart from the ones derived from Jewish (or Christian) concepts of the "religious other." This indeed is an important observation: using a single word to describe "paganism" essentially binds phenomena together that in the perception of their original adherents could not be subsumed under a single heading. It is only from the *outside* that an essentially plural world of beliefs and practices becomes unified (in contrast to today's "neopagans," who have adopted our modern terminology). Studying paganism brings one into contact with a world that is largely plural and phenomena that are local, particular, and have multifaceted. (This may even help one to recognize diversity within Christianity and Judaism, too.)

In the end, we should admit that our common vocabulary is inadequate and biased. With all these difficulties and problems in mind and for the sake of a readable text, I still dare to use the term *pagan* in its most neutral and descriptive sense. In that case, several observations must be stressed. First, pagan religions are no "subculture" per se but are an integral part of the private and public life of a respective society. Public and private life are intertwined in a complex world of living religiosity on multiple levels. We admire the beauty of temples erected as a pride of cities and rulers, and, on the other hand, we hear of sinister magic and bloody sacrificial rituals and are all too quick to separate the one from the other. However, we have no right to make quick judgments and no criteria to label the one practice as true religious devotion and the other as artificial and not serious. For the ancients, supposedly "prosaic" civil religion was not in contradiction with the inwardness of individual religious feelings. That means that supposedly "schematic" dedications on inscriptions or the performance of age-old sacrificial rituals must not be swiftly dismissed as simple show or political statements but should be examined with the same critical sympathy as, for example, a written personal prayer. We must acknowledge that for the people who performed these practices, they all had a religious significance.

Second, paganism should not be defined along ethnic boundaries either. This is an all too common picture. Because in biblical languages pagans in Palestine are often called "nations" or "Greeks," many people think that they were Greeks in an ethnic sense, implying that paganism was something alien to the region of biblical Palestine, imported from elsewhere along with goods brought in by ships to the thriving coastal cities. In addition, wherever we have temples in the classical style, many people assume that only Greeks worshiped in them. That is not entirely true. Pagans were not necessarily foreigners. Assuming that would mean to repeat the old ideologically constructed concept of disinheriting Palestinian pagans and rendering them "outsiders."

In antiquity, the relationship between *ethnos* (which should not simply be equated with what we call "ethnic" identity) and religious affiliation never was as clear-cut as we assume today, with one exception: in Jewish (and later also Christian) self-definition, a Jew by religion was at the same time a member of the Jewish people. "Pagans," however, belonged to many peoples, races, and ethnic groups. One did not have to be an ethnic Celt to worship the healing goddess Sirona at a sacred well. Isis was the savior of more people than just Egyptians. Religious affiliations did not necessarily overlap with ethnic entities, nor could they always be affixed to a specific place on a map or defined by means of material culture or language.

Third, paganism provided a nearly indefinite range of religious options. Interestingly, it is exactly this perplexing range of possibilities, choice, trends, affiliations, and devotions that makes paganism a very *individual* thing. Both the bewildering array of choices *and* the close emotional affiliation with one particular deity are unsurpassingly expressed in Apuleius's novel *Metamorphoses*. Paganism entailed a wide variety of religious means to practically express one's religion or *Weltanschauung*. Of course, many people may simply have followed the traditions and practices prevalent in their immediate society or region; the significant fact is that they did not have to.

Finally, pagans were not necessarily polytheists. Of course, there was a broad variety of names, images, and cultic sites in the pagan world, but there also was a growing feeling among the educated, and perhaps also the less literate, that these different names were just manifestations of the one great power, be it male, female, or "neutral," that ruled over the world and that could be invoked for help in all worrisome and happy contingencies of life. First propagated by philosophers, this conviction can also be detected in less mundane circles. An increasing number of inscriptions dedicated to *heis theos* and *theos hypsistos* attest this trend at least in the Roman period and may also remind us of the potential tendency of Semitic religions towards monolatry (if not monotheism). In general, the need to choose between many gods would often lead to a close relationship with one particular deity. The real difference between pagan monolatrists, on one hand, and Jews and Christians, on the other, is that pagans would never have required exclusive devotion to one personal God (although many might not actively have worshiped more than one) and flatly denied the existence of all others or denounced them as illegitimate objects of devotion.

"Pagans" in Biblical Language and Thinking

The widespread negligence of non-Jews and non-Christians in our perception of ancient Palestine certainly results from the fact that we also are heirs and part of that biblical tradition. Our perception of nonbiblical religions and the way to find an appropriate terminology is commonly shaped by biblical language and thinking, thus from texts written by Jewish or Christian authors who did not actually have a genuine interest in depicting the pagan "other" in neutral terms or for simply documentary purposes. Pagans feature in these texts, of course, but it is interesting to see how. From the time of the prophets onward, pagans in many ways embody a way of life that blatantly contradicts biblical commandments. Especially in Deuteronomistic theology warnings against idolatry and going "on the way of the nations" are combined with a call upon Israel to repent and keep the law. Biblical Israel in part defined itself as being different from other peoples. The rabbis modified this view in certain ways but followed the basic biblical principle that pagans were not interesting in themselves. Few Jews would enter into controversies about religion with pagans, but all Jews were, in the eyes of the rabbis, required to defend their faith when challenged by "outsiders." Granted, on the level of everyday life, there were many different ways to adjust to the practical needs of living together in a pagan or mixed city. In everyday practice, mere indifference seems to have prevailed in the attitude toward pagans. However, these adjustments probably never resulted in the renouncement of the claim that a Jew, as long as he or she kept to certain duties, was essentially different from his or her non-Jewish contemporaries. Of course, many texts expressed the hope the pagans would finally come to worship God and be saved, but this was not out of pure sympathy toward the pagan nations or out of respect for their cultural achievements but for the higher glory of the God of Israel. Moreover, it was something that basically no one expected for the near future but was associated with the ultimate last day to come. Many others, however, simply were content with the hope that in the end there would be no pagans at all, not because they had all converted but because God would have them destroyed as punishment for their aberration and idolatry.

The role of pagans at the eschatological margins of time equals their role on the margins of space. Despite the fact that there were many pagans in the land, and Jewish authors were well aware of that, for many ancient texts these pagans in a strict sense were without home. Although they might have been present in the land, they had no claim to it. Most of them were seen as living outside the land of Israel anyway, therefore being "outsiders" in the strictest sense. So, for many authors, Israel was essentially *and* symbolically *surrounded* by Gentile nations, while pagans existed essentially and symbolically on the *margins*.[1] Just as pagans would have no share in the world to come, they also lacked a place on the everyday map in the minds of many of those people whose texts frame our own perception of the religious world of Palestine until now.

It goes without saying that, to a large extent, this picture was also shared by early Christians. In the formative period of early Christianity, all Christian authors were convinced that the followers of Jesus (still) were true heirs to the biblical covenant, so they tried hard to avoid any notion that by no longer being proper "Jews" and uncircumcised, they were nothing but better pagans. With such a position, it is no wonder that until well into the late second century basic Christian attitudes toward pagans were more or less a reflection of the varieties of Jewish opinions.

Jewish rejection of paganism was matched by a distanced or even hostile attitude toward Jews on the side of Greeks and Romans. The peculiar self-definitions of both segments of the population in Palestine created a tense situation that was rather unique compared to other regions. For example, the fierce and often bloody confrontation between Celts and Romans was finally overcome, and by the conflation of both cultures a

---

[1] To what extent these two tenets still occupy even modern scholarly literature can be seen in Emil Schürer, *The History of the Jewish People in the Age of Jesus Christ (175 B.C.–A.D. 135)* (rev. and ed. G. Vermes, F. Millar, and M. Black; Edinburgh: T&T Clark, 1973–87), 2:52–53: "Hellenism in its religious aspect was driven out of the Jewish region proper by the Maccabean uprising and it was not until after the defeat of the Jewish nation in the wars of Vespasian and Hadrian that the Romans forced an entry for the pagan cults. ... The small Jewish territory was surrounded on almost all sides by Hellenistic regions." Schürer and his modern editors, however, rightly stress that this does not mean that Jews were unaffected by Hellenistic culture. However, Schürer goes on to say, "The Hellenized regions not only bordered Palestine on almost all sides but also existed within it" (2:75). Schürer clearly shows the aporias of an approach that conceptually concentrates on dividing pagan from Jewish culture. It might be better to see both as parts of one Hellenistic culture.

great part of the Latin West emerged. Moreover, the various peoples in Asia Minor finally succumbed to Greek culture and became a vital part of it. The situation in ancient Palestine was different. Here, from the very beginning, a need to manage irreducible cultural and religious plurality affected the deepest layers of ancient Palestinian history with all its violent tragedies. The religious situation in ancient Palestine was more pluralistic, the social situation more colorful, and the political situation more complex than in many other regions of the Greco-Roman world. Therefore, unlike in other parts of the ancient world, the presence of diverse religious cults did not mean more or less mutual respect and open competition between religious options of essentially equal value but at best a complicated cohabitation of groups who, at least in part, considered themselves as irreconcilable and mutually exclusive.

A study of pagan religious life in ancient Palestine can give us a better understanding of this mechanism and how defining oneself inevitably also entails constructing the other. It can help us to reconstruct and understand patterns of cohabitation as well as those of confrontation and tragedy. In that, the study of paganism constitutes an essential part in the study of the history and religious life in Palestine as a whole.

APPROACHING PAGANISM ON THE GROUND

In the following paragraphs I will sketch a few parameters that to me seem necessary to consider if one ventures into the largely unexplored field of ancient Palestinian paganism. Until now, my remarks were rather general and not limited to Palestine. There are two reasons for that. In the first place, from a pagan point of view, ancient Palestine would not have been seen as especially distinctive, apart from the large presence of Jews (and Christians). Despite all its peculiarities, Palestine was still part of the cultural world of the Eastern Mediterranean. Therefore, much of what can be said with regard to neighbouring regions probably was also true for ancient Palestine. Second, my remarks are rather general simply because paganism in ancient Palestine has never been comprehensively studied. As Israeli historian Joseph Geiger wrote in a recent survey of the evidence: "The history of the non-Jewish (and non-Samaritan) inhabitants of Palestine between the conquest of Alexander the Great and that of the Muslims is still a largely unexplored territory."[2] This is especially true for the immediate "New Testament period," better called the Late Hellenistic to Early

---

[2] Joseph Geiger, "Aspects of Palestinian Paganism in Late Antiquity," in *Sharing the Sacred: Religious Contacts and Conflicts in the Holy Land First–Fifteenth Century* (ed., A. Kofski and G. G. Stroumsa; Jerusalem:Yad Izhak Ben Zvi, 1998), 5.

Roman period. Despite a growing wealth of archaeological data from numerous digs in the region, only a few broader studies have examined and analyzed the material. As the study of ancient Palestine still has much to do with a desire to link one's own religious tradition back to persons, localities, and events connected with that region, paganism often comes into view only in connection or contrast with Judaism or early Christianity. Looking through relevant computer databases, it is perhaps not surprising to find numerous studies on the pagan-Christian controversy in late antiquity, on the conversion of a pagan empire to Christianity, on the role of pagan culture as represented in Christian apologetic literature, and on Jewish-pagan relations in the age of the Talmud. Of course, these studies are important in their own right because they show that, despite their differences, all groups in Palestine were in constant interaction. However, these studies are neither intended nor sufficient to fill the place of independent and comprehensive analyses of the growing evidence; even studies in pagan-Christian and pagan-Jewish relations need a solid database on the pagan side of the story.

A third reason for the difficulties in studying pagan culture in its own right is the regrettably widespread lack of literary sources. Few and often only passing reports in ancient geographic (Strabo, Pliny the Elder, Diodoros), historical (Tacitus, Dio Cassius), and philosophical (Damascius, Porphyry) literature can help identify and reconstruct pagan religious life. Most of the Jewish literature is not very reliable in depicting pagan religious activity, nor can one trust many of the Christian authors, although some fifth- and sixth-century authors provide valuable information on some sites (Procopius, Epiphanius, Sozomenos), but it always remains to be checked if their information can safely be used for earlier times. Strangely enough, Josephus is often our best and only source, even when it comes to the presence and behavior of pagans in the larger cities in and around Palestine in New Testament times. We know little about the history or architectural development of almost all of the pagan holy sites in ancient Palestine (the situation seems to be changing in regard to Caesarea Philippi), we have only scant information about the rituals that were performed at these sites (if they were any different from neighboring regions such as Syria or Egypt at all) or about the population they served, and usually we can only guess at the mythological world that surrounded the founding and maintenance of the particular site.

In the study of paganism, therefore, archaeology has a much larger role to play than in other fields of research on ancient Palestine. Stratigraphic excavation can show how a particular cult place was used and altered during its existence. The analysis of small finds such as pottery and coins may help identify the role of the cult in its former social, economic, and geographic environment. In collaboration with archaeology, epigraphy and numismatics can contribute most to our understanding of pagan culture. Written documents ranging from monumental inscriptions to personal graffiti often name deities and their worshipers, whose names would never otherwise turn up in literary sources. Such data indicate practices such as dedications or pilgrimages to holy sites. The analysis of coin inscriptions and images helps to identify cults that are not (yet) attested in the literary or epigraphic record. In short, the study of pagan religion in ancient Palestine calls for an approach that essentially breaks down traditional boundaries of disciplines; it inevitably needs to be more "archaeological" than text-oriented.

The greater role of archaeology, of course, has interesting methodological consequences. Because the study of paganism cannot rely on the availability of textual sources (because there are so few), we must be careful concluding that there were no pagans where we have no texts. Since monumental inscriptions are usually an element of urban culture, it is hard to reconstruct pagan life in rural areas where such sources are missing. Studying paganism means to get down to the level of "anonymous" artifacts such as lamps, pottery, and glass, which at most allow us to reconstruct general cultural influences. Considering the limited value of texts, it is also difficult to reconstruct pagan life from Jewish texts. Again, we must avoid concluding that in certain regions there were no pagans just because they are not mentioned in Jewish texts. In short, the study of paganism highlights the complicated problem of combining textual sources (or the lack of them) with archaeological evidence.

Let us dig a little deeper and include the factor of time in our scenario. Because Palestine was part of the ancient Eastern Mediterranean and historical and political events have always left their traces in the religious life of the region, paganism, too, was constantly in flux. What does that mean for the study of Palestinian paganism?

ASPECTS OF PAGAN LIFE IN PALESTINE

David Flusser is certainly right in starting his still-valuable survey with the programmatic phrase: "At no time in history was Judaism the only religion of Palestine."[3] And as I said before, paganism had been present for centuries and did not arrive with the Greeks. Though it is clear from the historical and archaeological sources that the two wars against Rome

---

[3] David Flusser, "Paganism in Palestine," in *The Jewish People in the First Century: Historical Geography; Political History; Social, Cultural, and Religious Life and Institutions* (ed. S. Safrai and M. Stern; CRINT 1; Assen: Van Gorcum; Philadelphia: Fortress, 1974–76), 1:1065.

brought about the most abrupt changes in the region, there had been influential factors before, such as the politics of Herod the Great and an
increase of Roman presence during the era of the procurators. The two
wars, moreover, affected the deep structures of the entire region by introducing many new settlers and relocating large groups of people within the
region. New cities were founded (Neapolis) and old ones altered
(Jerusalem); many Jews lost their lives or had to settle in places that previously were not so densely occupied (Darom, Galilee), thus forming new
centers of population and religion. While these two events caused cata-
strophic disruptions and an only gradual reconstruction of Jewish life in
Palestine, they usually led to an increase in pagan presence. From the
point of the non-Jewish population, however, the Romanization of Palestine in the wake of the two wars meant an acceleration of an otherwise
continuous process of integrating an important region into the religious
and political system of the pluralistic Eastern Empire.

Needless to say, the effects of the two revolts often make it impossible
to read back from later evidence and reconstruct the cultural profile of earlier habitation, unless the archaeological record comes up with conclusive
evidence to do so. While the overall picture shows generally gradual
changes, one still must avoid speaking of any continuity in terms of cult
and religious affiliation on a local level, especially for the time before and
after 70.

The complex nature of paganism opens a wide field for local, regional,
and social studies. Paganism had many faces. As Joseph Geiger sketches
the picture:

> local cults, still very much in their original guise, or beneath a thin or
> thicker veneer of interpretation Graeca, like those of Marnas-Zeus at Gaza,
> Greek cults proper like that of Dionysus at Scythopolis, Roman cults,
> headed by the cults of the Emperors, chiefly in the four Palestinian cities
> named after them, and the influx of the so-called oriental religions, evi-
> denced for instance by the Mithraeum in Caesarea, made up the
> complexity of what we'refer to, for a lack of a better term, as paganism.[4]

The evidence is unequally distributed over the whole of Palestine. We
have much more information on the religious life and various cults of the
cities, which were presumably largely Greek-speaking or bilingual, than
on the mostly Aramaic-speaking rural hinterland. There were pagans set-
tling at the fringes of predominately Jewish territories such as Nabateans
in the south and east, Phoenicians in the north and west, Itureans in the

---

[4] Geiger, "Aspects of Palestinian Paganism, " 5.

northeast, and Aramaic-speaking Syrians in the north. All these peoples or their ancestors have equally long histories of presence in ancient Palestine as the various branches of the biblical tradition. These groups testify to an indigenous, Semitic paganism that, alongside Jews and foreigners such as some Greeks and a few Romans, must have prevailed throughout antiquity not only around but also inside Palestine. Many of these cults were absorbed into Hellenistic culture and, like their Jewish neighbors, adopted a unique blend of architectural and artistic expression. Others might just have gathered around "holy men" such as Simon Magus or practiced their religion in their houses and villages in a way that has left little or no archaeological trace. There were even a few sites sacred to pagans and children of the biblical tradition alike (Mamre, Gerizim). Be that as it may, David Flusser again points out correctly: "Greeks and the Hellenized pagans living in Palestine did not feel they were strangers in the land, even from the religious point of view."[5]

Most likely, there were no clear geographical borders between Jewish and pagan populations, only regional differences in preponderance with regard to one population over against the other. There always was an overlap between these religious elements, at least in geographical terms, in urban centers possibly more than in rural areas, which by all that we actually know tended to be a bit more uniform in their cultural and ethnic composition. However, the latter is only an assumption, since most of our evidence (as I have said before) comes from cities, while the rural hinterland does not provide enough indisputably pagan material. Pagan religion, however, does not need temples, so we should not forget that many "cultural" and "religious indicators" in the countryside might long have disappeared like a fruit offering under a sacred tree or a whispered incantation at a holy spring. Studying pagan religion in Palestine can open up new angles on the relationship between town and countryside.

Given the small size of Palestine, trade and communication were constant factors that tied geographical microcosms to a larger entity. Nonetheless, geographical overlap does not mean that these groups had constant interaction with each other. Social behavior is not directed by geographical factors alone but is a result of religious and moral rules as well. Many Jewish texts (and a growing number of Christian) favored a clear restriction of social life to one's own kin. To have a pagan neighbor *next* to you did not mean one actually lived *with* him. However, since pagans and Jews seem to have used the same pots, the same coins, and the same glass vessels, archaeology may force us to challenge the certainty

---

[5] Flusser, "Paganism in Palestine," 1:1087.

with which we often hold textual rules of social behavior as being representative for actual everyday life. In that respect, the study of paganism supplements and deepens the concept of regionalism in Palestine and helps to prevent it from shaping "regions" only along predominately religious terms.

Finally, the presence of paganism is often seen as an indicator of the degree to which Palestine was Hellenized: the more pagans there were, the more Mediterranean (and the less Jewish) this region would be, and vice versa. A closer study of pagan culture will reveal, however, that this awkward alternative (Hellenistic-pagan versus non-Hellenistic–Jewish) must be abandoned. The presence of paganism cannot serve as an indicator for Hellenistic influence. Both factors have to be distinguished. In this way, the study of paganism confirms results of research that Eric Meyers and many others have carried out on the impact of Hellenism on Jewish culture in Palestine. Both Jews and pagans to various degrees profited from the increase of artistic and architectural options made possible through an all-encompassing influence of "Hellenism" in the East.

So, to summarize, there are four major reasons why is it necessary to include Palestinian paganism into biblical studies. First, we can better understand what the process of Hellenization in the East meant when we examine its impact on other Semitic traditions in Palestine apart from Judaism. Second, we can better perceive how diverse and complex the cultural, ethnic, and religious world of Judaism and early Christianity was and better understand why and how Jews and Christians reacted toward their environment as they did. Third, studying and mapping pagan sites in the classroom might help distinguish between regions with pagan population and those without. Our religious geography becomes more complex—and more realistic, too. Fourth, the study of pagan religion in Palestine, especially its Semitic components, can also contribute to the understanding of elements in Jewish and early Christian theology as well. I am far from repeating the tenets of the older *religionsgeschichtliche Schule* here, but recent research into concepts of monotheism and transcendent mediating figures has shown that paganism, Judaism, and early Christianity have certain features in common. Here the interesting questions begin: How can we explain these similarities? Is it sufficient to resort to old concepts of "syncretism" or to come to the conclusion that all religions are basically the same? Is it correct to see analogous features in different religious traditions as proof of "dependency"? Students, who often want to hear clear-cut answers when it comes to religion, might be invited to think in more differentiated terms. To speak about paganism is not to judge between true and false. On the contrary, students may learn to realize differences and at the same time accept that there can be similarities, too, if they are prepared to overcome the traditional way of opposing Judaism and Christianity against paganism. What do these differences and similarities mean for the religious, social, and intellectual formation of these groups? Finally, how do we today position our religious, social, and intellectual life in relation to these ancient examples?

In my opinion, silencing of the pagan voice leads to a major distortion of the cultural picture of ancient Palestine. In sum, in realizing the diversity in ancient Palestine we obtain a better notion of the religious heritage of ancient Judaism and early Christianity. In order to hear the voice of our fathers and mothers, we have to listen to the "others," too.

PUBLISHED RESOURCES ON THE STUDY OF ANCIENT PAGANISM

Since there is to date no comprehensive study on pagan religion(s) in Palestine in the Late Hellenistic/Early Roman period, the following list of resources is provided. Of the following, the most comprehensive study of the topic, masterly drawing from both literary and archaeological sources, is Nicole Belayche, *Iudaea-Palaestina*. To locate the numerous site reports dealing with pagan temples and shrines, see *NEAEHL* and *OEANE* under the respective entries.

Belayche, Nicole. *Iudaea-Palaestina: The Pagan Cults in Roman Palestine (Second to Fourth Century)*. Religions in the Roman Provinces 1. Tübingen: Mohr Siebeck, 2001.

Bowersock, Glen W. "Polytheism and Monotheism in Arabia and the Three Palestines." *Dumbarton Oaks Papers* 51 (1997): 1–11.

Cush, Denise. "Paganism in the Classroom." *British Journal of Religious Education* 19 (1997): 83–94.

DiSegni, Leah. "A Dated Inscription from Beth Shean." *SCI* 16 (1997): 139–61.

———. "*Heis Theos* in Palestinian Inscriptions." *SCI* 13 (1994): 94–115.

Feldman, Louis H. *Jew and Gentile in the Ancient World: Attitudes and Interactions from Alexander to Justinian*. Princeton: Princeton University Press, 1993, esp. 3–44.

Fine, Steven. "Non-Jews in the Synagogues of Late-Antique Palestine: Rabbinic and Archaeological Evidence." Pages 224–42 in *Jews, Christians, and Polytheists in the Ancient Synagogue: Cultural Interaction during the Greco-Roman Period*. Edited by S. Fine. London: Routledge, 1999.

Flusser, David. "Paganism in Palestine." Pages 1065–1100 in vol. 1 of *The Jewish People in the First Century: Historical Geography; Political History; Social, Cultural, and Religious Life and Institutions*. Edited by S. Safrai and M. Stern. CRINT 2. 2 vols. Assen: Van Gorcum; Philadelphia: Fortress, 1974–76.

Freyne, Sean. "Galileans, Phoenicians and Itureans: A Study of Regional Contrasts in the Hellenistic Age." Pages 182–215 in *Hellenism in the Land of Israel*. Edited by J. J. Collins and G. E. Sterling. Notre Dame, Ind.: University of Notre Dame Press, 2001.

Geiger, Joseph. "Aspects of Palestinian Paganism in Late Antiquity." Pages 3–17 in *Sharing the Sacred: Religious Contacts and Conflicts in the Holy Land First–Fifteenth Century*. Edited by A. Kofski and G. G. Stroumsa. Jerusalem: Yad Izhak Ben Zvi, 1998.

Goldenberg, Robert. *The Nation That Knows Thee Not: Ancient Jewish Attitudes toward Other Religions*. New York: New York University Press, 1998.

Hadas-Lebel, Mireille. "Le paganisme à travers les sources rabbiniques des IIe et IIIe siècles: Contribution à l'étude du syncrétisme dans lèmpire romain." *ANRW* 19.2:397–485.

Halbertal, Moshe. "Coexisting with the Enemy: Jews and Pagans in the Mishna." Pages 159–72 in *Tolerance and Intolerance in Early Judaism and Christianity*. Edited by G. N. Stanton and G. G. Stroumsa. Cambridge: Cambridge University Press, 1998.

Jacobs, Martin. "Pagane Tempel in Palästina: Rabbinische Aussagen im Vergleich mit archäologischen Funden." Pages 139–59 in *The Talmud Yerushalmi and Greco-Roman Culture II*. Edited by P. Schäfer and C. Hezser. Tübingen: Mohr Siebeck, 2000.

Kofski, Arieh. "Mamre: A Case of a Regional Cult?" Pages 19–30 in in *Sharing the Sacred: Religious Contacts and Conflicts in the Holy Land First–Fifteenth Century*. Edited by A. Kofski and G. G. Stroumsa. Jerusalem: Yad Izhak Ben Zvi, 1998.

MacMullen, Ramsay *Paganism in the Roman Empire*. New Haven: Yale University Press, 1981.

Meshorer, Ya'aqov. *City-Coins of Eretz-Israel and the Decapolis in the Roman Period*. Jerusalem: The Israel Museum, 1985.

Mitchell, Stephen. "The Cult of Theos Hypsistos between Pagans, Jews, and Christians," Pages 81–148 in *Pagan Monotheism in Late Antiquity*. Edited by P. Athanassidi and M. Frede. Oxford: Oxford University Press, 1999.

Porton, Gary G. "Forbidden Transactions. Prohibited Commerce with Gentiles in Earliest Rabbinism." Pages 317–35 in *To See Ourselves As Others See Us: Christians, Jews and "Others" in Late Antiquity*. Edited by J. Neusner and E. S. Frerichs. Chico, Calif.: Scholars Press, 1985.

_____. *Goyim: Gentiles and Israelites in Mishna-Tosefta*. BJS 155. Atlanta: Scholars Press, 1988.

Schürer, Emil. *The History of the Jewish People in the Age of Jesus Christ (175 B.C.–A.D. 135)*. Edited by G. Vermes, F. Millar, and M. Black. 3 vols. in 4. Edinburgh: T&T Clark, 1973–87.

Smith, Morton, "The Gentiles in Judaism 125 B.C.E.–66 C.E." Pages 263–319 in *Studies in Historical Method, Ancient Israel, Ancient Judaism.* Vol. 1 of *Studies in the Cult of Jahweh.* Edited by S. J. D. Cohen. Religions in the Graeco-Roman World 130. Leiden: Brill, 1996.

Teixidor, Javier. *The Pagan God: Popular Religion in the Greco-Roman Near East.* Princeton: Princeton University Press, 1977.

Tsafrir, Yoram. "The Fate of Pagan Cult Places in Palestine: The Archaeological Evidence with Emphasis on Beth Shean." Pages 197–218 in *Religious and Ethnic Communities in Later Roman Palestine.* Edited by H. Lapin. Bethesda: University Press of Maryland, 1998.

Veltri, Giuseppe. "Römische Religion an der Peripherie des Reiches: Ein Kapitel Rabbinischer Rhetorik." Pages 81–138 in *The Talmud Yerushalmi and Greco-Roman Culture II.* Edited by P. Schäfer and C. Hezser. Tübingen: Mohr Siebeck, 2000.

West, Michael. "Towards Monotheism." Pages 21–40 in *Pagan Monotheism in Late Antiquity.* Edited by P. Athanassidi and M. Frede. Oxford: Oxford University Press, 1999.

"HERE I AM AT KHIRBET CANA":
INTEGRATING BIBLICAL STUDIES AND ARCHAEOLOGY

Byron R. McCane
Wofford College

A recent commercial for a cruise line provides a good starting point for the topic of teaching archaeology and the Bible. Amid a rapid series of striking images from exotic places all around the world, and to the accompaniment of a driving rhythm section, the voice-over declares: "At last report the Acropolis of Athens had not yet been captured in a downloadable file, and a virtual tour of the great Alaskan ice field was, well, still virtual. The world may be getting smaller, but it still can't come to you. Get out there."

That, in a word, is the point of my contribution to this volume of essays on the topic of integrating biblical studies and archaeology: "Get out there." In this essay I intend to argue that if we want to integrate biblical studies and archaeology, we need to "get out there" with students. I make the case that the best—indeed, the *only*—way to teach students the appropriate relationship between biblical studies and archaeology is to get them "out there" for a season of digging. It is my view, and I hope to persuade the reader of its merit, that only students who have participated in the actual work of excavation will have had the experience they need in order adequately to integrate archaeology and biblical studies.

This essay is thus a discussion of pedagogy. Although academic papers on teaching are all too often not especially stimulating intellectually, I make no apology for choosing this topic for my essay. Unlike some discussions of pedagogy, this one does touch directly upon an intellectual issue of substantial import for all of us who work in and care about the fields of biblical studies and archaeology. For us, the problem of integrating biblical studies and archaeology is a question of considerable intellectual weight. Indeed, much of the history of the relationship between these disciplines during the twentieth century can be aptly summarized as a largely unsuccessful struggle to define and create a healthy interaction between them.

Through the first half of the twentieth century, for example, archaeology and biblical studies were *too integrated*. Under the influence of

195

William F. Albright and the "biblical archaeology" movement, material culture was viewed through such a thick lens of biblical content that distortion was inevitable and sometimes profound. "Solomon's stables" at Megiddo will forever stand as a monument to the wrong kind of integration between archaeology and the Bible. The second half of the century, by contrast, saw the rise of the so-called "New Archaeology," which encouraged students to treat material culture and the Bible as separate but equal sources of information about the past. Almost all of the contributors to this volume were trained in this method, and its agenda of segregating the Bible from archaeology has unquestionably been productive and positive, a necessary correction to the excesses of an earlier generation.

There are increasing indications, however, that the pendulum has swung back too far. Dis/integration has begun to produce dis/information. Recent debates about the history of Israel, for example, as well as the recent sensation of the James ossuary might well be taken as indications that in our day archaeology and the Bible are becoming *too segregated*. One need not wish for a return to the days of biblical archaeology in order to feel that we have apparently gone a little too far in the right direction. Today the task of finding a productive integration of biblical studies and archaeology is at the top of the agenda for those who work in both fields. Since the next generation of archaeologists and biblical scholars will come from students in our classes, it is essential that we introduce them to these issues intelligently, so as to prepare them for the problems and possibilities that lie ahead.

One way to prepare students to integrate the Bible and archaeology is by incorporating archaeological content into biblical studies courses. Certainly many professors include archaeology even in a beginning Bible course. The introductory course on the Hebrew Bible, for example, will typically devote at least one or two entire class sessions to the topic of Near-Eastern archaeology, covering the history of the discipline and describing the steady progress that has been made in methods of excavation. Several introductory textbooks include chapters on archaeology. Many professors supplement these texts by showing slides and videos, and some go so far as to pass representative sherds of pottery around the room. Later on, as the semester progresses, there are frequent references to material culture, introducing our students to four-roomed houses, lead figurines, fortified city gates, and the Tel Dan inscription. Our students are very impressed, so much so that on final exams they write impassioned essays extolling the inestimable value of archaeology for understanding the true meaning of the Bible. All of that is good, as far as it goes.

However, the fact is that it does not go nearly far enough. Perhaps at your school as well as mine, these introductory Bible courses are quite popular, regularly filling up with maximum enrollments. In the thirteen years that I have been teaching such courses at schools in the American southeast it has been my experience that few if any of those fresh faces that beam up at me from their desks on the first day of class actually know very much about the Bible. However, even if they cannot tell Genesis from Revelation, the students still bring into the course an unspoken presumption of the Bible's importance, a silent premise (however inchoate) that this book is special, unlike any other. Thus they come into our classes, and they sit for fifty minutes every Monday, Wednesday, and Friday in a room full of people, each of whom has a copy of this exceptional text, and they start turning pages. They learn to recognize the forms of Israelite literature, the techniques of poetic parallelism, and J, E, D, and P. Yet not one of them ever turns over even a trowel-full of dirt or sees a single artifact in its archaeological context. My point here is simply that the weight of a typical biblical studies course is tilted heavily in favor of the text. Both the individual class sessions and the course as a whole so privilege the text that archaeology, however compelling our presentation of it may be, can never be more than background. Thus we unwittingly perpetuate one of the errors of the biblical archaeologists, by treating material culture as secondary to the text.

To correct this error, some of us go further and teach an entire course on the subject of archaeology. Here many of the dangers of biblical archaeology are avoided, since a course on archaeology necessarily makes the recovery and interpretation of material culture its central focus of attention. The goal of this kind of course is for students to acquire a broad exposure to the discipline in its own right, learning, for example, how to read an archaeological report and how to recognize inappropriate uses of evidence. Students investigate particular sites, becoming familiar with typical problems at specific locations. Often they also review an archaeological period, gaining an appreciation for the breadth of evidence that excavations routinely produce. Certainly a student who has written a term paper on the typical architecture, ceramics, coins, lamps, and burial practices of a specific period will never again underestimate the weight and mass of the material data. Most important, in a course fully devoted to archaeology our students can perceive the discipline as a set of techniques that today are employed literally worldwide in the controlled recovery of information about the human past. All this is for the good, because it dramatically increases the likelihood that students will regard archaeology as an independent field, not simply as a stepchild to biblical studies.

Be that as it may, there still are significant problems with a course on archaeology. To begin, it runs a risk that lies at the opposite end of the spectrum from that of the biblical studies course: if those courses tend to privilege the Bible too much, archaeology courses may privilege it too little. It is not difficult to construct a course syllabus on "Principles of

Archaeology" that makes scant if any reference to the biblical text. Many of us have both taken and taught such courses, and when we do we rightly congratulate ourselves on giving the discipline of archaeology the autonomy that it has always deserved. Good for us—but in so doing have we met the challenge of *integrating* biblical studies and archaeology? Certainly a course on the archaeology of the American southeast or Maya civilization may not need to make much reference to literary sources, but in the archaeology of the ancient Near East it is harder to make the case that we do not need to interact critically with the biblical text, for the Bible itself is part of the evidence for the human past in our region and period. Indeed, if we are honest we will have to admit that the Bible is of such importance that without it hardly anyone would be very interested in the archaeology of Syro-Palestine. In the effort to integrate archaeology and biblical studies, then, the biblical text should have a role to play even in a course devoted to archaeology.

However, there is still another more serious problem with classroom courses on archaeology. It can be stated in the form of a question: Where's the beef? More specifically, where's the excavation? Isn't there something a little odd about a course on archaeology that never involves any excavation? Taking archaeology without excavating is rather like taking driver's education without getting behind the wheel. Here we have come close to the root of the difficulty in integrating these two disciplines, for we can now make explicit one of the deepest and most important differences between them. Biblical studies can be done in a classroom, with books and a blackboard and a teacher—but archaeology cannot. A course about archaeology is only that and nothing more: a course *about* archaeology. Unlike biblical studies, archaeology is not an indoor sport.

At this point it may seem as if this essay is taking on the aura of the old story about Goldilocks and the three bears: the first porridge was too hot, and the second porridge was too cold, so we must be coming to the porridge that is just right. Indeed we are, for I would like to put forward now the fairly modest proposal that we can best integrate archaeology and biblical studies by involving our students in the experience of field excavation. The field school, first pioneered by American archaeologists during the 1960s, offers the optimum educational environment for teaching a healthy relationship between archaeology and the Bible, for when a student participates in a season of excavation, he or she is unlikely to fall prey to the difficulties that can bedevil students in courses on either biblical studies or archaeology. Six weeks in the field—six weeks of filling gufas, sifting dirt, tagging buckets, drawing baulks and top plans, washing pottery, registering sherds—will effectively undermine any presumption of priority that may have adhered to the biblical text. Students will be able to perceive just how much of the story the Bible has left out. The sheer volume of the data will tilt the scale back toward equilibrium between archaeology and biblical studies. Exposure to the work of specialists—ceramicists, chemists, numismatists, epigraphers, paleobotanists—will demonstrate more convincingly than any lecture ever could that mere interpretation of the text is insufficient for the construction of biblical history. When they meet and see and hear archaeologists from countries in the region, our students will discover that they are involved in a project pursued not only by members of their own faith community or nationality but by thoughtful people from many perspectives the world over. Field experience will do all of this (and more) because excavation is, if I may coin a phrase, a total sensory learning environment. Students who have participated in a dig have not only read and thought and talked about biblical studies and archaeology, but they have lived it, worked it, sweated it, and tasted it. As one student succinctly put it in her evaluation of a season of excavations at Sepphoris, "On this trip I was learning 24/7, whether I wanted to or not."

Neither are students who participate in an excavation likely to make the opposite mistake of overlooking the Bible altogether, for there will be countless opportunities over the course of the season for sustained and thoughtful consideration of the relationship between the Bible and archaeology. In the field—where the area supervisor is the most strategic educator on the staff—and in the classes that take place during the evenings, as well as on weekend trips and tours, we can and will engage our students in extended and thoughtful conversation about the connections between biblical studies and archaeology. A student once peppered me with questions about the historical Jesus through most of a bus ride out to Masada, and another student's curiosity about the connections between Matthew, Sepphoris, and rabbinic Judaism consumed most of a dinner in East Jerusalem.These comments bring us to an important observation about the pedagogical value of field excavation. Earlier I remarked that archaeology is not an indoor sport. Indeed, considering the variety of challenges that it entails, participating in an excavation might rightly be described as the "X" Games of undergraduate education. As one student wrote of her season at Sepphoris, "I can't imagine any other experience which could offer so much—physically, intellectually, emotionally, spiritually." It is precisely the total demand of excavating, on body, soul, mind, and spirit, that opens up unusual opportunities for us as teachers. Over the course of the dig season, barriers come down that never could be surmounted on campus. Bonds of trust are formed, and we enter with our students into a teachable moment the likes of which never has and never will take place in a classroom.

Of course there are problems. In the same way that the pedagogical opportunities of field excavation are extraordinary, so too are the difficulties that can arise and the mistakes that can be made. Taking students into the field is expensive and time-consuming. We have to deal with all the annoyances of international travel: crowds, delays, airline food, missed connections, lost luggage, and jet lag. During a season of excavation we will routinely be faced with the challenges of fatigue, dehydration, homesickness, interpersonal conflicts, accidents, illness, injury, and intestinal distress. Still more seriously, the bonds of trust that I mentioned a moment ago—the connection between teacher and student that helps create an uncommon teachable moment—can themselves become occasions for difficulties of an emotional nature. Particularly in the closing days of a dig season, when a kind of group euphoria can develop that is strangely reminiscent of summer camp, we may well find our ethics and integrity being put to the test.

Is it at all surprising, however, if I state my honest opinion that these problems are more than outweighed by the benefits that come from involving students in the work of excavation? If our goal is to teach a productive interaction between the Bible and archaeology, in which the disciplines are neither too integrated nor too segregated, no pedagogical strategy is more effective. If we want to produce a generation of students (and subsequently a new generation of scholars) who can understand with clarity and subtlety that both archaeology and the Bible contribute to our comprehension of the human past in the Near East, there is no better way to do so than to let them get their hands dirty.

Yet I belabor the obvious. After all, who would seriously argue against the pedagogical value of taking our students into the field for a season of excavation? No one. Perhaps, then, it would be best to conclude this essay with some practical suggestions. In fact, there are some useful steps that can be taken as we prepare to bring students with us into the field. The first and most important is to *evaluate the field school* of the excavation. Before agreeing to participate in a dig, we should take some time to examine the educational program that the excavation will offer to students. Unfortunately, it cannot be assumed that each and every archaeological excavation will include a field school in which students will be trained to integrate archaeology and biblical studies. On the contrary, the quality of field-school programs can vary widely, with some excavations providing a coherent and comprehensive educational experience—complete with readings, classes, and tours—while others lack even basic orientation in elementary field techniques. Thus it will be important to talk with the director and ascertain how, when, and where the field school will be conducted. Ask for a copy of the syllabus (if there is one) or at least a schedule of the class sessions. Determine what texts the students will be reading and what writing assignments will be required. In particular, look for signs that the field school builds from basic archaeological knowledge toward higher-order reflection on broader questions of biblical and archaeological interpretation.

A strong field school will aim toward the goal we have been discussing here, namely, integrating archaeology and biblical studies. The academic program of the Sepphoris Acropolis Excavation, the syllabus of which is appended to this essay, can serve as an example of this type of field school. It begins with the basics, as students are taught to acquire and demonstrate competence in the techniques of field excavation. Each student, under the direction of his or her area supervisor, learns the fundamental tasks of excavation, starting with the very basic skill of baulk trimming. Students are also taught how to take elevations, draw top plans, take Munsell readings, record finds in the field notebook, and draw baulks. During the opening weeks of the excavation, evening class sessions reinforce the content of this training in the field. Under the rubrics of "What Are We Doing Here?" and "Why Do We Dig This Way?" class sessions introduce students to the rationale behind these techniques. Two sessions on the history of archaeology in Syro-Palestine, for example, acquaint students with the improvements in excavation methods that developed through the twentieth century. A class session on stratification and stratigraphy is especially important in helping students understand the importance of careful removal of successive layers. During this phase of the field-school program, the overall goal is for students to learn how and why archaeologists strive to "excavate under maximum control and record for maximum information retrieval."

As students begin to master the basic methods of field excavation, the content of the field-school sessions increases in sophistication and begins to engage students with questions of interpretation. Under the rubric of "What Can We Do with This Information?" students are now introduced to first-order questions of analysis and interpretation. Two sessions on gender provide a particularly compelling example of the ways in which archaeological evidence, in conjunction with theoretical perspectives, can generate productive information about the human past. Here the emphasis falls upon teaching students to be clear and conscious in the application of theoretical perspectives to archaeological data.

Finally, when students have acquired some familiarity with both method and interpretation in archaeology, the field school turns to higher-order questions of synthesis, and in the closing weeks of the excavation students are explicitly introduced to questions that call for the integration of biblical studies and archaeology. Under the rubric "What Are the Big Questions Here?" current controversies in biblical studies and archaeology—including, for example, issues of Israelite chronology and the historical Jesus—are introduced and discussed. Class sessions during this part of the field school are highly interactive, often taking the form of

panel discussions. Conversation ranges not only among panelists (typically members of the staff and other invited guests) but also between
students and panelists. In these conversations students and panelists
carry on the work of bringing archaeological material to bear on substantial questions of biblical studies. With fresh experience in field excavation
and disciplined control of archaeological method—not to mention three
or four weekends of touring important archaeological sites—students by
this point are uniquely situated to make coherent use of both archaeology and biblical studies. It has been my experience, in fact, that many
on-campus seminars struggle to attain to the level of engagement and
comprehension that frequently develops during these closing sessions of
the field school. Those moments are, in my judgment, the pedagogical
goal of the field school.

Two other brief suggestions may also be helpful at this point. When
taking students into the field for a season of excavation, *start small*. It is
not necessary—in fact, it is not even advisable—to gather a large group of
fifteen or twenty students. As a practical matter, a group of five to ten will
be much more manageable. Not only is a small group easier to travel with
(they can all fit into one van, for example), but also a small group allows
us to stay in closer touch with each student. In addition, *take along extra
money*. Everything always costs more than one thinks it will, and unexpected expenses have a way of popping up, so pad the budget with a little
extra for those surprises along the way. Each student's fee, in other words,
should include a small premium in order to provide a financial cushion.
That is not to say that we should dole out extra shekels to students who
have spent all of theirs on felafel and GoldStar, but it can be very helpful
to have some resources on hand when a weekend trip does not go exactly
according to plan. Finally, *put up a web site*. It may be only a few digital
photos and a bit of text to you, but to college students today it seems to be
the sign and seal of legitimacy. In their eyes, if you are on the Web, you
are real.

If by some chance you are still unconvinced of the merits of my argument that the best way to teach students to integrate archaeology and
biblical studies is to take them into the field for a season of excavation,
think for a moment of what would it mean if none of us brought any students along for the excavation. In that case, we on the staff would have to
do all the work: all the digging, sifting, pottery washing, and (heaven
forbid) rock removal. Perish the thought. As that cruise-line commercial
puts it, "The world may be getting smaller, but it still can't come to you.
Get out there."

APPENDIX: SYLLABUS OF THE FIELD SCHOOL: SEPPHORIS ACROPOLIS EXCAVATION

COURSE DESCRIPTION

The Field School of the Sepphoris Acropolis Excavation in a comprehensive course in the archaeology and history of Syro-Palestine. Through daily participation in field excavation, students will become proficient in standard methods of field archaeology, including recovery, recording, preservation, and interpretation of finds. Through daily attendance at lectures and discussions, students will become familiar with the major periods in the history of Syro-Palestine, including characteristic features and events in each period. Through weekend tours, students will visit important sites from each of these periods. The goal of the Field School is for students to acquire proficiency in field excavation (so that they would be able to serve as an assistant area supervisor on an excavation) and familiarity with the history of Syro-Palestine (so that they could participate constructively in historical and archaeological analyses of the region).

COURSE REQUIREMENTS

Participation in daily excavation activities is required. Excavation activities begin with departure to the site at 4:30 each weekday morning. Each student will be assigned to an area of the excavation, where the area supervisor will train the student in the methods of field excavation. Field excavation continues until 1:00 PM. "Daily excavation activities" include late-afternoon (4:00 pm) chores, i.e., pottery wash, bone wash, and artifact registration. Attendance at evening lectures and discussions is also required. Lectures and discussions convene at 7:00 PM, Monday–Thursday. Readings will be assigned in advance, and students are expected to have read the assignment ahead of time. Finally, participation in weekend tours is required. Tours will depart each Saturday morning at 8:30 AM and will last all day. Additional work (journal writing, final examination, etc.) may also be required by the student's academic institution.

TEXTBOOKS

Eric M. Meyers, ed. *Galilee through the Centuries*. Winona Lake, Ind.: Eisenbrauns, 1999.
Jerome Murphy-O'Connor, *The Holy Land*. Oxford: Oxford University Press, 1998.
In addition, each student will also receive a copy of the *Area Supervisor's Manual*.

SCHEDULE

Week 1: Getting Started: "What Are We Doing?"
    Class 1: Introduction to Field Excavation
    Class 2: Recognizing Typical Finds
    Class 3: History of Archaeology in Syro-Palestine (Part 1)
    Class 4: History of Archaeology in Syro-Palestine (Part 2)
    Weekend Tour: Beth She'arim, Megiddo, Caesarea

Week 2: Method: "Why Do We Dig This Way?"
    Class 1: Stratification and Stratigraphy
    Class 2: Bronze and Iron Age Syro-Palestine
    Class 3: Persian and Hellenistic Syro-Palestine
    Class 4: Roman and Byzantine Syro-Palestine
    Weekend Tour: Jerusalem (including Masada and Qumran)

Week 3: Interpretation: "What Can We Do with This Information?"
    Class 1: Ancient Societies: Technologies
    Class 2: Ancient Societies: Gender (Part 1)
    Class 3: Ancient Societies: Stratification
    Class 4: Ancient Societies: Death and the Dead
    Weekend Tour: Sea of Galilee, Capernaum, Gamla, Kursi

Week 4: History: "What Are the Big Questions Here?"
    Class 1: Early Israel: Issues of Chronology
    Class 2: Early Judaism: The Rabbis, Hellenism, and Sepphoris
    Class 3: Early Christianity: Jesus the Historical Galilean
    Class 4: Early Judaism and Christianity in Galilee
    Weekend Tour: Jerusalem

Week 5: Wrap-Up: "What Have We Accomplished?"
    Class 1: Results from Areas of Excavation
    Class 2: Integration and Interpretation
    Class #3: Objectives for Next Season
    Tour: Jordan (Amman, Petra, Madaba, Mount Nebo)

ANNOTATED BIBLIOGRAPHY FOR INTEGRATING ARCHAEOLOGY INTO BIBLICAL STUDIES

Melissa Aubin
Sepphoris Regional Project

For those who would like to read further on the many questions addressed in this volume, the following bibliography provides a starting point. Strictly introductory, this bibliography is limited in scope of topics covered and extent of annotation. The goal is to provide a list of materials that are (1) definitional, providing theoretical approaches and examples of works that integrate knowledge from Syro-Palestinian visual/material culture with biblical texts; (2) practical, introducing possible tools of various media for classroom use; and (3) introductory, allowing the reader to correlate more general works with particular studies mentioned in the contributions to this volume.

Several issues complicate the task of collecting resources for integrating material culture and biblical studies. While archaeological and literary knowledge of biblical cultures is as ripe for mutual recognition as it has ever been, the secondary sources often evidence tendencies toward either the absolute separation of archaeology and biblical studies, so that the reader is left to peruse one or the other and create reconstructions that draw from both fields, or overly facile harmonizing of archaeological and literary data. Instructors will realize that many of the books and other resources listed, which contain useful images or other archaeological information for the college student, may require critical analysis.

Particular issues that might warrant an instructor's attention include "popularizing" presentations that view archaeological discoveries with some degree of sensationalism; a presumption in favor of the historicity of biblical events and a linear narrative following the biblical books; methodological simplicity in identifying cultural groups or making social distinctions from archaeological data; and Christian biases, revealing tendencies to emphasize sites named in the New Testament but exhibiting only remains from later eras or to present a triumphalist viewpoint on non-Christian material.

These caveats aside, it is hoped that some of the following materials will assist the instructor to add archaeological knowledge to his or her constellation of disciplines and thus enable the student to experience a textured, and perhaps surprising, view on the cultures that produced the biblical texts.

ON PEDAGOGY AND ARCHAEOLOGY

Fagan, Brian M. "Education Is What's Left: Some Thoughts on Introductory Archaeology." *Antiquity* 74 (2000): 190–213. This article provides a pointed commentary on the need for "new delivery methods" in courses that employ archaeological data, with suggestions for the media elements that the course materials should contain. In addition, there are useful suggestions for the ways in which human diversity indicated in the archaeological record can be used to add appealing dimensions to the course from the students' points of view.

Jenkins, Clare. "Recording the Stones." *Times Educational Supplement* 4058 (8 April 1994): 10. The author documents an attempt to expose students to archaeological fieldwork in the United Kingdom in which students were required to record carefully and systematically the findings of their own excavation work.

MacKenzie, Robert, and Peter Stone. "Introduction: The Concept of the Excluded Past." Pages 1–14 in *The Excluded Past: Archaeology in Education.* Edited by P. Stone and R. MacKenzie. London: Unwin Hyman, 1990. This brief exposition explains why the "excluded pasts" of both preliterate societies and of minority or oppressed groups is an essential topic of study and how the discipline of archaeology is specially suited to address them.

Malone, Caroline. "Education in Archaeology." *Antiquity* 74 (2000): 122–26. This is the introductory article to an *Antiquity* issue devoted specifically to addressing aspects of archaeology in education, "from its use in primary and secondary school to colleges and universities and beyond into professional and teacher training." An international perspective is evidenced in the commentary of the contributors, as is an interest in developing both theoretical and practical knowledge.

Pretty, Kate. "Facts and Skills: Archaeology in Teacher Training." *Antiquity* 74 (2000): 214–18. Reflecting on her experience supervising interning teachers, the author explains how teachers of history who are comfortable working with literary sources can enrich their courses with archaeological resources. Even though teachers of history were not specialists in archaeology, their addition of material culture to curricula resulted in the augmentation of analytical techniques for students.

Smith, George S. "The Society for American Archaeology's 'Teaching Archaeology in the Twenty-First Century' Initiative." *Antiquity* 74 (2000): 186–89. This article describes the Society for American Archaeology's attempts to cure the decline in archaeological education through curriculum change.

Smith, K. C. "'Pathway to the Past: Archaeology Education in Precollegiate Classrooms." *The Social Studies* 89 (1998): 112–18. Documenting a recent upsurge in archaeology-based teaching resources, the author describes the pedagogical advantages of archaeology's hands-on nature, which prompts teachers to use visual culture and encourages students to participate in real or simulated excavations. An appendix includes a lists of myths about archaeological work that are successfully addressed in the classroom as well as sample assignments for students.

Wiseman, James. "Reforming Academic: Archaeological Advances Are Poorly Reflected in Curricula at Most American Universities." *Arch* 51 (1998): 27–31. The author reports on the problems encountered when pedagogical decisions regarding the teaching of archaeology are made by professionals outside of academia and calls for greater attention to contemporary concerns in the discipline of archaeology in its representation to students.

ADDRESSING DEFINITIONAL AND INTERPRETIVE PROBLEMS IN
"BIBLICAL ARCHAEOLOGY"

Bartlett, John R., ed. *Archaeology and Biblical Interpretation*. London: Routledge, 1997. This collection of essays aims at explaining the value of archaeology for illuminating Israelite religion, developments in Judaism and early Christianity, and the history of Roman and Byzantine Palestine. Particularly useful are the essays on Qumran and the Temple Mount.

Bunimovitz, Shlomo. "How Mute Stones Speak: Interpreting What We Dig Up." *BAR* 21/2 (1995): 58–67, 96. This is a valuable article for illustrating the problems and possibilities of interpreting archaeological data when biblical literary claims are involved. Especially constructive is the explanation of the historical and cultural contingency of goals of interpretation, and a historical overview of interpretive trends in Syro-Palestinian archaeology.

Meyers, Eric M. "Identifying Religious Groups through Archaeology." Pages 738–45 in *Biblical Archaeology Today: Proceedings of the Second*

208   BETWEEN TEXT AND ARTIFACT

International Congress on Biblical Archaeology. Edited by A. Biran and J. Aviram. Jerusalem: Israel Exploration Society, 1993. This study models the type of careful questioning that underlies well-informed conclusions regarding cultural questions that rest in part on archaeological data. This article should be read in conjunction with any fundamental text in "biblical archaeology."

Miller, Kevin D. "Did the Exodus Never Happen? How Two Egyptologists Are Countering Scholars Who Want to Turn the Old Testament into Myth." *Christianity Today* 42/10 (1998): 44–52. This article contrasts minimalist and maximalist approaches to interpreting archaeological evidence in light of biblical literature (and vice versa), taking as examples the case of Jericho and the historicity of the captivity and exodus. It is a valuable tool for exposing students to the interpretive decisions that contribute to the correlation of archaeological and literary evidence for historians of biblical cultures.

Pratico, Gary D. "Archaeology and Bible History." *BA* 57 (1994): 182–84. This useful, short introductory piece allows the introductory-level student to understand, on a basic level, the contributions and complications archaeological data presents for understanding biblical texts.

Sheler, Jeffery L. "Mysteries of the Bible: Archaeological Findings Related to the Bible. *U.S. News and World Report* 118/15 (1995): 60–68. This popularizing overview article considers the bearing of archaeological evidence from the Bronze and Iron Ages to the traditions of the patriarchs, exodus and conquest, and united monarchy. A short final section relates archaeological evidence from the Galilee region to questions about the historical Jesus.

Vaux, Roland de. "On Right and Wrong Uses of Archaeology." Pages 64–80 in *Near Eastern Archaeology in the Twentieth Century: Essays in Honor of Nelson Glueck.* Edited by J. A. Sanders. Garden City, N.Y.: Doubleday, 1970. A useful statement on the limits of archaeological research for the reconstruction of late ancient cultural history in Syro-Palestine.

SELECTED REFERENCE MATERIALS

"1995 Review of Study Bibles." *BAR* 21/6 (1995): 72–76. This comparative review in chart form of fifty-one study Bibles indicates, among other things, translation, indication of accompanying dictionary or encyclopedia entries, and maps.

Bienkowski, Piotr, and Alan Millard. *Dictionary of the Ancient Near East.* Philadelphia: University of Pennsylvania Press, 2000. Equipped with maps, black and white photos, and bibliographies, this resource addresses a period of 1.5 million years before the present until the fall of Babylon, covering the Levant, Mesopotamia, and the Caucausus.

Matthews, Victor H. and James C. Moyer, "The Use and Abuse of Archaeology in Current One-Volume Bible Commentaries." *BA* 53 (1990): 104–15. Focusing on four commentaries—*The New Jerome Bible Commentary, The Interpreter's Bible Commentary, the Eerdmans Bible Commentary, and Peake's Bible Commentary*—the authors note specific articles, maps, illustrations, and indices that allow the reader to incorporate archaeological information into thumbnail research on particular books or events. *The New Jerome Bible Commentary* was rated the most archaeologically informative. This is a good companion for teachers who wish to direct their students to pursue archaeological questions in libraries with holdings that are stronger in Bible reference than in archaeology.

————. "The Use and Abuse of Archaeology in Current Bible Handbooks." *BA* 48 (1985): 149–61. This article evaluates twelve Bible handbooks on the sophistication of their use of archaeological data in presentations of "biblical history." Presentations of the flood story and the fall of Jericho were selected for comparison.

Maxwell, John. "Intimidated No More: Bible Reference Tools." *Christianity Today* 37/12 (1993): 4–7. Maxwell includes some listings to archaeologically oriented resources for the nonspecialist.

Meyers, Eric M., ed. *Oxford Encyclopedia of Archaeology in the Near East.* 5 vols. New York: Oxford University Press, 1997. This is a tremendous five-volume resource. Entries cover a host of archaeological sites in the Near East, the principle figures and institutions in the discipline, geographic areas, and the broad cultural groups that occupied them. It is readily accessible to the lay reader, with charts linking archaeological phases to biblical chronology.

Murphy-O'Connor, Jerome. *The Holy Land: An Oxford Archaeological Guide from Earliest Times to 1700.* 4th ed. New York: Oxford University Press, 1998. This classic work offers a broad examination of the archaeology of Israel, West Bank, and Gaza from the prehistoric to early modern period in a site-by-site format. The author's own biases at times privilege sites or occupational phases with a Christian presence, but the volume provides an updated reference that is useful for the student or instructor seeking the archaeological summary of a particular site and, at times, its relationship to biblical or other ancient literary evidence.

Stern, Ephraim, ed. *The New Encyclopedia of Archaeological Excavations in the Holy Land.* 4 vols. Jerusalem: Israel Exploration Society; New York: Simon & Schuster, 1993. This reference work includes essays on sites excavated in the region of Israel, usually with a phase-by-phase description of the occupational history of the site.

INCORPORATING GENDER AS AN ANALYTICAL TOOL

Burtt, Fiona. "'Man the Hunter': Gender Bias in Children's Archaeology Books." *Archaeological Review from Cambridge* 6/2 (1987): 157–74. This offers an interesting presentation of the constructedness of gender as produced in the interpretation of archaeological data.

Conkey, Margaret W., and Ruth E. Tringham. "Cultivating Thinking/Challenging Authority: Some Experiments in Feminist Pedagogy and Archaeology." Pages 224–50 in *Gender and Archaeology.* Edited by R. P. Wright. Philadelphia: University of Pennsylvania Press, 1996. The authors offer a description of their attempts to build prehistory courses in ways that encourage students to critique reigning interpretive paradigms for archaeological knowledge production. Examples of syllabi for several types of gender-oriented courses are included.

Meyers, Carol. *Discovering Eve: Ancient Israelite Women in Context.* New York: Oxford University Press, 1988. This seminal text linking gender studies and Hebrew Bible also models the fruitful engagement of archaeological data with historical-critical approaches to literary evidence. The result is a rich reconstruction of women's historical roles in early Israelite culture.

————. "The Family in Early Israel." Pages 1–47 in *Families in Ancient Israel.* Edited by L. G. Perdue, J. Blenkinsopp, J. J. Collins, and C. Meyers. Library of Ancient Israel. Louisville: Westminster John Knox, 1997. An important "check" on the tendency to retroject modern notions of the family into understandings of the past, this essay provides insight into the social and economic importance of the family in early Israel.

————. "Recovering Objects, Re-visioning Subjects: Archaeology and Feminist Biblical Study." Pages 270–84 in *A Feminist Companion to Reading the Bible: Approaches, Methods and Strategies.* Edited by A. Brenner and C. Fontaine. Sheffield: Sheffield Academic Press, 1997. This essay, readily accessible to college students, offers sophisticated exposition of the many biases that have marked critical studies of the Bible and exemplifies corrective strategies for historicizing women with the tools of feminist theory, archaeology, and textual studies.

Romanowicz, J. V., and Rita P. Wright. "Gendered Perspectives in the Classroom." Pages 199–223 in *Gender and Archaeology*. Edited by R. P. Wright. Philadelphia: University of Pennsylvania Press, 1996. Beginning with a clear explanation for the need to include questions of gender in archaeology courses, the authors provide examples illustrating how the use of gender theory can alter conventional pedagogical scenarios. Suggestions for introductory and advanced archaeology course syllabi are offered.

Spector, Judith D., and M. K. Whelan. "Incorporating Gender into Archaeology Courses." Pages 36–50 in *Toward an Anthropology of Women*. Edited by R. Reiter. New York: Monthly Review Press, 1989. This is an important, early call to address bias in archaeology instruction; it provides guidance for theoretical approaches and addresses contexts outside the ancient Near East. ·

GENERAL RESOURCES FOR MATERIAL CULTURE IN HEBREW BIBLE AND NEW TESTAMENT

Bass, George F. "Nautical Archaeology and Biblical Archaeology." *BA* 53 (1990): 4–13. This article introduces ways in which underwater archaeology informs the reconstruction of cultures mentioned in biblical literature.

Biblical Archaeology Society. *Archaeology and Religion Slide Set*. Caption book by Dan P. Cole. Washington, D.C.: Biblical Archaeology Society, 1997. This collection gathers slides meant to illustrate contexts of religion for cults of the Neolithic period through the Roman period. Little attention is given in some places to the question of how one determines the cultic nature of a given site or implement, though the range of materials from Nabatean altars to Constantinian churches to the high places of Dan and Ashkelon provides a sense of the rich diversity of cultures in and surrounding the land of Israel within the phases represented (140 slides).

Biblical Archaeology Society. *The Archaeology of Jerusalem from David to Jesus*. Video 1: *From the Beginning to the Babylonian Destruction*. Video 2: *From the Return of the Exiles to the World of Jesus*. Washington D.C.: Biblical Archaeology Society, 1990. This set and its accompanying learner's guide examine highlights among the architecture, artifacts, and inscriptions from the Israelite, Judahite, and then Judean occupation of the city. Emphasis is placed on the changing boundaries of the city in its transition from Iron Age to Persian period to late antiquity. Although the narration tends toward a popularizing presentation, the footage is useful to provide a sense of the intersections and disjunctures between the archaeological and biblical records.

Biblical Archaeology Society. *Biblical Archaeology: From the Ground Down,* Parts 1 and 2. 90 minutes. Washington, D.C.: Biblical Archaeology Society, 1997. This series of two videos introduce practical aspects of field archaeology in the Near East, the history of the discipline, and several major finds from the last century of excavation. The narrator, Hershel Shanks, also introduces discrepancies between biblical claims and the archaeological record, using the problem of the Israelite conquest of Canaan as his central example.

Biblical Archaeology Society. *Biblical Archaeology Slide Set.* Caption book by Dan P. Cole. Washington, D.C.: Biblical Archaeology Society, 1997. This set has significant overlap with the *Mesopotamian Archaeology Slide Set* and the *Jerusalem Archaeology Slide Set,* in which subgroups of slides rather ahisorically illustrate remains from various cultural practices (domestic architecture, public architecture, writing, weapons, and tombs) represented in a wide range of chronological phases from the Bronze Age until the Roman period (134 slides).

Biblical Archaeology Society. *Galilee Archaeology Slide Set.* Caption book by James F. Strange. Washington, D.C.: Biblical Archaeology Society, 1997. In this set, slides depict architecture and landscapes from the Lower Galilee, Upper Galilee, and northern coastal region. The images (140 slides) depict materials that date from the Natufian until the Crusader period, so that the emphasis falls on late ancient Christian sites, though prehistoric (Chalcolithic ossuaries) and Iron age (images of Hazor) slides balance the distribution somewhat.

Biblical Archaeology Society. *Jerusalem Archaeology Set.* Caption book by Dan Bahat and Dan P. Cole. Washington, D.C.: Biblical Archaeology Society, 1997. The set (141 slides) provides a representative sample of architectural highlights from the best-attested phases of the city's history, from the Iron Age until the Islamic period. The set is particularly strong in the late Iron Age and Roman period.

Connolly, Peter, and Hazel Dodge. *The Ancient City: Life in Classical Athens and Rome.* New York: Oxford University Press, 1998. Peppered with plans, reconstructions, and maps, this volume is particularly useful for illuminating the Hellenistic and Roman contexts of formative Judaism and Christianity. Topics covered include city infrastructure, housing, and daily life.

DeVries, LaMoine F. *Cities of the Biblical World: An Introduction to the Archaeology, Geography, and History of Biblical Sites.* Peabody, Mass.: Hendrickson, 1997. This richly illustrated book provides a good companion to biblical studies courses, inasmuch as fifty cities in Mesopotamia, Aram/ Syria, Phoenecia, Anatolia, Egypt, Palestine, and provinces of the Roman world are presented. Descriptions emphasize the public aspects of these cities (trade, religion, defense, industry, and government).

Matthews, Victor H. *Manners and Customs in the Bible: An Illustrated Guide to Daily Life in Bible Times.* Peabody, Mass.: Hendrickson, 1988. Designed for the introductory audience, this book relies on comparative studies of Near Eastern cultures and archaeological data in order to reconstruct social practices in the periods stretching from the early second millennium B.C.E. through the second century C.E.. Five chapters (The Patriarchal Period, Exodus and Settlement Period, Monarchy Period, Exile and Return, and Intertestamental and New Testament Period) are arranged in a way that complements courses that proceed in a roughly chronological presentation of biblical literature.

Bible Atlases and Geography

Aharoni, Yohanan. *The Land of the Bible.* Rev. ed. Translated by A. F. Rainey. Philadelphia: Westminster, 1979. This is a landmark work in the historical geography of the land that hosted the cultures of the Bible. Though dated, the book provides useful information on the geographical and climactic setting, toponymy, and history of Syro-Palestine, from the Bronze Age to the Persian Period.

Aharoni, Yohanan and Michael Avi-Yonah. *Macmillan Bible Atlas.* New York: MacMillan, 1993. The strength of this volume is its multiple maps from particular regions and eras, illustrating reconstructions of trade routes, military campaigns, and cultural shifts. The maps are largely structured around events narrated in Hebrew Bible and New Testament texts, revealing a perspective that begins with the text and supplements it with a background that includes extrabiblical sources.

Bahat, Dan, with Chaim T. Rubinstein. *Illustrated Atlas of Jerusalem.* Translated by S. Ketko. New York: Simon & Schuster, 1990. This is a fine, concise historical atlas of Jerusalem based on recent field work and suitable for introductory students.

May, Herbert G. *Oxford Bible Atlas.* 3d ed. Rev. by John Day. New York: Oxford University Press, 1984. Richly illustrated topographical maps trace shifting borders and routes from the Bronze to Roman periods, including commentaries that address geography, climate, and the general historical archaeological context.

Matthews, Victor H., and James C. Moyer. "Bible Atlases: Which Ones Are Best?" *BA* 53 (1990): 220–31. The authors examine reference Bible atlases and student Bible atlases, evaluating the usefulness and accuracy of maps, gazetteers, captions, and charts. The authors share a concern that the atlases reflect information gained from recent archaeological discoveries. *The Moody Atlas of Bible Lands, Facts on File Atlas of the Bible,* and *Harper's Atlas of the Bible* rated highly on content and presentation.

Textbooks and Readers

Albright, William F. *The Archaeology of Palestine*. New York: Pelican, 1961. Convinced to a surprising degree of the historical reliability of biblical literature, the author engages archaeology often as a resource for expanding on the biblical portrait. Albright's knowledge of epigraphy and ancient languages enhance the volume, which stands as an important installation in the development of the discipline.

Ben-Tor, Amnon., ed. *The Archaeology of Ancient Israel*. Translated by R. Greenberg. New Haven: Yale University Press, 1994. This comprehensive introduction to the topic includes contributions from noted scholars, each of which includes an overview of the occupational history of Syro-Palestine and highlights artifacts from public and private life, intercultural relationships, and long-term cultural change. The vivid photographs and maps are well-integrated with the sophisticated, straightforward commentary.

Currid, John D. *Doing Archaeology in the Land of the Bible: A Basic Guide*. Grand Rapids: Baker, 1999. This book is designed to explain the basic principles of archaeology to newcomers to the subject. The author discusses the formation and excavation of tell sites; the surveying, excavation, and excavation of sites; and the interpretation of the stratified results of excavation. There are rich examples to illustrate building materials and patterns, and there is an application of the principles to the site at Bethsaida. Despite some inconsistencies, the volume is a valuable introduction to archaeology that draws entirely from the culture and history of ancient Israel.

Drinkard, Joel F., Jr., Gerald L. Mattingly, and J. Maxwell Miller, eds. *Benchmarks in Time and Culture: An Introduction to Palestinian Archaeology Dedicated to Joseph A. Callaway*. SBLABS 1. Atlanta: Scholars Press, 1988. This series of essays, designed as a textbook, is a Festschrift in honor of archaeologist and biblical scholar Joseph A. Callaway. The twenty-three essays provide information in the history of the development of Western archaeological schools in Israel, the methods and techniques used in contemporary archaeological research, and selected examples of how archaeological knowledge has figured in historical and cultural syntheses.

Frank, Harry Thomas. *Discovering the Biblical World*. Revised by James F. Strange. Maplewood, N.J.: Hammond, 1987. The initial volume and its revision were designed as introductory works for those interested in understanding the cultural history and geography intertwined with biblical narratives. Thus, the volume is necessarily driven by biblical literary sources, though the many resources (maps, color photos of sites, archaeological data, and data from nonbiblical literary sources) awaken the reader to broader cultural horizons than those presumed in many biblical studies textbooks. The revised edition contains updated information on the Dead Sea Scrolls, an expanded bibliography, and new data from sites such as Sepphoris, Capernaum, and Mount Ebal.

Fritz, Volkmar. *Introduction to Biblical Archaeology*. 2d ed. Translated by B. Manz-Davies. JSOTSup 172. Sheffield: JSOT Press, 1996. Approximately half of this book presents introductory issues, such as geography, history of the discipline, methodology, and chronology. The emphasis on the occupational history of Israel falls in the late Bronze and Iron Ages, with brief attention to the Hellenistic and Roman periods.

Kenyon, Kathleen M. *Archaeology in the Holy Land*. New York: Praeger, 1960. An important early overview of the archaeology of Syro-Palestine, from the Neolithic to the Persian period, this book represents a significant attempt to narrate the history of the region through archaeological analysis, independently, when possible, from the biblical portrait.

Lapp, Paul W. *Biblical Archaeology and History*. New York: World, 1969. Drawn from lectures, the book provides a useful statement on the limits of historical reconstructions for those who would take the biblical narratives as a starting point for archaeological research. It is aimed at an undergraduate audience.

Laughlin, John C. H. *Archaeology and the Bible*. London: Routledge, 2000. This is a careful methodological and substantive overview of fieldwork in Syro-Palestine and the history of the discipline as well as an introduction to the major Neolithic to Late Iron Ages sites. Throughout the book, the author addresses problems of periodization and linking literary narratives with historical sequences based on archaeology. It is a very useful starting point for introductory students.

Levy, Thomas L., ed. *The Archaeology of Society in the Holy Land*. London: Leicester University Press, 1995. This is a tremendous overview of not only the material culture of Syro-Palestine but also the socioeconomic and cultural forces that figure in the historical contours of the region. Chapters range from the Neolithic to modern periods, with a particularly useful initial section entitled "Approaches to the Past."

Mazar, Amihai. *Archaeology of the Land of the Bible: 10,000–586 B.C.E.* New York: Doubleday, 1990. This is a standard text presenting reconstructions of the various phases in the occupational history of Syro-Palestine, from the Neolithic period to the Babylonian conquest, divided when possible along periods drawn from biblical chronology. It presents a wealth of data from excavation sites, placing the focus of the book on archaeological and extrabiblical evidence.

Rast, Walter E. *Through the Ages in Palestinian Archaeology: An Introductory Handbook*. Philadelphia: Trinity Press International, 1992. This straightforward introductory text emphasizes problems in "traditional" approaches that would attempt to harmonize archaeology and the Bible. The strengths of this volume are its broad overviews of archaeological phases reaching from the Epipaleolithic to the medieval eras and its inclusion of Transjordanian sites.

Thompson, Henry O. *Biblical Archaeology: The World, the Mediterranean, the Bible*. New York: Paragon House, 1987. This introductory text includes chapters on the method and history of archaeology in the lands of the Bible, archaeology and science, daily life in biblical times, and archaeology and religion. The section entitled "Archaeology Illuminates the Bible" summarizes the contributions of archaeological data for our understanding of biblical literature from ancient Israel to developing Christianity.

Wright, G. Ernest. *Biblical Archaeology*. 2d ed. Philadelphia: Westminster, 1962. Heavily reliant on the biblical narrative, the author views archaeology as a supplement to a presumably historically unproblematic biblical text. It is a useful contrast to more recent works, such as Laughlin's *Archaeology and the Bible* (see above).

Wright, G. Ernest, Edward F. Campbell, and David Noel Freedman, eds. *The Biblical Archaeologist Reader*. 4 vols. Garden City, N.Y. and New York: Doubleday 1961–83. Selected articles from past issues of *BA* (now *NEA*) provide highlights of reports and syntheses. When the anthologies are examined together, they leave the reader with some sense of methodological changes in the discipline over time.

MATERIAL CULTURE AND HEBREW BIBLE

Backhouse, Robert. *The Kregel Pictorial Guide to the Temple.* Edited by Tim Dowley. Grand Rapids: Kregel, 1996. This brief book aims to present a history for the Jerusalem temple, from its prehistory as a tent of meeting until its destruction in 70 C.E. The short presentation of Solomon's temple is greatly overshadowed by the description of the model of the Herodian temple, which makes up half of the book. The illustrations are vivid, including perspectives from the ground and from the air.

Berlin, Andrea. "Between Large Forces: Palestine in the Hellenistic Period." *BA* 60 (1997): 2–51. This overview of the political history and material culture of Hellenistic Palestine provides a rich backdrop for study of the later documents in the Hebrew Bible.

Biblical Archaeology Society. *Dead Sea Scrolls Slide Set.* Caption book by Dan P. Cole. Washington, D.C.: Biblical Archaeology Society. 1997. The narrative and selection of slides reflect the Essene hypothesis, which locates the region of the production of the scrolls at Qumran and assumes that the authors were Essenes. The set is useful not only for illustrating the material culture of the Qumran settlement and selections from the scrolls corpus but also for teaching the history of Roman period Palestine and manuscript production in antiquity.

Biblical Archaeology Society. *Mesopotamian Archaeology Slide Set.* Caption book by Marie-Henriette Gates. Washington, D.C.: Biblical Archaeology Society, 1997. This set (140 slides) is of particular use for teaching the Near Eastern civilizations of the Bronze Age and for illustrating the highlights of the material culture of the Neo-Babylonian and Persian periods during and after the period of the exile. Also of interest are the overviews and details of Sennacherib's siege of Lachish.

Dever, William G. *Recent Archaeological Discoveries and Biblical Research.* Seattle: University of Washington Press, 1990. Comprised of four papers delivered as popular lectures, this book is useful for a general audience and can serve as a tool for exposing the complexities in using archaeological data to arrive at historical and cultural syntheses that also engage material from biblical literature. The first chapter offers a negative evaluation of "biblical archaeology," and the three other chapters illustrate how archaeology can contribute to a more nuanced understanding of the biblical world, focusing on the Israelite settlement in Canaan, the monumental art and architecture of the united monarchy, and the religion of Israel.

Finkelstein, Israel, and Neil A. Silberman. *The Bible Unearthed: Archaeology's New Vision of Ancient Israel and the Origin of Its Sacred Texts.* New York: Free Press, 2001. Treating archaeological evidence as the primary source for the history of Israel, the authors argue for a late dating of the Deuteronomistic History and challenges biblical representations of history for the nonspecialist audience.

Fritz, Volkmar. *The City in Ancient Israel.* BibSem 29. Sheffield: Sheffield Academic Press, 1995. The language and format of the book suggest that it is intended for a popular or undergraduate audience. Despite the title, the book devotes chapters to village and city life, including Canaanite cities, Israelite villages, and Israelite cities. The author presents an interpretation of the nature of the Israelite city and the reasons for its development and includes descriptions of what life was like in the cities around the tenth century B.C.E.

Hendel, Ronald S. "Finding Historical Memories in the Patriarchal Narratives." *BAR* 21/4 (1995): 53–59, 70–71. This article reviews attempts to date the patriarchal period and a critical analysis of how history might be constructed on the basis of the patriarchal narratives and Bronze Age artifacts.

Herr, Larry G. "The Iron Age II Period: Emerging Nations." *BA* 60 (1997): 115–83. This is a thorough review of Late Iron Age material culture in the nations occupying the Levant and critical engagement of social history and archaeology.

Leonard, Albert L., Jr. "The Late Bronze Age." *BA* 53 (1989): 2–39. The author offers an overview of Late Bronze Age sites in Palestine and a presentation of the state of the question in Late Bronze Age research.

McCarter, P. Kyle. *Ancient Inscriptions: Voices from the Biblical World* (with accompanying slide set). Washington, D.C.: Biblical Archaeology Society, 1996. A richly illustrated introduction to inscribed artifacts (scrolls, coins, pottery, reliefs, stelae), primarily from Israel, Mesopotamia, and Egypt, this set of 140 slides provides a resource for introducing biblical manuscript texts and extrabiblical texts dating from the Bronze Age until the medieval period.

Silberman, Neil A. "Digging in the Land of the Bible." *Arch* 51 (1998): 36–47. Silberman offers a thumbnail overview of the role of archaeology in revisionist history of biblical cultures.

Stiebing, William H. *Out of the Desert? Archaeology and the Exodus/ Conquest Narratives.* Buffalo: Prometheus, 1989. This survey for the layperson reviews a wide variety of theories concerning the settlement of Canaan, draws together archaeological and literary evidence, but acknowledges radically differing syntheses based on the same historical data.

Westenholz, Joan Goodnick. ed. *Royal Cities of the Biblical World.* Jerusalem: Bible Lands Museum, 1996. This lavishly illustrated catalogue for the Bible Lands Museum's exhibit "Jerusalem—A Capital for All Times, Royal Cities of the Biblical World," contains a series of essays on the archaeology and history of eight Near Eastern cities (Ur, Tanis, Akhenaten, Jerusalem, Nineveh, Hattusha, Babylon, and Susa).

MATERIAL CULTURE AND NEW TESTAMENT

Biblical Archaeology Society. *New Testament Archaeology Slide Set.* Caption book by Dan P. Cole. Washington, D.C.: Biblical Archaeology Society, 1997. Despite the tendencies toward positivism and romanticism in the accompanying captions, the set offers a broad overview of sites associated with the development and spread of Christianity. The slides cover images of landscapes, architecture, and artifacts from Greco-Roman Palestine and sites associated with the missionary journeys of Paul (as reconstructed from Acts and the undisputed letters).

Biblical Archaeology Society. *Supplemental New Testament Archaeology Slide Set.* Caption book by Dan P. Cole. Washington, D.C.: Biblical Archaeology Society, 1997. This set (105 slides) augments its predecessor by adding more slides illustrating Greco-Roman Palestine, though the slides that might date to the period of the historical Jesus are outnumbered by the many images illustrating developments in late ancient Christianity (e.g., church architecture, early Christian art).

Finegan, Jack. *The Archaeology of the New Testament: The Life of Jesus and the Beginning of the Early Church.* Princeton: Princeton University Press, 1992. Often taking the biblical text at face value, this book surrounds the events reported in the New Testament books with stones, coins, and pottery, offering a contextualized view of the New Testament stories without complicating the historicity of the stories themselves.

Freyne, Sean. "Archaeology and the Historical Jesus." Pages 160–82 in *Galilee and Gospel: Collected Essays.* Edited by S. Freyne. Tübingen: Mohr Siebeck, 2000. This circumspect discussion of the value of archaeological data in the reconstruction of earliest Christian history would serve the introductory New Testament student well.

Hanson, K. C., and Douglas E Oakman. *Palestine in the Time of Jesus: Social Structures and Social Conflicts.* Minneapolis: Fortress, 1998. This is a valuable attempt to reconstruct the social and cultural context of Palestine during the Jesus movement, drawing from archaeology, social-scientific theory, geography, and philology. The author emphasizes kinship, politics, economics, and religion, areas in which an interdisciplinary approach can help to bridge the cultural gap between the modern reader and the first-century Palestinians.

Harrison, Roland K. *Archaeology of the New Testament.* New York: Association, 1964. This early attempt to use archaeology to contextualize the Jesus movement gives little attention to methodological perspectives that criticize the historical value of unanalyzed New Testament narratives.

Meyers, Eric M. "Early Judaism and Christianity in Light of Archaeology." *BA* 51 (1988): 69–79. Meyers offers an instructive synthesis of archaeological and literary evidence addressing controversies in the reconstruction of earliest Christian communities in Palestine.

Meyers, Eric M. and L. Michael White. "Jews and Christians in a Roman World." *Arch* 42 (1989): 26–33. This is a useful example for any audience of the important corrective archaeology may provide when developing a history of Jewish and Christian communities and their interrelationships during the first and second centuries.

Millard, Alan. *Discoveries from the Time of Jesus.* Oxford: Lion, 1990. Written for a popular audience, with nontechnical text and no footnotes, Millard's book summarizes the archaeological record in Second Temple Palestine. The book is arranged thematically into six sections: Daily Life, Rules of the Land, Religion, Death and Burial, Writers, and Gospel Records (which includes a discussion of text as artifact, with an overview of textual criticism).

Reed, Jonathan L. *Archaeology and the Galilean Jesus: A Reexamination of the Evidence.* Harrisburg, Pa.: Trinity Press International, 2000. Among the best recent treatments of archaeological data for New Testament studies, this book demonstrates how settlement patterns and material culture of Galilean sites point to links between Galilee and Judea in the first century and discusses the impact of urbanization in the Galilee on agrarian populations. The author reviews the state of the question on archaeological research in Sepphoris and Capernaum and draws clear connections between archaeological analysis and historical-critical perspectives on New Testament texts.

Stephens, William H. *The New Testament World in Pictures*. Nashville: Broadman, 1987. This volume comprises 884 black and white photos and four color plates, largely from museum materials. The major divisions are: The Emperors, Military, People, City, Business, Professions and Trades, Religion, Leisure Time, Home and Hearth. The volume draws together images from the broad expanse of the early empire, though it is biased toward the western provinces, and some of the objects clearly postdate the period of the development of New Testament traditions.

Strange, James F. "Some Implications of Archaeology for New Testament Studies." Pages 23–59 in *What Has Archaeology to Do with Faith?* Edited by J. H. Charlesworth and W. P. Weaver. Philadelphia: Trinity Press International, 1992. Offering a pragmatic perspective on the limits and the value of archaeology for understanding the Bible and for faith, the author urges the integration of archaeological data in reconstruction of earliest Christian history, so that a textured historical perspective might enrich the possibilities for understanding formative Christian texts.

Unger, Merrill Frederick. *Archaeology and the New Testament*. Grand Rapids: Zondervan, 1962. A literalist view of New Testament texts allows the author to select only archaeological evidence that appears to illuminate the picture drawn in the texts. The book is a clear example of an approach that has been, for the most part, abandoned, and it serves as an illustrative counterexample to more recent work, such as that of Jonathan Reed, James Strange, or Eric Meyers.

ON ELECTRONIC RESOURCES

Silberman, Neil A. "Digitizing the Ancient Near East: CD-ROMs and World Wide Web Sites." *Arch* 48 (1996): 86–89. The author provides a critical review of easily accessible CD-ROM electronic books and World Wide Web sites germane to contextualizing biblical and parabiblical literature within the material culture of the ancient Near East. Programs that generate tailored Bible maps receive special attention, and there is a positive assessment of the electronic book, *Dead Sea Scrolls Revealed*.

Younger, John. "Caught in the Net: Electronic Opportunities in Archaeology." *BA* 59 (1996): 191–93. This is one teacher's narrative of an attempt to encourage students to engage electronic sources in their own critical reflection on material culture. Students' work included three projects. In the first, students were assigned to design a course of their own, relying on a slide collection. The second project required students to locate sites pertaining to archaeology of various cultures through search engines, and the third project involved pursuing specific classical archaeological sites. The instructor reaffirms the importance of library research as an important companion to Web research. Later issues of *BA* continue this feature, addressing other aspects of on-line resources.[1]

---

[1] Of the recent publications that have appeared since the completion of this annotated bibliography, one noteworthy addition to our understanding of the material culture of the Hebrew Bible should be particularly interesting to biblical scholars: Oded Borowski, *Daily Life in Biblical Times* (SBLABS 5; Atlanta: Society of Biblical Literature; Leiden, Brill: 2003).

BIBLIOGRAPHY

Abu El-Haj, Nadia. *Facts on the Ground: Archaeological Practice and Territorial Self-Fashioning in Israeli Society.* Chicago: University of Chicago Press, 2001.

Adams, Robert McC. *Heartland of Cities: Surveys of Ancient Settlement and Land Use on the Central Floodplain of the Euphrates.* Chicago: University of Chicago Press, 1981.

———. *Land behind Baghdad: A History of Settlement on the Diyala Plains.* Chicago: University of Chicago Press, 1965.

Adams, Robert McC., and Hans J. Nissen. *The Uruk Countryside: The Natural Setting of Urban Societies.* Chicago: University of Chicago Press, 1972.

Adan-Bayewitz, David. *Common Pottery in Roman Galilee: A Study of Local Trade.* Ramat-Gan, Israel: Bar-Ilan University Press, 1993.

Aharoni, Yohanan. *The Archaeology of the Land of Israel from the Prehistoric Beginnings to the End of the First Temple Period: Monotheism and the Historical Process.* Translated by A. F. Rainey. Philadelphia: Westminster, 1982.

———. *Ha-Archeologiyah Shel Eretz Yisrael.* Jerusalem: Shikmona Publishing Company, 1978.

———. *The Land of the Bible: A Historical Geography.* Translated by A. F. Rainey. London: Burns & Oates, 1967.

Ahlström, Gösta W. *The History of Ancient Palestine.* Edited by Diana Edelman. Minneapolis: Fortress, 1994.

Albright, William F. *Archaeology and the Religion of Israel: The Ayer Lecture of the Colgate-Rochester Divinity School, 1941.* Baltimore: Johns Hopkins University Press, 1942.

———. *The Archaeology of Palestine and the Bible.* New York: Revell, 1932.

———. *The Archaeology of Palestine.* Harmondsworth Middlesex: Penguin, 1949.

———. *The Archaeology of Palestine.* Rev. ed. London: Penguin, 1954.

———. *From the Stone Age to Christianity: Monotheism and the Historical Process.* Baltimore: Johns Hopkins University Press, 1940.

———. *History, Archaeology, and Christian Humanism.* New York: McGraw-Hill, 1964.

———. "The Impact of Archaeology on Biblical Research–1966." Pages 1–16 in *New Directions in Biblical Archaeology.* Edited by D. N. Freedman and J. C. Greenfield. Garden City, N.Y.: Doubleday, 1971.

Amiran, Ruth. *Ancient Pottery of the Holy Land from Its Beginning in the Neolithic Period to the End of the Iron Age.* Rutgers N.J.: Rutgers University Press, 1970.

———. "Some Observations on Chalcolithic and Early Bronze Age Sanctuaries and Religion." Pages 47–53 in *Temples and High Places in Biblical Times.* Edited by A. Biran. Jerusalem: Hebrew Union College, 1981.

Arnal, William E. *Jesus and the Village Scribes: Galilean Conflicts and the Setting of Q*. Minneapolis: Fortress, 2001.

Aubin, Melissa A. "Gendering Magic in Late Antique Judaism." Ph.D diss., Duke University, 1998.

Avigad, Nahman. *Bullae and Seals from a Post-Exilic Judean Archive*. Qedem 4. Jerusalem: Hebrew University, Institute of Archaeology, 1976.

———. "The Inscribed Pomegranate from the 'House of the Lord.'" Pages 128–37 in *Ancient Jerusalem Revealed*. Edited by H. Geva. Jerusalem: Israel Exploration Society, 1994.

Avner, Uzi. "Ancient Agricultural Settlement and Religion in the Uvda Valley in Southern Israel." *BA* 53 (1990): 125–41.

Baramki, Dimitri C. *The Art and Architecture of Ancient Palestine: A Survey of the Archaeology of Palestine from Earliest Times to the Ottoman Conquest*. Beirut: Palestine Liberation Organization Research Center, 1969.

Barber, Elizabeth Wayland. *Women's Work—The First Twenty Thousand Years: Women, Cloth, and Society in Early Times*. New York: Norton, 1994.

Barbour, Ian G. *Religion and Science: Historical and Contemporary Issues*. New York: HarperCollins, 1997.

Bartlett, John R. "The Archaeology of Qumran." Pages 67–94 in *Archaeology and Biblical Interpretation*. Edited by J. Bartlett. London: Routledge, 1997.

———, ed. *Archaeology and Biblical Interpretation*. London: Routledge, 1997.

Bates, Ülku U., Sarah B. Pomeroy, Virginia Held, Florence L. Denmark, and Dorothy O. Helly (Hunter College Women's Studies Collective). *Women's Realities, Women's Choices: An Introduction to Women's Studies*. 2d ed. New York: Oxford University Press, 1995.

Beck, Pirhiya. "The Drawings from Horvat Teirman (Kuntillet ʿAjrud)." *TA* 9 (1982): 3–68.

Beit-Arieh, Itzhaq, and Pirhiya Beck. *Edomite Shrine: Discoveries from Qitmit in the Negev*. Jerusalem: Israel Museum, 1987.

Benoit, Pierre. "French Archaeologists." Pages 63–86 in *Benchmarks in Time and Culture: An Introduction to Palestinian Archaeology Dedicated to Joseph A. Callaway*. Edited by J. F. Drinkard Jr., G. L. Mattingly, and J. M. Miller. SBLABS 1. Atlanta: Scholars Press, 1988.

Ben-Tor, Amnon. "Notes and News: Excavations and Surveys, Tel Hazor, 1996." *IEJ* 46 (1996): 262–69.

———, ed. *The Archaeology of Ancient Israel*. Translated by R. Greenberg. New Haven: Yale University Press; Tel Aviv: Open University of Israel, 1992.

———. *Mavo la-arkhe'ologyah shel Erets-Yisra'el bi-tekufat ha-Mikra*. Tel Aviv: Open University of Israel, 1991.

Berlin, Andrea M. "Archaeological Sources for the History of Palestine: Between Large Forces: Palestine in the Hellenistic Period." *BA* 60 (1997): 2–51.

Bernett, Monika, and Othmar Keel. *Mond, Stier und Kult am Stadttor: Die Stele von Betsaida (et-Tell)*. OBO 161. Göttingen: Vandenhoeck & Ruprecht, 1998.

Binford, Lewis R. *An Archaeological Perspective*. Studies in Archeology. New York: Academic, 1972.

Biran, Avraham. "Sacred Spaces: Of Standing Stones, High Places and Cult Objects at Dan." *BAR* 24/5 (1998): 38–45, 70.

Biran, Avraham, and Joseph Aviram, eds. *Biblical Archaeology Today, 1990: Proceedings of the Second International Congress of Biblical Archaeology, Jerusalem, June–July 1990.* Jerusalem: Israel Exploration Society and the Israel Academy of Sciences and Humanities, 1993.

Bird, Phyllis. "The Place of Women in Israelite Cultus," Pages 397–419 in *Ancient Israelite Religion: Essays in Honor of Frank Moore Cross, Jr.* Edited by P. D. Miller Jr., P. D. Hanson, and S. D. McBride. Philadelphia: Fortress, 1987.

Block-Smith, Elizabeth, and Beth-Alpert Nakhai. "A Landscape Comes to Life: The Iron I Period." *NEA* 62 (1999): 62–92, 101–27.

Bohmbach, Karla G. "Names and Naming in the Biblical World." Pages 33–39 in *Women in Scripture: A Dictionary of Named and Unnamed Women in the Hebrew Bible, the Apocryphal/Deuterocanonical Books, and the New Testament.* Edited by C. Meyers, T. Craven, and R. S. Kraemer. Boston: Houghton Mifflin, 2000.

Bonani, Georges, Susan Ivy, Willy Wölfli, Magen Broshi, Israel Carmi, and John Strugnell. "Radiocarbon Dating of the Dead Sea Scrolls." *Atiqôt* 20 (1991): 27–32.

Bright, John. *A History of Israel.* 3d ed. Philadelphia: Westminster, 1981.

Broshi, Magen. "Was Qumran, Indeed, a Monastery? The Consensus and Its Challengers: An Archaeologist's View." Pages 19–37 in *Caves of Enlightenment: Proceedings of the American Schools of Oriental Research Dead Sea Scrolls Jubilee Symposium (1947–1997).* Edited by J. H. Charlesworth. North Richland Hills, Tex.: Bibal, 1998.

Burnette-Bletsch, Rhonda. "Women after Childbirth (Lev 12:1–8)." Pages 173–74 in *Women in Scripture: A Dictionary of Named and Unnamed Women in the Hebrew Bible, the Apocryphal/Deuterocanonical Books, and the New Testament.* Edited by C. Meyers, T. Craven, and R. S. Kraemer. Boston: Houghton Mifflin, 2000.

Callaway, Joseph A. "'Ai." *NEAEHL* 1:39–45.

Callaway, P. R. *The History of the Qumran Community: An Investigation.* JSPSup 3. Sheffield: JSOT Press, 1988.

Campbell, Edward F. "Wright, George Ernest." *OEANE* 5:350–52.

Carter, Charles E. *The Emergence of Yehud in the Persian Period: A Social and Demographic Study.* JSOTSup 294. Sheffield: Sheffield Academic Press, 1999.
———. "Ethnoarchaeology." *OEANE* 2:280–84.

Catron, Janice. "Digging for Truth: Archeological Studies Are Shedding New Light On Biblical Accounts." *Presbyterians Today* (2002): 10–15.

Chancey, Mark A. *The Myth of a Gentile Galilee.* SNTSMS 118. Cambridge: Cambridge University Press, 2002.

Chancey, Mark A., and Eric M. Meyers. "How Jewish Was Sepphoris in Jesus' Time?" *BAR* 26/4 (2000): 18–33, 61.

Chancey, Mark A., and Adam Porter. "The Archaeology of Roman Palestine." *NEA* 64 (2001): 164–203.

Charlesworth, James H. "Archaeology, Jesus, and Christian Faith," Pages 1–22 in *What Has Archaeology to Do With Faith?* Edited by J. H. Charlesworth and W. P. Weaver. Faith and Scholarship Colloquies. Philadelphia: Trinity Press International, 1992.

Cohen, Shaye J. D. *The Beginnings of Jewishness: Boundaries, Varieties, Uncertainties.* Berkeley and Los Angeles: University of California Press, 1999.

Coogan, Michael. "Archaeology and Biblical Studies: The Book of Joshua." Pages 19–32 in *The Hebrew Bible and Its Interpreters.* Edited by W. H. Propp, B. Halpern and D. N. Freedman. Biblical and Judaic Studies from the University of California, San Diego, 1. Winona Lake, Ind.: Eisenbrauns, 1990.

———, ed.; *The Oxford History of the Biblical World.* New York: Oxford University Press, 1998.

Cooley, Robert E. "'Ai." *OEANE* 1:32–33.

Costin, Cathy Lynne. "Exploring the Relationship Between Gender and Craft in Complex Societies: Methodological and Theoretical Issues of Gender Attribution." Pages 114–40 in *Gender and Archaeology.* Edited by R. P. Wright. Philadelphia: University of Pennsylvania Press, 1994.

Counihan, Carole M. "Introduction—Food and Gender: Identity and Power." Pages 1–21 in *Food and Gender: Identity and Power.* Edited by C. M. Counihan and S. L. Kaplan. Amsterdam: Harwood Academic Publishers, 1998.

Crossan, John Dominic, and Jonathan L. Reed. *Excavating Jesus: Beneath the Stones, Behind the Texts.* San Francisco: HarperSanFrancisco, 2001.

Crown, Alan D., and Lena Cansdale. "Qumran: Was It an Essene Settlement?" *BAR* 20/2 (1994): 24–35, 73–78.

Currid, John. *Doing Archaeology in the Land of the Bible: A Basic Guide.* Grand Rapids: Baker, 1999.

Daviau, P. M. Michèle. "Family Religion: Evidence for the Paraphernalia of the Domestic Cult." Pages 199–229 in *The World of the Arameans II: Studies in History and Archaeology in Honour of Paul-Eugène Dion.* Edited by P. M. M. Daviau, J. M. Wevers, and M. Weigl. JSOTSup 325. Sheffield: Sheffield Academic Press, 2001.

———. *Houses and Their Furnishings in Bronze Age Palestine.* JSOT/ASOR Monograph Series 8. Sheffield: Sheffield Academic Press, 1993.

Davies, Graham I. "British Archaeologists." Pages 37–62 in *Benchmarks in Time and Culture: An Introduction to Palestinian Archaeology Dedicated to Joseph A. Callaway.* Edited by J. F. Drinkard Jr., G. L. Mattingly, and J. M. Miller. SBLABS 1. Atlanta: Scholars Press, 1988.

Davies, Philip R. *The Damascus Covenant.* JSOTSup 25. Sheffield: JSOT Press, 1983.

———. "How Not to Do Archaeology: The Story of Qumran." *BA* 51 (1988): 203–7.

———. *Qumran.* Cities of the Biblical World. Guildford, Surrey: Lutterworth, 1982.

Dessel, J. P. "Reading between the Lines: William Foxwell Albright 'In' the Field and 'On' the Field." *NEA* 65 (2003): 43–50.

———. Review of E. Stern, *Archaeology of the Land of the Bible, Volume II: 732–332 B.C.E. BAR* 28/6 (2002): 58–59.

Dever, William G. "Archaeology, Syro-Palestinian and Biblical." *ABD* 1:354–67.

———. "Asherah, Consort of Yahweh? New Evidence from Kuntillet ʿAjrud," *BASOR* 255 (1984): 21–37.

———. "Biblical Archeology." *OEANE* 1:315–19.

———. "Biblical Archaeology: Death and Rebirth?" Pages 706–22 in *Biblical Archaeology Today, 1990: Proceedings of the Second International Congress on Biblical Archaeology, Jerusalem, June–July 1990.* Edited by A. Biran and J. Aviram. Jerusalem: Israel Exploration Society; 1993.

———. "Biblical Theology and Biblical Archaeology: An Appreciation of G. Ernest Wright." *HTR* 73 (1980): 1–15.

———. "Gezer." *OEANE* 2:396–400.

———. "Impact of the 'New Archaeology,'" Pages 337–352 in *Benchmarks in Time and Culture: An Introduction to Palestinian Archaeology Dedicated to Joseph A. Callaway*. Edited by J. F. Drinkard Jr., G. L. Mattingly, and J. M. Miller. SBLABS 1. Atlanta: Scholars Press, 1988.

——— "Israel, History of (Archaeology and the 'Conquest')." *ABD* 3:545–58.

———. "On Listening to the Text—and the Artifacts." Pages 1–23 in *The Echoes of Many Texts: Reflections on Jewish and Christian Traditions: Essays in Honor of Lou H. Silberman*. Edited by W. G. Dever and J. E. Wright. Atlanta: Scholars Press, 1997.

———. *Recent Archaeological Discoveries and Biblical Research.* Seattle: University of Washington Press, 1990.

———. "Retrospects and Prospects in Biblical and Syro-Palestinian Archaeology." *BA* 45 (1982): 103–7.

———. "The Silence of the Text: An Archaeological Commentary of 2 Kings 23." Pages 143–68 in *Scripture and Other Artifacts: Essays on the Bible and Archaeology in Honor of Philip J. King*. Edited by M. D. Coogan, J. C. Exum, and L. E. Stager. Louisville: John Knox, 1994.

———. "Syro-Palestinian and Biblical Archaeology." Pages 31–74 in *The Hebrew Bible and Its Modern Interpreters*. Edited by D. A. Knight and G. M. Tucker. Chico, Calif.: Scholars Press, 1985.

———. *What Did the Biblical Writers Know and When Did They Know It? What Archaeology Can Tell Us about the Reality of Ancient Israel*. Grand Rapids: Eerdmans, 2001.

——— "What Remains of the House That Albright Built?" *BA* 56 (1993): 25–35.

Donceel, R., and P. Donceel-Voûte. "The Archaeology of Khirbet Qumran." Pages 1–38 in *Methods of Investigation of the Dead Sea Scrolls and the Khirbet Qumran Site: Present Realities and Future Prospects*. Edited by Michael O. Wise et al. Annals of the New York Academy of Sciences 722. New York: New York Academy of Sciences, 1994.

Dothan, Trude, and Seymour Gittin. "Miqneh, Tel." *OEANE* 4:30–35.

Doudna, Greg. "Dating the Scrolls on the Basis of Radiocarbon Analysis." Pages 430–71 in volume 1 of *The Dead Sea Scrolls after Fifty Years: A Comprehensive Assessment*. Edited by P. W. Flint and J. C. VanderKam. Leiden: Brill, 1998.

Drinkard, Joel F., Jr., Gerald L. Mattingly, and J. Maxwell Miller, eds. *Benchmarks in Time and Culture: An Introduction to Palestinian Archaeology Dedicated to Joseph A. Callaway*. SBLABS 1. Atlanta: Scholars Press, 1988.

Edwards, Douglas. "First Century Urban/Rural Relations in Lower Galilee: Exploring the Archaeological and Literary Evidence." Pages 169–82 in *SBL Seminar Papers, 1988*. Edited by D. Lull. SBLSP 27. Atlanta: Scholars Press, 1988.

———. "The Socio-economic and Cultural Ethos of Lower Galilee in the First Century: Implications for the Nascent Jesus Movement." Pages 53–73 in *The Galilee*

in Late Antiquity. Edited by L. I. Levine. New York: Jewish Theological Semi-
    nary, 1992.

Elder, Linda Bennet. "The Woman Question and Female Ascetics among Essenes."
    BA 57 (1994): 220–34.

Eshel, Hanan, Magen Broshi, Richard Freund, and Brian Schultz. "New Data on the
    Cemetery East of Khirbet Qumran." *DSD* 9 (2002): 135–65.

Eshel, Hanan, and Zvi Greenhut. "Ḥiam el-Sagha, a Cemetery of the Qumran Type,
    Judaean Desert." *RB* 100 (1993): 252–59.

Exum, J. Cheryl, and David J. A. Clines, eds. *The New Literary Criticism and the
    Hebrew Bible*. Valley Forge, Pa.: Trinity Press International, 1993.

Falk, Nancy A., and Rita M. Gross "In the Wings: Rituals for Wives and Mothers."
    Pages 57–58 in *Unspoken Words: Women's Religious Lives*. Edited by N. A. Falk
    and R. M. Gross. 3d ed. Belmont, Calif.: Wadsworth, 2001.

———, eds. *Unspoken Words: Women's Religious Lives*. 3d ed. Belmont, Calif.:
    Wadsworth, 2001.

Faust, Avraham. "The Rural Community of Ancient Israel in the Iron Age." *BASOR*
    317 (2000): 17–39.

Finkelstein, Israel. *The Archaeology of the Israelite Settlement*. Jerusalem: Israel
    Exploration Society, 1988.

——— "The Great Transformation: The 'Conquest' of the Highlands Frontiers and
    the Rise of the Territorial States." Pages 349–65 in *The Archaeology of Society in
    the Holy Land*. Edited by T. E. Levy. New York: Facts on File, 1995.

Finkelstein, Israel, and Nadav Na'aman, eds. *From Nomadism to Monarchy: Archae-
    ological and Historical Aspects of Early Israel*. Jerusalem: Israel Exploration
    Society, 1994.

Finkelstein, Israel, and Neil Asher Silberman. *The Bible Unearthed: Archaeology's
    New Vision of Ancient Israel and the Origin of Its Sacred Texts*. New York: Free
    Press, 2001.

Finley, Moses I. "The Ancient City: From Fustel de Coulanges to Max Weber and
    Beyond." *Comparative Studies in Society and History* 19 (1977): 305–32.

Flusser, David. "Paganism in Palestine." Pages 1065–1100 in vol. 1 of *The Jewish
    People in the First Century: Historical Geography; Political History; Social, Cul-
    tural and Religious Life and Institutions*. Edited by S. Safrai and M. Stern.
    CRINT 1. 2 vols. Philadelphia: Fortress, 1976.

Fontaine, Carole R. "Wife (Prov 5:18–19; 12:4; 18:22; 19; 13–14; 21:9,19; 25:24;
    27:15–16; 30:23; 31:10–31)." Pages 303–4 in *Women in Scripture: A Dictionary
    of the Named and Unnamed Women in the Hebrew Bible, the Apocryphal/
    Deuterocanonical Books, and the New Testament*. Edited by C. Meyers, T. Craven,
    and R. S. Kraemer. Boston: Houghton Mifflin, 2000.

Frerichs, Ernest S., and Leon H. Lesko, eds. *Exodus: The Egyptian Evidence*. Winona
    Lake, Ind: Eisenbrauns, 1997.

Freyne, Sean V. "Archaeology and the Historical Jesus." Pages 117-44 in *Archaeology
    and Biblical Interpretation*. Edited by J. R. Bartlett. London: Routledge, 1997.

———. *Galilee, Jesus and the Gospels: Literary Approaches and Historical Investi-
    gations*. Philadelphia: Fortress, 1988.

———. "Galilee-Jerusalem Relations according to Josephus' *Life*." *NTS* 33 (1987):
    600–9.

Fritz, Volkmar. 1994. *An Introduction to Biblical Archaeology*. JSOTSup 172. Sheffield: JSOT Press, 1994.

Gal, Zvi. *Lower Galilee during the Iron Age*. Winona Lake, Ind.: Eisenbrauns, 1992.

Garnett, Lucy M. S. *The Women of Turkey and Their Folklore*. 2 vols. London: David Nutt, 1890–91.

Geiger, Joseph. "Aspects of Palestinian Paganism in Late Antiquity." Pages 3–17 in *Sharing the Sacred: Religious Contacts and Conflicts in the Holy Land First–Fifteenth Century*. Edited by A. Kofski and G. G. Stroumsa. Jerusalem: Yad Izhak Ben Zvi, 1998.

Geraty, Lawrence T. "The Khirbet el Kôm Bilingual Ostracon." *BASOR* 220 (1975): 55–61.

Gerkin, Charles V. *The Living Human Document: Re-visioning Pastoral Counseling in a Hermeneutical Mode*. Nashville: Abingdon, 1984.

Gero, Joan M., and Margaret W. Conkey, eds. *Engendering Archaeology: Women and Prehistory*. Oxford: Basil Blackwell, 1991.

Geva, Hillel, ed. *Ancient Jerusalem Revealed*. Jerusalem: Israel Exploration Society, 1992.

Gilchrist, Roberta P. *Gender and Archaeology: Contesting the Past*. London: Routledge, 1999.

Ginsburg, Christian D. *The Essenes: Their History and Doctrines*. London: Longman, Green, Longman, Roberts & Green, 1864.

Gitin, Seymour, and William G. Dever, eds. *Recent Excavations in Israel: Studies in Iron Age Archaeology*. AASOR 49. Winona Lake, Ind.: Eisenbrauns, 1989.

Golb, Norman. "Khirbet Qumran and the Manuscript Finds of the Judaean Wilderness." Pages 51–72 in *Methods of Investigation of the Dead Sea Scrolls and the Khirbet Qumran Site: Present Realities and Future Prospects*. Edited by Michael O. Wise et al. Annals of the New York Academy of Sciences 722. New York: New York Academy of Sciences, 1994.

———. "Khirbet Qumran and the Manuscripts of the Judean Wilderness: Observations on the Logic of Their Investigation." *JNES* 49 (1990): 103–14.

Goshen-Gottstein, Moshe Henry. "Tanakh Theology: The Religion of the Old Testament and the Place of Jewish Biblical Theology." Pages 617–44 in *Ancient Israelite Religion: Essays in Honor of Frank Moore Cross, Jr.* Edited by P. D. Miller Jr., P. D. Hanson, and S. D. McBride. Philadelphia: Fortress, 1987.

Gottwald, Norman K. *The Tribes of Yahweh: A Sociology of the Religion of Liberated Israel, 1250–1050 B.C.E.* Maryknoll, N.Y.: Orbis, 1979.

Grabbe, Lester L. *The Persian and Greek Periods*. Vol. 1 of *Judaism from Cyrus to Hadrian*. Minneapolis: Fortress, 1992.

———, ed. *Can a "History of Israel" Be Written?* JSOTSup 245. Sheffield: Sheffield Academic Press, 1997.

Graf, David F. "Palestine in the Persian through the Roman Period." *OEANE* 4:222–28.

Granqvist, Hilma. *Birth and Childhood among the Arabs: Studies in a Mohammedan Village in Palestine*. Helsingfors: Sodörström, 1947.

Greenspoon, Leonard J. "Between Alexandria and Antioch: Jews and Judaism in the Hellenistic Period." Pages 421–66 in *The Oxford History of the Biblical World*. Edited by M. D. Coogan. New York: Oxford University Press, 1998.

Gross, Rita M. *Feminism and Religion: An Introduction*. Boston: Beacon, 1996.

Gruber, Mayer I. "Women in the Religious System of Qumran." Pages 173–96 in *The Judaism of Qumran: A Systemic Reading of the Dead Sea Scrolls*. Part 5 of *Judaism in Late Antiquity*. Edited by A. J. Avery-Peck, J. Neusner, and B. D. Chilton. Handbook of Oriental Studies, The Near and Middle East 56. Leiden: Brill, 2001.

Haak, Robert D. "Altars." *OEANE* 1:80–81.

Hachlili, Rachel. "Burial Practices at Qumran." *RevQ* 16 (1993): 247–64.

Hallo, William W. "Albright and the Gods of Mesopotamia." *BA* 56 (1993): 18–24.

Halpern, Baruch. "The Baal (and the Asherah?) in Seventh-Century Judah: Yhwh's Retainers Retired." Pages 115–54 in *Konsequente Traditionsgeschichte: Festschrift für Klaus Baltzer zum 65. Geburtstag*. Edited by R. Bartelmus. Göttingen: Vandenhoeck & Ruprecht, 1993.

Hanson, K. C. "The Galilean Fishing Economy and the Jesus Tradition." *BTB* 27 (1997): 99–111.

Harrison, Robert K. "Hellenization in Syria-Palestine: The Case of Judaea in the Third Century B.C.E." *BA* 57 (1992): 98–108.

Helly, Dorothy O., and Susan M. Reverby, eds. *Domains: Rethinking Public and Private in Women's History*. Ithaca, N.Y.: Cornell University Press, 1992.

Herr, Denise Dick, and Mary P. Boyd. "A Watermelon Named Abimelech." *BAR* 28/1 (2002): 34–37, 62.

Herr, Larry G. "The Iron II Period: Emerging Nations." *BA* 60 (1997): 114–83.

Hestrin, Ruth. "Understanding Asherah—Exploring Semitic Iconography." *BAR* 17/5 (1991): 50–58.

Hodder, Ian. *Reading the Past: Current Approaches to Interpretation in Archaeology*. Cambridge: Cambridge University Press, 1986.

Hoerth, Alfred J. *Archaeology of the Old Testament*. Grand Rapids: Baker, 1988.

Hoffmeier, James K. *Israel in Egypt*. New York: Oxford University Press, 1997.

Hoglund, Kenneth. *Achaemenid Imperial Administration in Syria-Palestine and the Missions of Ezra and Nehemiah*. SBLDS 25. Atlanta: Scholars Press, 1992.

Holladay, John S., Jr. "The Kingdoms of Israel and Judah: Political and Economic Centralization in the Iron II A–B (ca. 1000–750 B.C.E.)." Pages 368–98 in *The Archaeology of Society in the Holy Land*. Edited by T. E. Levy. New York: Facts on File, 1995.

———. "Religion in Israel and Judah under the Monarchy." Pages 249–99 in *Ancient Israelite Religion: Essays in Honor of Frank Moore Cross, Jr.* Edited by P. D. Miller Jr., P. D. Hanson, and S. D. McBride. Philadelphia: Fortress, 1987.

Holland, Thomas. "Jericho." *OEANE* 3:220–24.

Horsley, Richard. *Archaeology, History and Society in Galilee: The Social Context of Jesus and the Rabbis*. Valley Forge, Pa.: Trinity Press International, 1996.

———. "Social Conflict in the Synoptic Sayings Source Q." Pages 37–52 in *Conflict and Invention: Literary, Rhetorical, and Social Studies on the Sayings Gospel Q*. Edited by J. S. Kloppenborg. Valley Forge, Pa.: Trinity Press International, 1996.

Humbert, Jean-Baptiste, and Alain Chambon. *Fouilles de Khirbet Qumrân et de Aïn Feschkha*. Vol. 1. Novum Testamentum et Orbis Antiquus Series Archaeologica 1. Fribourg: Éditions Universitaires; Göttingen: Vandenhoeck & Ruprecht, 1994.

Hunsinger, Deborah van Deusen. *Theology and Pastoral Counseling: A New Inter-disciplinary Approach*. Grand Rapids: Eerdmans, 1995.

Isserlin, B. S. J. *The Israelites*. London: Thames & Hudson, 1988.

Jenkins, Nancy Harmon. "Food Matters." *Wellesley* 85 (2002): 21–25.

Joffe, Alexander H., J. P. Dessel, and Rachel S. Hallote. "The 'Gilat Woman': Female Iconography, Chalcolithic Cult and the End of Southern Levantine Prehistory." *NEA* 64 (2001): 8–23.

Kaiser, Werner. "Elephantine." *OEANE* 2:234–36.

Kempinski, Aharon, and Michael Avi-Yonah. *Syria-Palestine II: From the Middle Bronze Age to the End of the Classical World (2200 B.C.–324 A.D.)*. Translated by J. Hogarth. Geneva: Nagel, 1979.

Kenyon, Kathleen M. *Archaeology in the Holy Land*. London: Benn, 1960, 1979.

———. *Archaeology in the Holy Land*, 4th ed. London: Benn; New York: Norton, 1979.

———. "Jericho." *NEAEHL* 2:674–81.

King, Philip J. *American Archaeology in the Mideast: A History of the American Schools of Oriental Research*. Philadelphia: American Schools of Oriental Research, 1983.

———. "The Influence of G. Ernest Wright on the Archaeology of Palestine." Pages 15–30 in *Archaeology and Biblical Interpretation: Essays in Memory of D. Glenn Rose*. Edited by L. G. Perdue, L. E. Toombs, and G. L. Johnson. Atlanta: John Knox, 1987.

King, Philip J., and Lawrence E. Stager. *Life in Biblical Israel*. Louisville: Westminster John Knox, 2001.

Klein, Michele. *A Time to Be Born: Customs and Folklore of Jewish Birth*. Philadelphia: Jewish Publication Society, 1998.

Kletter, Raz. *The Judean Pillar-Figurines and the Archaeology of Asherah*. BARIS 636. Oxford: Archaeopress, 1996.

Knight, Douglas A. "Foreword." Pages xvii–xviii in *Life in Biblical Israel,* by Philip J. King and Lawrence E. Stager. Louisville: Westminster John Knox, 2001.

Kramer, Carol. "Pots and People." Pages 99–112 in *Mountains and Lowlands: Essays in the Archaeology of Greater Mesopotamia*. Edited by L. D. Levine and T. C. Young Jr. BMes 6. Malibu: Undena, 1977.

Lamphere, Louise. "The Domestic Sphere of Women and the Public Sphere of Men: The Strengths and Limitations of an Anthropological Dichotomy." Pages 67–77 in *Gender in Cross-Cultural Perspective*. Edited by C. B. Brettell and C. F. Sargent. Englewood Cliffs, N.J.: Prentice Hall, 1992.

LaRocca-Pitts, Elizabeth C. *"Of Wood and Stone": The Significance of Israelite Cultic Items in the Bible and Its Ancient Interpreters*. HSM 61. Winona Lake Ind.: Eisenbrauns, 2001.

Laughlin, John C. H. *Archaeology and the Bible*. London: Routledge, 2000.

Leith, Mary Joan Winn. "Israel among the Nations: The Persian Period." Pages 367–420 in *The Oxford History of the Biblical World*. Edited by M. D. Coogan. New York: Oxford University Press, 1997.

LeMaire, Andre. "Who or What Was Yahweh's Asherah? Startling New Inscriptions from Two Different Sites Reopen the Debate about the Meaning of Asherah." *BAR* 10/6 (1984): 42–51.

Levine, Lee. I. *Judaism and Hellenism in Antiquity: Conflict or Confluence?* Samuel and Althea Stroum Lectures in Jewish Studies. Seattle: University of Washington Press, 1998.

Levy, Thomas E. "Preface." Pages x–xvi in *The Archaeology of Society in the Holy Land.* Edited by T. E. Levy. New York: Facts on File, 1995.

———, ed. *The Archaeology of Society in the Holy Land.* New York: Facts on File, 1995.

Lipschits, Oded, and Joseph Blenkinsopp, eds. *Judah and the Judeans in the Neo-Babylonian Period.* Winona Lake, Ind.: Eisenbrauns, 2003.

Long, Burke O. "Mythic Trope in the Autobiography of William Foxwell Albright." *BA* 56 (1993): 36–45.

———. *Planting and Reaping Albright: Politics, Ideology, and Interpreting the Bible.* University Park: Pennsylvania State University Press, 1997.

Machinist, Peter. "William Foxwell Albright: The Man and His Work." Pages 385–403 in *The Study of the Ancient Near East in the Twenty-First Century: The William Foxwell Albright Centennial Conference.* Edited by J. S. Cooper and Glenn M. Schwartz. Winona Lake, Ind.: Eisenbrauns, 1996.

Magness, Jodi. *The Archaeology of Qumran and the Dead Sea Scrolls.* Studies in the Dead Sea Scrolls and Related Literature. Grand Rapids: Eerdmans, 2002.

———. "Qumran Archaeology: Past Perspectives and Future Prospects." Pages 47–77 in volume 1 of *The Dead Sea Scrolls after Fifty Years: A Comprehensive Assessment.* Edited by P. W. Flint and J. C. VanderKam. Leiden: Brill, 1998.

———. "A Villa at Khirbet Qumran?" *RevQ* 16 (1994): 397–419.

Malbon, Elizabeth Struthers. *In the Company of Jesus: Characters in Mark's Gospel.* Louisville: Westminster John Knox, 2000.

Marcus, Amy Dockser. *The View from Nebo: How Archaeology Is Rewriting the Bible and Reshaping the Middle East.* New York: Little, Brown & Company, 2000.

Mazar, Amihai. *Archaeology of the Land of the Bible: 10,000–586 B.C.E.* ABRL. New York: Doubleday, 1990.

———. "Bronze Bull Found in Israelite 'High Place' from the Time of the Judges." *BAR* 9/5 (1983): 34–40.

———. "Israeli Archaeologists." Pages 109–28 in *Benchmarks in Time and Culture: An Introduction to Palestinian Archaeology Dedicated to Joseph A. Callaway.* Edited by J. F. Drinkard Jr., G. L. Mattingly, and J. M. Miller. SBLABS 1. Atlanta: Scholars Press, 1988.

McCarter, P. Kyle, Jr. *Ancient Inscriptions: Voices from the Biblical World.* Washington, D.C.: Biblical Archaeology Society, 1996.

———. "Aspects of the Religion of the Israelite Monarchy: Biblical and Epigraphic Data." Pages 137–55 in *Ancient Israelite Religion: Essays in Honor of Frank Moore Cross, Jr.* Edited by P. D. Miller Jr., P. D. Hanson, and S. D. McBride. Philadelphia: Fortress, 1987.

McKenzie, Steven L., and Stephen R. Haynes, eds. *To Each Its Own Meaning: An Introduction to Biblical Criticisms and Their Application.* Rev. ed. Louisville: Westminster John Knox, 1999.

McNutt, Paula M. *Reconstructing the Society of Ancient Israel.* Knoxville: Westminster John Knox, 1999.

Meshel, Ze'ev. "Kuntillet ʿAjrud," *OEANE* 3:310–12.

Meyers, Carol. *Discovering Eve: Ancient Israelite Women in Context.* New York: Oxford University Press, 1988.

———. "Engendering Syro-Palestinian Archaeology." *NEA* (forthcoming).

———. "The Family in Early Israel." Pages 1–47 in *Families in Ancient Israel,* by L. G. Perdue, J. Blenkinsopp, J. J. Collins, and C. Meyers. Louisville: Westminster John Knox, 1997.

———. "From Household to House of Yahweh: Women's Religious Culture in Ancient Israel." Pages 277–303 in *Congress Volume: Basel, 2001.* Edited by A. Lemaire. VTSup 92. Leiden: Brill, 2002.

———. "Having Their Space and Eating There Too: Bread Production and Female Power in Ancient Israelite Households." *Nashim* 5 (2002): 14–44.

———. "Kinship and Kingship, The Early Monarchy." Pages 165–205 in *The Oxford History of the Biblical World.* Edited by M. D. Coogan. New York: Oxford University Press, 2001.

———. "Material Remains and Social Relations: Women's Culture in Agrarian Households of the Iron Age." Pages 425–44 in *Symbiosis, Symbolism, and the Power of the Past: Canaan, Ancient Israel, and Their Neighbors from the Late Bronze Age through Roman Palestine.* Edited by W. G. Dever and S. Gitin. Winona Lake, Ind.: Eisenbrauns, 2003.

———. "Women of the Neighborhood (Ruth 4:17)." Page 254 in *Women in Scripture: A Dictionary of the Named and Unnamed Women in the Hebrew Bible, the Apocryphal/Deuterocanonical Books, and the New Testament.* Edited by C. Meyers, T. Craven, and R. S. Kraemer. Boston: Houghton Mifflin, 2000.

Meyers, Carol. L., and Eric M. Meyers. "Expanding the Frontiers of Biblical Archaeology." *ErIsr* 20 (1989): 140–47.

———. *Haggai, Zechariah 1–8.* AB 25B. Garden City N.Y.: Doubleday, 1987.

———. *Zechariah 9–14.* AB 25C. Garden City, N.Y.: Doubleday, 1993.

Meyers, Eric M. "Jewish Culture in Greco-Roman Palestine." Pages 135–79 in volume 1 of *Cultures of the Jews: A New History.* Edited by D. Biale. New York: Random House/Schocken, 2002.

———. "The Persian Period and the Judean Restoration: From Zerubbabel to Nehemiah." Pages 509–21 in *Ancient Israelite Religion: Essays in Honor of Frank Moore Cross, Jr.* Edited by P. D. Miller Jr., P. D. Hanson, and S. D. McBride. Philadelphia: Fortress, 1987.

———. "Sepphoris on the Eve of the Great Revolt (67–68 C.E.): Archaeology and Josephus." Pages 109–22 in *Galilee through the Centuries.* Edited by E. M. Meyers. Winona Lake, Ind.: Eisenbrauns, 1999.

———. "Sepphoris, The Ornament of All Galilee." *BA* 49 (1986): 4–19.

———. "The Shelomith Seal and the Judean Restoration: Some Additional Considerations." *ErIsr* 18 (1985): 33–38.

———, ed. *The Oxford Encyclopedia of Archaeology in the Near East.* 5 vols. New York: Oxford University Press, 1997.

Miller, J. Maxwell. "Reading the Bible Historically: The Historian's Approach." Pages 17–34 in *To Each Its Own Meaning: An Introduction to Biblical Criticisms and Their Application.* Edited by S. L. McKenzie and S. R. Haynes. Rev. and exp. ed. Louisville: Westminster John Knox, 1999.

Miller, J. Maxwell, and John H. Hayes. *A History of Ancient Israel and Judah*. Philadelphia: Westminster, 1986.

Monson, John. "The New Ain Dara Temple: Closest Solomonic Parallel." *BAR* 26/3 (2000): 20–35, 67.

Moorey, Peter R. S. *A Century of Biblical Archaeology*. Cambridge: Lutterworth, 1991.

———. "Kathleen Kenyon and Palestinian Archaeology." *PEQ* 111 (1979): 3–10.

Morgenstern, Julian. *Rites of Birth, Marriage, Death and Kindred Occasions among the Semites*. Cincinnati: Hebrew Union College Press, 1966.

Nakhai, Beth Alpert. "What's a Bamah? How Sacred Space Functioned in Ancient Israel," *BAR* 20/3 (1994): 18–29.

Negbi, Ora. *Canaanite Gods in Metal: An Archaeological Study of Ancient Syro-Palestinian Figurines*. Tel Aviv: Tel Aviv University Institute of Archaeology, 1976.

Nelson, Sarah M. *Gender in Archaeology: Analyzing Power and Prestige*. Walnut Creek, Calif.: Altamira, 1997.

Nickelsburg, George W. E. "Currents in Qumran Scholarship: The Interplay of Data, Agendas, and Methodology." Pages 79–99 in *The Dead Sea Scrolls at Fifty: Proceedings of the 1997 Society of Biblical Literature Qumran Section Meetings*. Edited by R. A. Kugler and E. Schuller. SBLSymS 15. Atlanta: Scholars Press, 1999.

Perdue, Leo. *The Collapse of History: Reconstructing Old Testament Theology*. Minneapolis: Fortress, 1994.

Perdue, Leo, Lawrence E. Toombs, and Gary L. Johnson, eds. *Archaeology and Biblical Interpretation: Essays in Memory of D. Glenn Rose*. Atlanta: John Knox, 1987.

Perrot, Jean. *Syria Palestine I: From the Origins to the Bronze Age*. Translated by J. Hogarth. Geneva: Nagel Verlag, 1979.

Petersen, Allan Rosengren. "The Archaeology of Khirbet Qumran." Pages 249–60 in *Qumran between the Old and New Testaments*. Edited by F. H. Cryer and T. L. Thompson. JSOTSup 290. Sheffield: Sheffield Academic Press, 1998.

Porten, Bezalel. "Egyptian Aramaic Texts." *OEANE* 2:213–29.

Price, Randall. *The Stones Cry Out: What Archaeology Reveals about the Truth of the Bible*. Eugene, Ore.: Harvest House, 1997.

Pritchard, James B. *The Ancient Near East: An Anthology of Texts and Pictures*. Princeton: Princeton University Press, 1973.

Puech, Emile. "The Necropolises of Khirbet Qumrân and 'Ain el-Ghuweir and the Essene Belief in Afterlife." *BASOR* 312 (1998): 21–36.

Qedar, Shraga. "Two Lead Weights of Herod Antipas and Agrippa II and the Early History of Tiberias." *Israel Numismatic Journal* 9 (1989): 66–75.

Rapoport, Amos. "Spatial Organization and the Built Environment." Pages 460–502 in *Companion Encyclopedia of Archaeology*. Edited by T. Ingold. London: Routledge, 1994.

Rast, Walter E. *Through the Ages in Palestinian Archaeology: An Introductory Handbook*. Philadelphia: Trinity Press International, 1992.

Redmount, Carol. "Bitter Lives: Israel in and out of Egypt." Pages 58–89 in *The Oxford History of the Biblical World*. Edited by M. D. Coogan. New York: Oxford University Press, 2001.

Reed, Jonathan L. *Archaeology and the Galilean Jesus*. Harrisburg, Pa.: Trinity Press International, 2000.

Reif, Stefan C. "The Damascus Document from the Cairo Genizah: Its Discovery, Early Study and Historical Significance." Pages 109–31 in *The Damascus Document: A Centennial of Discovery: Proceedings of the Third International Symposium of the Orion Center for the Study of the Dead Sea Scrolls and Associated Literature, 4–8 February, 1998*. Edited by J. M. Baumgarten, E. G. Chazon, and A. Pinnick. STDJ 34. Leiden: Brill, 2000.

Renfrew, Colin, and Paul Bahn. *Archaeology: Theories, Methods and Practice*. 3d ed. London: Thames & Hudson, 2000.

Rhoads, David, Joanna Dewey, and Donald Michie. *Mark As Story: An Introduction to the Narrative of a Gospel*. 2d ed. Minneapolis: Fortress, 1999.

Richardson, Peter. *Herod: King of the Jews and Friend of the Romans*. Minneapolis: Fortress, 1999.

Röhrer-Ertl, Olav, Ferdinand Rohrhirsch, and Dietbert Hahn. "Über die Gräberfelder von Khirbet Qumran, insbesondere die Funde der Campagne 1956.I: Anthropologisch Datenvorlage und Erstauswertung aufgrund der Collectio Kurth." *RevQ* 19 (1999): 3–47.

Rosaldo, Michelle Z. "Women, Culture, and Society: A Theoretical Overview." Pages 23–35 in *Women, Culture, and Society*. Edited by M. Z. Rosaldo and L. Lamphere. Stanford, Calif.: Stanford University Press, 1974.

Rose, D. Glen. "The Bible and Archaeology: The State of the Art." Pages 53–64 in *Archaeology and Biblical Interpretation*. Edited by L. G. Perdue, L. E. Toombs, and G. L. Johnson. Atlanta: John Knox, 1987.

Rosenthal, Renate, and Renee Sivan. *Ancient Lamps in the Schloessinger Collection*. Qedem 8. Jerusalem: Hebrew University Institute of Archaeology, 1978.

Running, Leona Glidden, and David Noel Freedman. *William Foxwell Albright: A Twentieth-Century Genius*. New York: Two Continents, 1975.

Safrai, Ze'ev. *The Economy of Roman Palestine*. London: Routledge, 1994.

Sanday, Peggy. "Female Status in the Public Domain." Pages 189–206 in *Women, Culture, and Society*. Edited by M. Z. Rosaldo and L. Lamphere. Stanford, Calif.: Stanford University Press, 1974.

Sasson, Jack M. "Albright As an Orientalist." *BA* 56 (1993): 3–7.

Sasson, Jack M., ed. *Civilizations of the Ancient Near East*. 4 vols. New York: Charles Scribner's Sons, 1995.

Sawicki, Marianne. *Crossing Galilee: Architectures of Contact in the Occupied Land of Jesus*. Harrisburg, Pa.: Trinity Press International, 2000.

Schiffman, Lawrence H. *Reclaiming the Dead Sea Scrolls: The History of Judaism, the Background of Christianity, the Lost Library of Qumran*. Philadelphia: Jewish Publication Society, 1994.

Schmidt, Karl Ludwig. *Der Rahmen der Geschichte Jesu: Literarkritische Untersuchungen zur ältesten Jesusüberlieferung*. Berlin: Trowitzsch, 1919.

Schuller, Eileen. "Women in the Dead Sea Scrolls." Pages 117–44 in volume 2 of *The Dead Sea Scrolls after Fifty Years: A Comprehensive Assessment*. Edited by P. W. Flint and J. C. VanderKam. Leiden: Brill, 1998.

Schürer, Emil. *The History of the Jewish People in the Age of Jesus Christ: (175 B.C.– A.D. 135)*. Revised and edited by G. Vermes, F. Millar, and M. Black. 3 vols. in 4. Edinburgh: T&T Clark, 1973–87.

Seger, Joe D. "Shechem." *OEANE* 5:19–23.

Sered, Susan Starr. *Women As Ritual Experts: The Religious Lives of Elderly Jewish Women in Jerusalem*. Oxford: Oxford University Press, 1992.

Shanks, Hershel. "Who Lies Here? Jordan Tombs Match Those at Qumran." *BAR* 25/5 (1999): 48–53, 76.

———, ed. *Ancient Israel: From Abraham to the Roman Destruction of the Temple*. Rev. ed. Washington D.C.: Biblical Archaeology Society and Prentice Hall, 1999.

Sharistanian, Janet. *Beyond the Public/Private Dichotomy*. Westport, Conn.: Greenwood, 1987.

Sheridan, Susan Guise. "Scholars, Soldiers, Craftsmen, Elites? Analysis of French Collection of Human Remains from Qumran." *DSD* 9 (2002): 199–248.

Silberman, Neil Asher. *Between Past and Present: Archaeology, Ideology, and Nationalism in the Modern Middle East*. New York: Henry Holt, 1989.

———. *Digging for God and Country: Exploration, Archeology, and the Secret Struggle for the Holy Land, 1799–1917*. New York: Knopf, 1982.

———. *A Prophet from amongst You: The Life of Yigael Yadin: Soldier, Scholar, and Mythmaker of Modern Israel*. New York: Addison-Wesley, 1993.

———. "Visions of the Future: Albright in Jerusalem, 1919–1929." *BA* 56 (1993): 8–16.

Stager, Lawrence E. "The Archaeology of the Family in Ancient Israel." *BASOR* 260 (1985): 1–35.

———. "When Canaanites and Philistines Ruled Ashkelon." *BAR* 7/2 (1990): 24–31, 35–37, 40–43.

Stegemann, Hartmut. *The Library of Qumran: On the Essenes, Qumran, John the Baptist and Jesus*. Grand Rapids: Eerdmans; Leiden: Brill, 1998.

Stern, Ephraim. *Archaeology of the Land of the Bible, Volume II: The Assyrian, Babylonian, and Persian Periods (732–332 B.C.E.)*. ABRL. New York: Doubleday, 2001.

———. "The Bible and Israeli Archaeology." Pages 31–40 in *Archaeology and Biblical Interpretation: Essays in Memory of D. Glenn Rose*. Edited by L. G. Perdue, L. E. Toombs, and G. L. Johnson. Atlanta: John Knox, 1987.

———, ed. *The New Encyclopedia of Archaeological Excavations in the Holy Land*. 4 vols. Jerusalem: Israel Exploration Society and Carta; New York: Simon & Schuster, 1993.

Stohl, Marten. *Births in Babylon and the Bible: Its Mediterranean Setting*. Cuneiform Monographs 14. Groningen: STYX, 2001.

Strange, James F. "Some Implications of Archaeology for New Testament Studies." Pages 23-59 in *What Has Archaeology to Do with Faith?* Edited by J. H. Charlesworth and W. P. Weaver. Philadelphia: Trinity Press International, 1992.

Szinovacz, Maximiliane M. "Family Power." Pages 651–93 in *Handbook of Marriage and the Family*. Edited by M. B. Sussman and S. K. Steinmetz. New York: Plenum, 1987.

Tadmor, Miriam. "Female Cult Figurines in Late Canaan and Early Israel: Archaeological Evidence." Pages 139–73 in *Studies in the Period of David and Solomon and Other Essays*. Edited by T. Ishida. Winona Lake, Ind.: Eisenbrauns, 1982.

Taylor, Joan E. "The Cemeteries of Khirbet Qumran and Women's Presence at the Site." *DSD* 6 (1999): 285–323.

Thompson, Henry O. *Biblical Archaeology: The World, The Mediterranean, The Bible*. New York: Paragon House, 1987.

Toombs, Lawrence E. "The Development of Palestinian Archeology As a Discipline." *BA* 45 (1982): 89–91.

———. "A Perspective on the New Archaeology." Pages 41–52 in *Archaeology and Biblical Interpretation: Essays in Memory of D. Glenn Rose*. Edited by L. G. Perdue, L. E. Toombs, and G. L. Johnson. Atlanta: John Knox, 1987.

Tov, Emanuel. "Scribal Practices and Physical Aspects of the Dead Sea Scrolls." Pages 9–33 in *The Bible As Book: The Manuscript Tradition*. Edited by J. L. Sharpe III and K. van Kampen. London: British Library; Newcastle, Del.: Oak Knoll Press, in association with the Scriptorium, Center for Christian Antiquities, 1998.

———. "Scribal Practices Reflected in the Texts from the Judaean Desert." Pages 403–29 in volume 1 of *The Dead Sea Scrolls after Fifty Years: A Comprehensive Assessment*. Edited by P. W. Flint and J. C. VanderKam. Leiden: Brill, 1998.

Tushingham, A. D. "Kenyon, Kathleen Mary." *OEANE* 3:279–80.

Uehlinger, Christoph. "Anthropomorphic Cult Statuary in Iron Age Palestine and the Search for Yahweh's Cult Images." Pages 97–155 in *The Image and the Book: Iconic Cults, Aniconism, and the Rise of Book Religion in Israel and the Ancient Near East*. Edited by K. van der Toorn. Leuven: Peeters, 1997.

Ussiskin, David. "Megiddo." *OEANE* 3:460–69.

Van Beek, Gus W. "William Foxwell Albright: A Short Biography." Pages 7–15 in *The Scholarship of William Foxwell Albright: An Appraisal*. Edited by G. Van Beek. HSS 33. "Papers Delivered at the Symposium 'Homage to William Foxwell Albright,' The American Friends of the Israel Exploration Society, Rockville, Maryland, 1984. Atlanta: Scholars Press, 1989.

———, ed. *The Scholarship of William Foxwell Albright: An Appraisal*. HSS 33. "Papers Delivered at the Symposium 'Homage to William Foxwell Albright,' The American Friends of the Israel Exploration Society, Rockville, Maryland, 1984. Atlanta: Scholars Press, 1989.

VanderKam, James C. *An Introduction to Early Judaism*. Grand Rapids: Eerdmans, 1999.

Van der Toorn, Karel. *From Her Cradle to Her Grave: The Role of Religion in the Life of the Israelite and the Babylonian Woman*. Translated by S. J. Denning-Bolle. BibSem 23. Sheffield: JSOT Press, 1995.

Vaughn, Andrew G., and Ann E. Killebrew. *Jerusalem in Bible and Archaeology: The First Temple Period*. SBLSymS 18. Atlanta: Society of Biblical Literature; Leiden: Brill, 2003.

Vaux, Roland de. *Archaeology and the Dead Sea Scrolls*. Rev. ed. The Schweich Lectures of the British Academy 1959. London: Oxford University Press, 1973.

Vermes, Geza, and Martin D. Goodman, eds. *The Essenes according to the Classical Sources*. Oxford Centre Textbooks 1. Sheffield: JSOT Press, 1989.

Weippert, Helga. *Palästina in vorhellenistischer Zeit*. Munich: Beck, 1988.

Weippert, Manfred, and Helga Weippert. "German Archaeologists." Pages 87–108 in *Benchmarks in Time and Culture: An Introduction to Palestinian Archaeology Dedicated to Joseph A. Callaway*. Edited by J. F. Drinkard Jr., G. L. Mattingly, and J. M. Miller. SBLABS 1. Atlanta: Scholars Press, 1988.

Willis, W. Waite, Jr. "The Archaeology of Palestine and the Archaeology of Faith: Between a Rock and a Hard Place." Pages 75–111 in *What Has Archaeology to Do with Faith?* Edited by J. H. Charlesworth and W. P. Weaver. Faith and Scholarship Colloquies. Philadelphia: Trinity Press International, 1992.

Wise, Michael O., Norman Golb, John J. Collins, and Dennis G. Pardee, eds. *Methods of Investigation of the Dead Sea Scrolls and the Khirbet Qumran Site: Present Realities and Future Prospects.* Annals of the New York Academy of Sciences 722. New York: New York Academy of Sciences, 1994.

———. "'Qumran Type' Graves in Jerusalem: Archaeological Evidence of an Essene Community." *DSD* 5 (1998): 158–71.

Wright, G. Ernest. *Biblical Archaeology.* Philadelphia: Westminster, 1957.

——— *Biblical Archaeology.* Abridged ed. Philadelphia: Westminster: 1960.

———. *Biblical Archaeology.* Rev. ed. Philadelphia: Westminster, 1962.

———. *The Pottery of Palestine from the Earliest Times to the End of the Early Bronze Age.* New Haven: American Schools of Oriental Research, 1937.

Wright, Rita P., ed. *Gender and Archaeology.* Philadelphia: University of Pennsylvania Press, 1996.

Yadin, Yigael. "Biblical Archaeology Today: The Archaeological Aspect." Pages 21–27 in *Biblical Archaeology Today: Proceedings of the International Congress on Biblical Archaeology Jerusalem, April 1984.* Edited by J. Amitai. Jerusalem: Israel Exploration Society, 1985.

———, ed. *Jerusalem Revealed: Archaeology in the Holy City, 1968–1974.* Jerusalem: Israel Exploration Society 1975.

Yeivin, Shmuel. "On the Use and Misuse of Archaeology in Interpreting the Bible." *American Academy for Jewish Research Proceedings* 34 (1966): 141–54.

Zangenberg, Jürgen. "Between Jerusalem and the Galilee: Samaria in the Time of Jesus." In *Jesus and Archaeology.* Edited by J. H. Charlesworth. Grand Rapids: Eerdmans, forthcoming.

———. "Bones of Contention: 'New' Bones from Qumran Help Settle Old Questions (and Raise New Ones)—Remarks on Two Recent Conferences." *QC* 9 (2000): 51–76.

———. "Opening Up Our View: Khirbet Qumran in a Regional Perspective." In *Religion and Society in Roman Palestine.* Edited by D. R. Edwards. London: Routledge, forthcoming.

Zayadine, Fawzi. "Iraq el-Amir." *OEANE* 2:177–81.

Zevit, Ziony. "Three Debates about Bible and Archaeology." *Bib* 83 (2002): 1–27.

Zias, Joseph E. "The Cemeteries of Qumran and Celibacy: Confusion Laid to Rest?" *DSD* 7 (2000): 220–53.

Zissu, Boaz. "Odd Tomb Out: Has Jerusalem's Essene Cemetery Been Found?" *BAR* 25/2 (1999): 50–55, 62.

———. "'Qumran Type' Graves in Jerusalem: Archaeological Evidence of an Essene Community." *DSD* 5 (1998): 158–71.

INDEX OF MODERN AUTHORS

CONTRIBUTORS

Melissa Aubin is Senior Staff member on the Sepphoris Regional Project.

Shannon Burkes is Assistant Professor of Religion at Florida State University, Tallahassee, Florida.

J. P. Dessel is Assistant Professor in the Department of History and the Steinfeld Program in Judaic Studies at the University of Tennessee, Knoxville.

Daniel K. Falk is Assistant Professor of Religious Studies at the University of Oregon, Eugene, Oregon.

Ann E. Killebrew is Assistant Professor of Classics and Ancient Mediterranean Studies and Jewish Studies at The Pennsylvania State University, University Park, Pennsylvania.

Beth LaRocca-Pitts is Adjunct Assistant Professor of Religion at the University of Georgia, Athens, Georgia.

John C. H. Laughlin is Professor and Chair, Department of Religion, at Averett University, Danville, Virginia.

Byron R. McCane is Professor and Chair, Department of Religion, at Wofford College, Spartanburg, South Carolina.

Carol Meyers is Mary Grace Wilson Professor of Religion at Duke University, Durham, North Carolina.

Eric M. Meyers is Bernice and Morton Lerner Professor of Judaic Studies at Duke University, Durham, North Carolina.

Milton C. Moreland is Assistant Professor of Religious Studies at Rhodes College, Memphis, Tennessee.

Scott R. A. Starbuck is the Pastor of Manito Presbyterian Church in Spokane, Washington, and Adjunct Assistant Professor at Gonzaga University and Whitworth College, Spokane, Washington.

Jürgen Zangenberg is Wissenschaftlicher Assistent for New Testament at Bergische Universität-Gesamthochschule, Wuppertal, Germany.

Printed in the United States
1399200005B/102